Beyond Craft

ALSO AVAILABLE FROM BLOOMSBURY

The *Research in Creative Writing* series

Titles include:
Craft Consciousness and Artistic Practice in Creative Writing, by Benjamin Ristow
The Place and the Writer, edited by Sam Meekings and Marshall Moore

Beyond Craft:

An Anti-Handbook for Creative Writers

STEVE WESTBROOK AND JAMES RYAN

BLOOMSBURY ACADEMIC
LONDON • NEW YORK • OXFORD • NEW DELHI • SYDNEY

BLOOMSBURY ACADEMIC
Bloomsbury Publishing Plc
50 Bedford Square, London, WC1B 3DP, UK
1385 Broadway, New York, NY 10018, USA

BLOOMSBURY, BLOOMSBURY ACADEMIC and the Diana logo are trademarks of Bloomsbury Publishing Plc

First published in Great Britain 2020

Cover design: Eleanor Rose
Cover images © Getty Images

A catalogue record for this book is available from the British Library.

Library of Congress Cataloging-in-Publication Data
Names: Westbrook, Steve, 1973– author. | Ryan, James (James William), author.
Title: Beyond craft : an anti-handbook for creative writers /
Steve Westbrook and James Ryan.
Description: New York : Bloomsbury Academic, 2020. | Includes bibliographical references. |
Identifiers: LCCN 2020010490 (print) | LCCN 2020010491 (ebook) |
ISBN 9781350152021 (paperback) | ISBN 9781350119451 (hardback) |
ISBN 9781350119468 (ebook) | ISBN 9781350119475 (epub)
Subjects: LCSH: Creative writing.
Classification: LCC PN145 .W433 2020 (print) | LCC PN145 (ebook) | DDC 808.02–dc23
LC record available at https://lccn.loc.gov/2020010490
LC ebook record available at https://lccn.loc.gov/2020010491

ISBN: HB: 978-1-3501-1945-1
PB: 978-1-3501-5202-1
ePDF: 978-1-3501-1946-8
eBook: 978-1-3501-1947-5

Typeset by RefineCatch Limited, Bungay, Suffolk
Printed and bound in Great Britain

To find out more about our authors and books visit www.bloomsbury.com and sign up for our newsletters.

Contents

Figures

All Illustrations by Steve Westbrook

Acknowledgments

James would like to thank his first reader, sounding board, social conscience, and life partner, Heidi Weston for all her work as a resonator and reviewer. Further thanks to Trent Hergenrader, Stephanie Vanderslice, and Rachel Haley Himmelheber for their professional support and their work on Creative Writing Studies Organization, Journal of Creative Writing Studies, and the Creative Writing Studies Conference, institutions without which the publication of this book would not be possible. Thanks, too, to Bloomsbury and to all the editors and readers serving the Creative Writing Studies Organization.

Steve would like to echo James's appreciation for the members of the Creative Writing Studies Organization, whose tireless work expands possibilities for creative writers on a daily basis. He would also like to offer a few special shout-outs. Thank you to the Montsalvat Artists' Community, where early ideas for this project took shape, and to the members of Cal State Fullerton's English 515: Professional Editing and Journal Production class, who provided feedback on sections of this manuscript. Thanks to Janae Dimick for her wisdom, compassion, and conscientiousness; Janelle Adsit for her incredible vision and tenacity; Lucy Brown for her editorial savvy; and Steve North for being Steve North. Finally, thanks to Sequoia for having patience with her dad's weird, time-consuming writing project.

AN INTRODUCTION

By Way of Boxes and Paradoxes (and Too Many Lines About Felines)

The text you are currently reading is and is *not* another creative writing handbook. In this sense, it's a little bit like the famous paradox of Schrödinger's cat from the field of quantum physics. In this thought experiment, a cat is imagined to be hidden from view in a closed box. Along with the cat is a certain amount of poison that—depending on a chance event—may or may not be released into the atmosphere. Within this context, the cat is said to be simultaneously alive and not alive (in what physicists call a state of "superposition") until an observer opens the box, looks inside, and determines the animal's status as definitively one or the other: living or dead. We are tempted to extend this comparison and suggest that turning each new page of this book might be akin to opening Schrödinger's box. In other words, as you read, it is up to you as our observer and collaborator to determine whether the text you encounter is or is not, in fact, a creative writing handbook.

For what it's worth, we enjoy the seeming impossibility of states of superposition, and we are perfectly comfortable considering our text simultaneously a handbook and not a handbook. Hence, we have chosen (here and throughout the book) to leave most of the decision-making to you. But we fear we may have begun with too strange and potentially morbid an image. While we enjoy the idea of suspending ourselves in paradox and possibility—of swapping the restrictions of *either/or* for the generosity of *both/and*, of rewriting Hamlet's famous soliloquy as "to be *and* not to be"—neither one of us particularly likes the idea of trapping a cat in a box with hydrocyanic acid, even if only theoretically. As far as we know, Erwin Schrödinger never actually performed this experiment, but merely treated it as a conceptual problem. Regardless, we certainly don't want you to worry about encountering corpses of felines, however real or imagined, as you move from page to page. Nor do we want you to fear coming upon a vengeful attack cat who has been cultivating his rage while trapped in a box for too long. Perhaps we should scrap the comparison to Schrödinger's cat altogether and start over. Maybe this handbook against handbooks is more like quantum physics as a whole or, to use a more commonplace simile, like a friend's relationship status: i.e., *it's complicated*.

On a more serious note, we should admit that our decision to keep things complicated is a deliberate one. Frankly, this project grew out of our collective frustration—Steve as a professor and James as a graduate student—with our inability to find substantial, progressive approaches to the study of creative writing despite the scores of pedagogical materials on the market. We discovered that while there seem to be as many handbooks as breeds of cats in the world, there are few that manage not to radically oversimplify the idea of writing creatively. Most handbooks do so by offering a rather narrow and dated perspective on what creative writing is, who creative writers are, how they go about their processes of writing, and what they need to know. In fact, the vast majority seem to suggest that the only thing emerging authors should study is *craft*, *craft*, and more *craft*.

We are not the only ones to launch this complaint. Poet Dean Young has famously expressed his frustration with the field of creative writing's crafty treatment of his preferred genre. In his book, *The Art of Recklessness: Poetry as Assertive Force and Contradiction*, he offers the most vehement rejection of craft-centered pedagogy we've encountered yet, screaming across the page in all caps, "THE WRITING OF POETRY IS NOT A CRAFT!" (47). While we share Young's obvious frustration (and in doing so represent a minority in what is otherwise apparently a craft-centered universe), we have a significantly different perspective from his, albeit one that might be expressed through only a slight editorial change and a little less screaming: we would suggest that creative writing is not ONLY a craft.

Before we further explain what we mean, we have to admit that, perhaps unlike Young, in many ways we understand creative writing's obsession with craft. We get it: emerging authors need to be aware of the materials and techniques that comprise the foundation of their artistic pursuits. We think fiction and creative nonfiction writers should be concerned with how to sequence their narratives through linear and nonlinear modes of construction, how to create dialogue that manipulates readers while sustaining an illusion of natural speech, how to decide upon the appropriate point-of-view for their stories, and how to choose viewpoint characters effectively. Poets should develop their understanding of how to control rhythm and emphasis through line lengths and line breaks, how to develop emotional resonance through tone and image, how to construct metaphors that offer the delight of unexpected comparisons and thereby challenge readers to move beyond their habitual ways of thinking. No emerging writer would want to offer readers a poorly constructed story with flat characters and an underdeveloped plot or a poem full of arbitrary rhymes and clichés. Who would want to equate beauty with a sunrise or a flower when the world has already experienced the wonder of Lautreamont's famous simile: "as beautiful as the chance meeting of a sewing machine and an umbrella on a dissecting table"? In short, studying devices of craft makes a whole lot of sense to us.

To our thinking, the problem lies not in the concern with craft itself but in the exclusion of nearly everything else. Too often issues of craft are not placed in relation to a whole host of other subjects. In fact, the impression most handbook authors give is that the discipline of creative writing seeks to somehow artificially isolate formal issues of craft from larger contexts, concerns, and functions related to writing. In establishing these parameters of separation, they effectively trap emerging authors in boxes of their own. To be clear, we are not necessarily suggesting this sort of boxing in is done maliciously, conspiratorially, or even consciously. What we're talking about appears to be less of a nefarious agenda item and more of an ideological practice—the seemingly normal, inherited way of doing things for people who write handbooks.

Let us explain what we mean through an example. Robert DeMaria's *The College Handbook of Creative Writing* represents a typical treatment of the problem. In his introduction, DeMaria establishes the province of craft as creative writers' appropriate subject of study. He states, "*Writers* usually study the craft of writing in order to understand, pragmatically, how certain devices work. Their primary goal is to produce work that is aesthetically effective" (1 his italics). While we are not particularly surprised by DeMaria's conventional treatment of craft, we are curious about his rhetorical strategy of introducing the subject. Before issuing this statement, he demarcates restrictive lines between creative writers and three other groups within the field of literary studies to suggest precisely who creative writers *are not* and what they *do not* study. Specifically, he suggests that writers do not do the work of "scholars," who, he claims, "tend to emphasize the biographical and historical context of a literary work." Nor do they pursue the interests of "critics," who, he suggests, "are interested in . . . linguistic significance" (1). DeMaria invents a rather strange label to describe the identity of the third group to which creative writers supposedly stand in opposition: "special interest readers." He states, "*Special interest readers* who have politicized the study of literature are preoccupied with such things as race, ethnicity, and gender" (1 his italics). He then goes on to explain that in contrast to the work of these three groups, his handbook decidedly "takes the writer's approach. It deals with the practical aspects of the craft" (1). And he organizes the content of his book accordingly, devoting chapters to theme, setting, characters, plot, point of view, dialogue, description, images, tone and style while avoiding what he has deemed the appropriate subjects for others.

When we pursue the example of one of these groups of others, we quickly uncover problems with DeMaria's system. Let's take a look at the so-called "special interest readers." Even if we somehow overlook the pejorative tone with which DeMaria dismisses the seriousness of cultural representation as a mere "preoccupation" of this "special interest" group, we are still faced with a fallacious attempt at demarcation. By inventing the very notion of specialized readers who "politicize" literature, DeMaria suggests that politics is something that is imposed onto an existing piece of writing from the outside rather than inevitably inherent to the process of its creation. In his view, a minority of readers concern themselves with issues of representation; creative writers do not. The implications of this division would suggest that creative writers have no need, for example, to actively contemplate how they construct the ethnic or sexual identities of the characters in their work, nor the issue of how their own biases may affect these representations, nor how their audiences might react upon encountering them. When we push this way of thinking to its logical extreme, it leads us to ask seemingly absurd but insightful questions. Would DeMaria have advised Ralph Ellison to write *The Invisible Man* without pursuing the "special interest" of race? Would he have suggested that Adrienne Rich purge her poetry of overt feminist impulses or that Gloria Anzaldúa rid *Borderlands* of its concern with representations of Chicana identity: i.e., leave these issues for politicizing readers to somehow uncover or invent for themselves? Framed this way, DeMaria's attempt at separating special interests from creative writers' interests—issues of culture from issues of craft—seems an outlandish proposition. Nonetheless it represents a rational extension of the approach he outlines, one that reduces creative writing to an isolated, oversimplified artistic pursuit.

We don't mean to single out DeMaria here. As we have suggested, his approach is commonplace within the field of creative writing, indicative of many handbooks' treatment of fiction and poetry. At the risk of being perhaps too cynical, we'd suggest that most handbooks have such similar perspectives on craft you could exchange one for another without noticing much of a difference. For instance, you might swap Janet Burroway's *Writing Fiction: A Guide to Narrative Craft* for Ursula LeGuin's *Steering the Craft* or Douglas Bauer's *The Stuff of Fiction: Advice on Craft* and find radically similar theoretical orientations, minimal variations in subject matter, and only slight disparities in approach. One book might offer a more substantial discussion on point of view or character development, for example; otherwise, their restrictive concentration on elements of craft remains remarkably similar.

Frankly, we find that writers of handbooks or guidebooks not only offer incredibly similar approaches to craft but also go out of their way to isolate creative writing from other pursuits in radically similar ways. Novelist Francine Prose offers insight to this problem in *Reading Like a Writer: A Guide for People Who Love Books and for Those Who Want to Write Them*. When reflecting on her teaching career, Prose advises readers that one of her favorite classroom experiences involved conducting a "seminar for MFA students who wanted to be writers *rather than* scholars, which meant that it was all right for us to fritter away our time talking about books rather than politics or ideas" (10 our italics). Indeed, throughout her guidebook, Prose recommends approaches to study that allow writers to pleasantly "fritter away" their time by decidedly not doing the work of scholars or politicians or philosophers (among others) in language eerily akin to DeMaria's. For what it's worth, we too like to fritter away our time talking about books, but we're not sure we've ever been able to do so without also talking about ideas. In fact, our favorite conversations about books tend to involve big ideas—whether they intersect with scholarship or politics or philosophy or religion or science or economics or physics or cultural studies or architecture or robotics or the seemingly infinite intertextual representations of Schrödinger's cat. We're not sure, but we suspect that maybe the most interestingly bookish conversation we could possibly have would somehow cover all of these subjects. We are sure that the kind of insular mentality represented in the handbooks we've been discussing—an *either/or* approach to study that has been pervasive in the field of creative writing for too long—is exactly what we'd like to disrupt.

And we are not alone. For some time, contemporary authors have insisted on the need to disrupt this insularity because of its marginalizing effect—specifically on writers of color. In 2014, Junot Díaz famously identified the implicit racism in traditional, craft-centered pedagogy. His essay "MFA vs POC," which examined the conflict he experienced as a Person of Color (POC) enrolled in Cornell University's Master of Fine Arts (MFA) creative writing program, was reprinted in the *New Yorker*, where it garnered much attention. In the essay, Díaz states the problem this way:

> In my workshop we never explored our racial identities or how they impacted our writing—at all. Never got any kind of instruction in that area—at all. Shit, in my workshop we never talked about race except on the rare occasion someone wanted to argue that 'race discussions' were exactly the discussion a serious writer should *not* be having.

He goes on to suggest that if he and the two other writers of color enrolled in the program attempted to expand workshop conversations to issues of racial representation they would "be seen as politicizing the Pure Art and betraying the (White) Universal (no race) ideal of True Literature." Faced with this kind of discrimination, he and his colleagues of color felt ostracized. They were placed in a position of remaining silent, disrupting the ideological prohibitions of the workshop, or dropping out. Díaz admits to considering this final option nearly every day of the semester and laments the decision of one of his peers to do just that. Instead, Díaz finished the program and also co-founded an arts organization, Voices of Our Nation, designed specifically to support writers of color who might otherwise feel silenced or "othered" by traditional creative writing pedagogy. Whatever your feelings about Díaz (who was publicly implicated in sexual misconduct allegations at the time of this writing) there is no denying that when it appeared in the *New Yorker*, "MFA vs POC" brought significant public attention—perhaps more attention than ever before—to a problem that had been plaguing creative writing programs for decades.

Of course, the problem Díaz describes in his essay has not been limited to the context of MFA programs in the US. British poet Daljit Nagra recently suggested that he and other writers of color in the UK often feel pressure to "bleach ourselves to fit in" (qtd. in Flood). Novelist and professor Aminatta Forna, who has been instrumental in cultivating transnational approaches to creative writing at Bath Spa University, has called decisions *not* to discuss issues of race, sexuality, and gender in writing workshops "a dereliction of moral and creative duty" while deeming such avoidance an act of "implicit cowardliness" (qtd. in Flood).

Whether intended or not, the marginalizing *effect* of creative writing's prohibitive ideology—its *either/or* way of thinking—can be detrimental to emerging writers, particularly those who don't conform to the dominant or historical culture of the workshop. The intentional or inadvertent reproduction of this ideology in the vast majority of creative writing handbooks has real consequences; as you must have surmised by now, we'd like to offer a more inviting and inclusive approach to study. In fact, we've designed our anti-handbook specifically to provide a *both/and* alternative to the *either/or* way of thinking we feel is holding creative writers back from exploring greater possibilities of identity, innovation, and experimentation. If permitted enough poetic license to borrow (and bastardize) that wonderfully weird term from physics, we might, indeed, define our approach as "superpositional," in the sense that it asks emerging authors to construct inclusive identities for themselves, to imagine they are *both* creative writers *and* what other handbook authors have defined as *not* creative writers: that is, to imagine being writers *and* scholars, writers *and* critics, writers *and* "special interest readers," writers *and* politicians, writers *and* philosophers, writers *and* citizens of the world (among other identities). To this end, in the forthcoming pages, we place creative writing in relation to a range of broader subjects and contexts that include academic and popular culture, publishing markets, histories of ideas, composition scholarship, and interrogations of personal, professional, and larger social motivations for writing.

We don't shy away from addressing big ideas or asking big questions and we encourage you to examine a broad array of big issues as you engage with the book. In fact, we allow a mix of critical interrogation and creative thinking—as well as a significant amount of irreverence—to define our overall approach. As we do so, we often find ourselves inviting you to help us demythologize the strange restrictions, prohibitions, and inherited bits of misinformation that continue to confine creative writers to rather uncomfortable boxes. In some ways, our book is about this very process of unboxing and demythologizing, in the sense that much of its function is to untangle the lore we've inherited so that we can move forward more expansively. Through this process, we hope to reimagine "creative writing" and, along the way, liberate Schrödinger's cat from his conceptual confinement, allowing our furry friend a little more comfort and freedom.

In Section 1, we begin our project by asking you to reflect critically on where creative writing comes from. In the first chapter of this section, we explain how creative writing came to be considered a restrictive craft by examining the history of its development as an academic field of study. What may sound a little dry is really a sordid history of impossible beauty, propaganda wars, and strange pyramid schemes. (You'll see what we mean.) In Chapter 2, we examine where creative writing comes from in a more immediate and personal sense: i.e., where writers get inspiration and how they may or may not use this inspiration to develop their work. Along the way, we try to debunk the debilitating notion of spontaneous genius by examining the truth behind several Romantic creation myths. In Chapter 3, we place these creation myths in relation to contemporary theories of composition in an effort to determine more accurately how writers actually invent their poems and stories (less through impromptu visitations from a muse and more through deliberate processes of labor). Throughout this section, our discussion also includes forays into subjects that range from cinematic representations of authors to drug addiction, from genetic determinism to the fine art of bullshitting.

In Section 2, which consists of Chapters 4 and 5, we ask you to critically examine who creative writers are (or, at least, who they are *represented* as being) and how authorship functions in both theory and practice. By exploring the collaborative relationships between a number of historical and contemporary writers, we question the very idea or myth of single authorship to reveal the ways in which writers rely on others somewhat paradoxically to produce their own signature work. As we delve into this conversation, we draw from the fields of philosophy, literary theory, and composition-rhetoric to survey different kinds of implicit and explicit forms of collaboration. We also focus on readers' roles as authorial collaborators.

In Section 3, we shift our focus to offer an investigation of the ethics and economics of the literary marketplace. Too often we find that students go through an entire creative writing program without being offered an honest, extensive, and critical examination of the publishing industry. Here, we try to provide such a perspective to help you successfully navigate the worlds of journal and book publishing in ways that do not gloss over the darker sides of the industry or neglect the most recent beneficial developments in technology, production, and distribution. In Chapter 6, we address the question of how a great book is made a Great Book not simply by an author but by a whole network of people working in publishing and related industries. Then, building on this discussion, we devote the following three chapters to examining three major contexts for contemporary book and journal publishing. In Chapter 7, we look at the context of commercial publishing, discussing how authors become successful in this market. We examine strategies for finding an agent, networking with others, and marketing literature. In Chapter 8, we switch to the context of small, independent, and university-affiliated literary publishing. In this chapter, we survey typical acceptance rates, offer suggestions for placement strategies, and investigate the ethics of literary contests. In Chapter 9, we discuss options for self-publishing in relation to the market for ebooks. Here, we examine the stories of several writers who managed to make successful leaps from self- to commercial publishing and vice versa, paying heed to the rationale underlying the decisions that led them to move in either direction. We also compare authors' royalty rates and examine the increasing importance of social media on book sales.

In Section 4, which consists of one final chapter, we look toward the future of creative writing. Chapter 10 focuses specifically on how rapid developments in technology are expanding possibilities for understanding what exactly creative writing is and what functions it fulfills. Here, we look at how enhanced ebooks, augmented reality, global positioning systems, and other technologies have influenced writers to produce work that challenges and expands the genres of poetry, fiction, and creative nonfiction. We also discuss the social utility of this work, as we reveal how it is inspiring others to engage in more immediate action in the world.

Although we emphasize expansion and inclusion throughout our work, we need to confess our practical limitations. As we think we've made clear, what you will *not* find in the chapters described above is a conventional approach to the crafts of fiction and poetry. Because hundreds of creative writing handbooks already address formal issues of craft perfectly adequately, we did not feel a need to try to replicate their work here. In an effort to avoid redundancy, we have not attempted to offer any sort of "how-to" guide to the genres traditionally affiliated with creative writing. We recognize this may be too glaring an absence for some readers, and we suggest that if you are looking for such a guide, you supplement this book with a conventional handbook of your choice. A simple search on Google or Amazon or your library's databases will reveal dozens and dozens of options. Our work here is more about critically examining a subject of study in which students of creative writing are already engaged. In fact, we anticipate that the readers who will benefit most from this book are those who have already gained some experience with the kind of craft-driven pedagogy that dominates most introductory creative writing courses. In this sense, *Beyond Craft* is perhaps most suitable for a variety of upper division and graduate-level classrooms. It may also be useful for emerging writers who are not necessarily enrolled in a creative writing program but seek to understand more about the art and the industry of the enterprise. Similarly, it might be useful for those who have already graduated from an MFA program but find themselves still seeking to gain perspective on subjects they may not have discussed in their craft-dominated courses of study. Of course, we'd like think the book is suitable for just about anyone who would appreciate an honest look at the relationships among writing, authorship, and publishing.

Regardless of where exactly you find yourself in your pursuit of creative writing, we ask that you approach the issues raised in the following pages with an open mind and as much critical as creative faculty. As you've probably gathered by now, for us, being creative does not mean avoiding critical inquiry. In fact, we align ourselves with multitudes of writers throughout history who have used what we now call creative genres for critical purposes: novelists like Uptain Sinclair, who used fiction to reveal the plight of the working poor and effectively reform safety conditions in the US food industry, and poets like Anne Waldman and Jerome Rothenberg, who used poetry to criticize formal traditions of Western verse that refused to make room for verbal improvization, shamanistic turns of thought, and ritual chanting. Of course, we also align ourselves with the exceedingly few writers-turned-handbook-authors whose highly innovative work has challenged the prohibitions of mainstream creative writing pedagogy: writers like Rob Pope, whose handbook, *Textual Intervention*, extended the courtesy of cultural and political intervention to creative writing students through innovative rewriting exercises, and the late great June Jordan, whose *Poetry for The People* re-conceptualized the writing and performance of poetry as a form of co-taught grassroots community activism.

All of this is to say that like the authors we've just mentioned, we don't consider it particularly useful to discriminate between critical and creative forms of writing; instead, we find it preferable to merge the two into a critical-creative or creative-critical totality. And we'd like to invite you to use *Beyond Craft* for this express purpose. To that end, we've decided to conclude each of our chapters with an apparatus that asks you to respond creatively and critically to what you have just read. We've provided a sample of the apparatus below. As you'll notice, we offer several categories of response, including Discussion Questions, Writing Experiments, and Deep Readings. Within this context, we've opted not to restrict your responses to a particular genre. We feel that doing so would be unnecessarily confining, especially in an era of hybrid texts, hypertext, blogs, Tweets, cell phone novels, video poems, and increasingly frequent multimedia experiments that challenge creative writing's traditional classificatory systems on a regular basis. Instead, we tend to offer loose suggestions and let you choose what form or genre would work best for your needs. As we suggested earlier, we'd like to leave most of the major decision making to you.

That said, we do, of course, have our own biases and tastes and skewed perspectives, which permeate our work. We realize we'd be real hypocrites if we spent entire chapters being critical of others and their takes on the enterprise of creative writing without inviting you to be critical of us. For this reason, we've left a designated space between the discussion questions and writing experiments for you to insert your own questions and comments, which you might use to offer a dissenting opinion, point to problems in our work, raise an issue we neglected to discuss, or reflect on whatever issues you find relevant to the readings. We welcome your collaboration in this regard, as we hope our anti-handbook (which *is* and *isn't* a handbook) can move beyond a state of simply existing as a bound object or static screen to transform into a productive tool for dialogue and debate.

Discussion Questions

1. How have your previous experiences with creative writing handbooks or classes been reinforced or challenged by the ideas you've encountered here? Explain your thoughts on this issue—maybe through a list of innovative similes?

2. Throughout our introduction, we've called attention to some handbook authors' suggestions that creative writers should not consider themselves scholars, critics, or political activists. If you were a handbook author, would you feel comfortable issuing emerging authors this kind of advice? What about established writers? Why or why not? What issues of authority are at stake in your decision?

3. If you had to be a bit reductionist, what would you say is *the* most important thing creative writers need to learn or gain exposure to as they extend their studies and embark on their careers? In other words, what sort of material *should* creative writing handbooks cover?

Your Turn: Questions, Concerns & Creative-Critical Comments

1. ____________________

____

____

____

2. ____________________

____

____

____

3. ____________________

____

____

____

Writing Experiment

Develop a piece of creative writing—poem, story, or whatever genre you see fit—that remains exclusively concerned with craft. In other words, the work you produce must refrain from engaging with what DeMaria calls "special interests" and what Prose deems "politics or ideas." Better yet, it should remain entirely isolated from larger cultural arenas. While it may comment on its own use of aesthetic devices, it must not be seen as participating in scholarly pursuits, critical discourse, philosophical inquiry, or issues of argument/debate. Even if you think this is an impossible task, please do your best and produce some sort of text: i.e., come as close as you can to the ideal of aesthetic neutrality with something other than a blank page. After you've produced a draft, reflect on your work and try to determine (a) how and why you may have been able or unable to accomplish this goal and (b) how you felt during your process of writing. When you return to your class or your writing group, share your draft with others and ask if they can locate any areas of text that evoke issues transcending the boundaries of craft. After you've finished, reflect critically on this experience with your peers.

Deep Reading

1. We've provided a bleak outlook on the state of contemporary creative writing handbooks; in our estimation, very few adequately connect issues of craft to issues of culture. But maybe we've overlooked a number of resources or maybe more progressive handbooks have been published since the time of our writing. We certainly hope so, and we'd like to suggest you conduct some research of your own to affirm or contest our findings. Go online or to your library and peruse handbooks. Then, choose two or three that we haven't discussed here and read them critically. Note the structure and focus of each book. How many chapters address issues of craft (point-of-view, metaphor, plot, and so on) and how many appear to connect these issues to larger social and intellectual contexts? How different do the overall arrangements appear to be from book to book? How does each conceptualize the cultural value of writing creatively? Do the handbooks include any prohibitions akin to those found in the work of DeMaria and Prose? Ultimately, what do these texts suggest creative writers should or should not do?

2. If you are interested in further exploring what Díaz has characterized as the "MFA vs POC" conflict, we recommend Matthew Salesses's four-part serial essay, "Pure Craft is a Lie," on the *Pleiades* website. In each entry, Salesses uses a different lens to discuss the impossibility of genuinely isolating something

called "craft" from something called "culture." He not only explores the problem of workshop pedagogy from a minority perspective but also offers useful suggestions for change. You can find the first installment here: http://www.pleiadesmag.com/pure-craft-is-a-lie-part-1/. If hypertext installments aren't your thing, you can access the essay in Janelle Adsit's edited collection, *Critical Creative Writing*.

3. For a longer and more theoretical study of craft, you might consider Ben Ristow's *Nurturing Craft Consciousness and Artistic Practice in Creative Writing*. Ristow's views on craft differ substantially from the ideas we've presented here; he argues that an alternate understanding of craft—as a disruptive force in the arts—may lead toward a productive future for creative writing studies.

SECTION ONE

Where Creative Writing Comes From

1

From Art for Art's Sake to Craft for Craft's Sake:

Our Love-Hate Relationship with the Academic History of Creative Writing

You may have heard the phrase "art for art's sake" before, perhaps in a literature, art, or philosophy class. Maybe you associate the phrase with the work of Oscar Wilde, who famously quipped that "all art is quite useless" in his preface to *The Picture of Dorian Gray* (4). Maybe you've come across the idea in the philosophy of Kant, who is often credited for formally developing theories of artistic autonomy. And, whether you realize it or not, you've probably seen it at the movies many times: the Latin version of the phrase—*Ars Gratia Artis*—flanks the head of another famous cat: Metro Goldwyn Mayer's Leo, the roaring lion.

Clearly there are numerous articulations of this phrase (and its underlying suppositions) in academic and popular culture. While aestheticism was popularized in the latter half of the nineteenth century by writers like Oscar Wilde, Edgar Allan Poe, and Victor Cousin, who were reacting against the pervasiveness of didacticism and sentimentalism in the literature of their time, it has since come to represent a theory that suggests art should not necessarily be concerned with its own participation in larger cultural arenas. Art should simply exist. In other words, a theory of pure aesthetics treats what DeMaria calls "the highest kind of importance: the creation of beauty" (2) as an end in itself. Artists and writers who subscribe to this philosophy often claim that they are making art or creating beauty *instead of* participating in social, political, and economic arenas; they are artists, *not* ideologues.

And therein lies the beauty of paradox, or rather the paradox of beauty, as it were. To believe that an art like fiction or poetry exists only for the sake of being beautiful is, in fact, to subscribe to a kind of ideological belief. If we claim we are writing a poem, say, to express beauty as an end itself (a perfectly admirable motive), we are affiliating ourselves with a particular way of thinking that is not neutral, that has its own contested biases and historical traditions, and that also has its share of detractors and opponents. Indeed, whether we know it or not, the poem we write may echo the work of a previous advocate of aestheticism, say Archibald Mac Leish. His "Ars Poetica" famously argues that rather than engage in worldly communicative exchanges or cultural practices, a poem should remain as "mute / As a globed fruit" (1–2), a still and silent object of display that is to be properly admired and appreciated solely for the artistry of its construction—much like a still life painting. Or, as MacLeish states succinctly in his final couplet, "A poem should not mean / But be" (23–24). At the same time we may be echoing MacLeish, we may also be evoking a counter-position to his aestheticism, perhaps a figure like Chinua Achebe, who in the later twentieth century insisted that art is inevitably useful—as it fulfills functional purposes for the development of community—and who famously expressed his disdain for aestheticism in language equally poetic and crass: "*art for art's sake is just another piece of deodorized dog shit*" (29, his italics). Whether we intend to or not, we are conjuring up these positions and counter-positions (in some cases with alarming appeals to our senses). Through the practice of writing our hypothetical poem, we are entering into a dialogue with others—of different races, genders, classes, nationalities, and historical epochs than our own—who may have expressed similar or different ways of thinking. In no way are we able to isolate our pursuit of beauty, for in this pursuit we are inevitably collaborating with these

others or, at the very least, affiliating ourselves with their work in one way or another. Depending on how literally you take Achebe's words, you might say we are inadvertently stepping in a pile of it.

Whether we name our affiliation a political or "politicized" one, it inevitably affects and is affected by contested cultural arenas. In fact, we like to compare the paradox of aestheticism to the issue of attempted nonparticipation in democratic elections. Choosing not to affiliate art with politics is inevitably to make a political statement the way that choosing not to vote is inevitably to engage in a political act. Regardless of their intentions, citizens who do not cast their ballots affect the outcome of an election. In these cases, the very absence of individuals' votes may wind up being the determining factor in who is or is not elected. This, of course, is the reason that some candidates and organizations try to encourage low voter turnout through covert means of disenfranchisement when preliminary poll numbers do not appear to be in their party's favor. More simply put, trying to suggest that art can be isolated is sort of like trying to write the word *nonparticipation* without including its last five syllables.

Before we get too much further into our line of argument, we'd like to be clear about one thing: we love beauty. Seriously, we like to think that we pursue beauty relentlessly, not only in the paintings we choose to hang on our walls, in our (failed) efforts at feng shui, but also in the things we create: our gardens, our (failed) attempts to bake perfect cardamom-spiced carrot cakes, and, yes, our creative writing. That being said, when we think critically about beauty, especially as applied to writing or art, we don't quite understand how it can supposedly exist in a cultural vacuum or (to return to our unfortunate initial metaphor) be trapped like a cat inside a box. Here is the catch: Unlike the experiment of Schrödinger's cat, art for art's sake presupposes that beauty can be said to exist (or not exist) without the necessary consideration and complication of participant-observers: i.e., beholders looking into the box, people who occupy specific positions in culture and make decisions about what is and is not beautiful in this world based largely on their positions.

All of this is our rather longwinded way of saying that no matter how much proponents of aestheticism may want to walk or, better yet, dance right past the ballot boxes of the present or the salons, town squares, and agoras of the past, their waltzes and foxtrots—however artful and however seemingly isolated—have a larger effect in the world. Ultimately, art for art's sake (like a state of superposition) is a beautiful impossibility in a world that extends beyond the parameters of closed boxes. We might like to dwell in this mythology—in fact, the phrase *beautiful impossibility* has a utopian ring to our ears—but despite our best efforts we can't sustain the kind of isolation it would require. It simply is not possible. Of course, this hasn't stopped creative writing teachers from trying. As the paradox of Schrödinger's cat has set a precedent for experimentation in quantum physics, the beautiful impossibility of art for art's sake has defined the mythology of creative writing from its academic inception. In fact, the strength of aestheticism's foundational influence on creative writing serves to explain why the philosophy has had such a lingering effect—despite the impossibility of its assertions—on the discipline, its teaching materials, and its obsession with craft.

A Beautiful Impossibility: On Creative Writing's Formative Influences

Although the origins of creative writing in US academies may be traced as far back as the late nineteenth century, its modern history as an institutionalized fine art is usually located in the founding of the University of Iowa Writers' Workshops and the proliferation of New Criticism in the late 1930s. At Iowa, creative writing (known at the time as "imaginative literature") was initially instituted as a component of the university's PhD program in English, which, scholars have pointed out, offered a generous approach to study that also included language, literary history, and criticism (see Foerster, Graff, Mayers, and Myers). Students enrolled in the program attended a range of classes in these four areas and entered into a field of specialization only in their final year of coursework. As D G Myers states in *The Elephants Teach*, the program was designed for different "types of students—teachers, scholars, critics, *and* writers" (133, his italics).

However, shortly after creative writing appeared in the PhD curriculum, it was relocated to a new Master of Fine Arts program. Important to note here is the material and symbolic shift from the philosophical arena (a *both/and* approach to study) to the studio arts model (an *either/or* approach), which severed creative writing from other branches of inquiry, restricting the curriculum largely to poetry and fiction workshops designed exclusively for emerging poets and fiction writers. It was within the MFA program, a curricular model that had been the province of the visual and performing arts, that creative writing began to be formally practiced and conceptualized more exclusively as an artistic craft. In fact, the term *craft* seemed to enjoy a sudden omnipresence shortly after this shift. According to Wilbur Schramm, who directed the Iowa Writer's Workshops from 1939 to 1942, the new MFA program allowed students to approach one another's poems and stories "with the intelligent understanding of a fellow *craftsman* in order to see how others have met the common problems of the *craft* and to estimate the effectiveness of their solution" (165, our italics). This kind of specialization, perhaps useful and innovative, nonetheless signaled a defining separation of more narrowly focused issues of craft from larger theoretical issues of culture: it forced students to opt quite literally, in choosing their degree, for *either* fine art (MFA) *or* other forms of philosophical, cultural, and critical study (PhD).

The shift toward aestheticism that coincided with creative writing's attempt to establish its own separate identity was made possible by the work of the New Critics, a group of writers including Cleanth Brooks, Robert Penn Warren, John Crowe Ransom, Allen Tate, Donald Davidson, and others, who essentially made aestheticism into a way of understanding literature. Within the context of the 1930s, the New Critics reconceptualized literary studies (and in doing so helped to establish the discipline of creative writing) in part by pursuing two goals. First, they sought to effectively isolate "imaginative literature" from what they called the "contamination" of sentimentality, didacticism, and political discourse, or what they often referred to collectively as "propaganda." In this sense, they might be said to have extended the work of late nineteenth century aesthetes, although they were, of course, reacting to the literature and philosophy of their time. As Gerald Graff has pointed out, the 1930s "generated theories of art so crudely propagandistic that they made the separation of art from politics seem an attractive or even a necessary position" (146). For example, some Marxists of the time argued that all art should serve a political purpose, one that would, in the words of Bolshevik poet Vladimir Mayakovsky, "pull the republic out of the mud" (150).

Second, the New Critics sought to eliminate the excessive pedantry, or what they often referred to as "scientism," that in their view was corrupting the academic study of literature. By the way, if they could somehow time-travel into the present, they would surely detest our foray into physics; they'd likely try to stuff Schrödinger's cat back into his box, duct tape the lid shut, slap a stamp on the top, and mail him back to the Department of Natural Sciences and Mathematics.

At the time, however, their reaction against scientism may have made a little more sense. When it came to literature, English departments tended to offer what Jed Rasula calls "a philologically disposed" form of "historical scholarship" (74), a method of analysis that treated literary texts more as artifacts of linguistic, etymological, and historical interest than carefully crafted artistic texts worthy of study in their own right. In other words, scholars seemed to approach literary texts more as archaeological evidence—i.e., dead things used by scientists to understand dead cultures—than the soulful stuff of current human experience: artistic texts written by actual living, breathing people. Alan Tate's famous complaint reflected their position: "We study literature today from various historical points of view as if nobody intended to write any more of it" (qtd. In Schramm 179). By shifting the focus of analysis away from external factors and onto the ways in which authors used internal structural devices to produce what they deemed variously the "total effect" or "organic unity" of a piece of literature, New Critics like Tate helped to establish a field that would allow students to write more literature. However, in doing so, they also established trends that, in conjunction with the program at Iowa, would lead to the further isolation of craft.

Although the New Critics' approach may not have been as insular during its own era as it appears from a distance of history, it nonetheless had the effect of severing texts from their social and communicative contexts. This effect was achieved largely through an exclusive focus on the internal conventions or unity of "the text itself," a phrase that would become a New Critical mantra. Brooks and Warren articulated this approach in *Understanding Poetry* (1938), an influential anthology/textbook that functioned largely as a default creative writing handbook in an era when few handbooks existed (at least as we know them today). Explaining their approach, they write, "criticism and analysis as modestly practiced in this book and more grandly elsewhere by other hands, is ultimately of value *only insofar as it can return readers to the poem itself*" (16, their italics). To this end, they focus on devices of craft, or what they deemed "crucial elements": "metaphor, rhythm, and statement," for example, "absorbed into a vital unity" (11). After offering this orientation, they go on to downplay the communicative functions of poetry, opting instead to conceptualize the genre as if its quest for beauty or formal perfection begins and ends on the page: "The poem in its vital unity is a 'formed' thing, a thing existing in itself, and its vital unity, its form, embodies—is—its meaning" (11). In this fashion, they draw a symbolic border or box around the text, sustaining the illusion that in its aesthetic form, a poem can and should remain untarnished by social, political, cultural, or argumentative discourse, simple didactic interpretation, and the complications of worldly communicative exchange. In doing so, they echo Archibald MacLeish's "Ars Poetica," suggesting that internal artistic form trumps all.

Brooks rearticulates this ideology in his own scholarly writings. In *Modern Poetry and the Tradition*, he argues that "privacy and obscurity . . . are inevitable in all poetry" (60). He also faults poets who attempt to clearly address public concerns—to reach outside the closed box of the text itself—for corrupting their poetry. When discussing the work of W H Auden, for example, he states the following: "In general, Auden's poetry weakens as he tries to rely upon an external framework—a doctrine or ideology" (126). This might seem relatively tame, but Brooks even goes so far as to label poets like Langston Hughes and Genevieve Taggard, who attempted to use their work to intervene in social affairs, as "propagandists" (51). In fact, he "convicts" them for being "*preoccupied* with the inculcation of a particular message" (49 our italics)—much the way DeMaria would, decades later, fault "special interest readers" for being "*preoccupied*" with representations of race, ethnicity, and gender. While we don't want to exaggerate the influence of New Critical thinking, we find ourselves awed by the extent of its reach across decades: the echoes here are strikingly evident (even down to the level of diction).

In fact, we find the New Critics' "convicting" of "propagandists" a foundational example of the kind of discrimination that Junot Diaz and other writers of color would find still lingering in late twentieth and early twenty-first century articulations of the creative writing workshop. In other words, the example of Brooks ostracizing a gay man (Auden), a black man (Hughes), and a socialist woman (Taggard) represents what would result in the legacy that Daljit Nagra, Aminatta Forna, Matthew Salesses and many other writers have deemed a discrediting of minority authors under the guise of Art. You might say that the history of the Iowa/New Critical alliance, indeed, laid the groundwork for the "MFA vs POC" conflict.

Let's Make this Personal, or at Least More Personal Than a Proselytizing Machine

Although we find it somewhat astonishing that Brooks's rallies against larger social discourse can be unconsciously rearticulated roughly 75 years later in nearly the exact phrasing, we do not find it particularly surprising that the combined force of New Criticism and the Iowa Workshops had such a profound influence on the early stages of creative writing's development. As writers ourselves, we understand how appealing a focus on the internal aesthetic devices of literature must have been to aspiring fiction writers and poets who were attempting to learn their craft under the auspices of "scientism" and without the support of a writer-friendly systematized form of study—the kind of creative writing track or program you can find today at most universities. In a sense, the shift New Criticism offered was rather revolutionary—perhaps ironically revolutionary for a group that attempted to isolate the study of imaginative literature from larger cultural practices—and the implementation of this approach at Iowa seemed to fill a significant educational need.

But we grew up in a different era, during the radical expansion of creative writing, and entered the profession after the system established at Iowa had already become, in the words of D G Myers, "a machine for creating more and more creative writing programs" (146) through a system that he refers to as "institutionalized proselytism" (164). With a tone that combines the echoes of Fordist industrialism with the language of religious conversion, Myers may appear to exaggerate the trajectory of expansion; nonetheless, his statement reflects the pace and fervor with which creative writing workshops based on the Iowa model spread throughout the country. In "How Iowa Flattened Literature," Eric Bennet describes the phenomenon this way: "More than half of the second-wave programs, about 50 of which appeared by 1970, were founded by Iowa graduates." He continues: "Third- and fourth- and fifth-wave programs, also Iowa scions, have kept coming ever since." In other words, programs based on the Iowa model and New Critical paradigm were reproduced, some might say (adopting a slightly different tone), *ad nauseam*.

Perhaps we are being too harsh in our choice of words. We are certainly being too Latin. But the judgment of what might be deemed creative writing's overexpansion, however deserved or undeserved, is not limited to our perspective. It has been suggested by Iowa insiders. Reflecting on his experience as director of the Iowa Workshops, Donald Justice describes the phenomenon this way: "Those who went through Iowa went out and took part in other writing programs—a kind of pyramid scheme it seems now, looking back" (qtd. in Myers 164–165). This "pyramid scheme" is an apt way to characterize the phenomenal growth of the craft-dominated workshop. Between 1967 and 2013, the institutional membership of the Association of Writers and Writing Programs (i.e., the number of colleges and universities with creative writing programs that signed on as AWP members) grew from 12 to over 500 ("Our History"). Currently, the total number of creative writing programs (whether affiliated or unaffiliated with AWP) exceeds 800 ("Guide"). 203 of these are MFA programs, which range in size from 7 to 200 students and collectively graduate thousands of new MFAs each year ("MFA Programs"). Regardless of whether these numbers point to a wildly successful enterprise or what will soon be an approaching bubble and subsequent crash, they make it is easy to see how a system of expansion that at least one former director has likened to a Ponzi scheme would buttress the authority of the Iowa Workshop model and spread the influence of its approach to craft.

Beyond Aesthetic Ascetics & Their Pyramid Schemes

Although Iowa's approach to craft became the dominant paradigm for creative writing in the US, its authority has been at least somewhat decentralized. As you might suspect, even if many creative writing programs were founded by Iowa graduates and based on New Critical approaches to learning, some must surely have evolved into their own distinct identities and begun to reproduce variant approaches to study. It would seem difficult for Iowa to retain control of its pyramid scheme, given the proliferation of other programs and their potential growth away from the foundational model. And, in fact, a kind of diversification began taking place near the end of the twentieth century when reformers started producing scholarship that reacted to the limitations of creative writing's restrictive focus on craft. Edited collections of this time period were mostly comprised of reflections on creative writing pedagogy (Moxley, Bishop and Ostrom), and evidenced a group of scholars concerned with advancing the theory and practice of teaching. Further scholarship treated creative writing as a complex site of scholarly inquiry, mapping out the history, politics, and processes of the field (Bishop, Haake, Myers).

Several articles from the 1990s reveal the tenor of the early reform movement. In "Notes from a Cell: Creative Writing Programs in Isolation," Eve Shellnut criticized creative writing for attempting to maintain a purely craft-driven, aesthetic approach to study and called for workshop instructors to collaborate with theorists in composition-rhetoric and literary studies in order to better examine "the methods by which subtle social and political affects are or can be expressed in imaginative writing" (19). In "The Book in the World," Valerie Miner advocated a generous both/and approach to study that combined the Iowa workshop model with what she called "literary fieldwork." In the class she described, titled Social Issues in Publishing, students divided their time between classroom days and fieldwork days. During the former, they would discuss conventions of craft in their own and each other's writing, and during the latter they would observe and investigate the culture of the book publishing industry first-hand by working as what might be described as intern-ethnographers. By performing their assigned duties at various presses or literary nonprofits and writing field notes based on their experiences, they gained a practical understanding not only of the business and economics of creative writing, but also of the collaboration among writers, agents, editors, and publishers, which functions to produce books within specific cultural networks. Finally, in his playfully titled "Emily Dickinson, Madonna, Boomers, Busters, the Old Criterion, and the New Millennium," Martin Schecter argued in favor of more expansive approaches to learning as applied to the genre of fiction. He sought to emphasize connections between the craft of narrative and what he called "concerns of economic, class, or cultural positioning" (15)—precisely those out-of-the-box issues that had been relegated too quickly to other specialties.

Although met with resistance, these and other reformers created scholarship that called for a shift in the way creative writing might be conceived for the new millennium. Taken collectively, their efforts led gradually toward bolder experiments with creative writing pedagogy and a more extensive body of scholarship in the discipline. As inquiry into the teaching and practice of creative writing grew and diversified, it developed into a field of its own: "Creative Writing Studies." This slight but significant change in terminology signified a more self-reflective, theoretically-informed, and expansive understanding of creative writing, in which scholar-practitioners wrote—and *researched*—creatively.

These scholar-practitioners built on the the work of earlier reformers through diverse and variegated approaches to study: some dug deeper into the history of creative writing programs in the United States (McGurl, Glass, Bennet), while others analyzed the institutional position of creative writing (Mayers, Shivani). Still others worked to update the field's understanding of its relationship to ever evolving technologies (Clark et. al., Koehler, Hergenrader, Farman), or built on early critiques of the politics of the workshop to examine creative writing through an intersectional lens, studying the ways cultural identities (e.g., race, class, gender, orientation, ability) matter to writers and the writing process (Mura, Rankine et al, Quan-Lee, Adsit). Of course, many scholars continued in the tradition of early researchers and advanced the field's understanding of pedagogy (Ritter and Vanderslice, Leahy, Peary and Hunley).

While these (mostly) American authors were expanding the scholarly study of creative writing, educators in Australia and the UK were professionalizing the field, leading to the production of peer-reviewed journals like *TEXT* and *NEW WRITING*, and to the launch of *New Writing Viewpoints*, a peer-reviewed book series. Professionalization of creative writing in the United States has largely been overseen by the Association of Writers and Writing Programs (AWP), which, historically, has taken a dim view of the utility of scholarship and theory for creative writers (see Fenza or, more recently, Leahy "Against"). But recent developments outside of the AWP have pushed US-based Creative Writing Studies in a scholarly direction. The peer-reviewed *Journal of Creative Writing Studies* launched in 2016, with the support of the newly formed *Creative Writing Studies Organization* (CWSO) and its annual conference. Shortly thereafter, Bloomsbury Academic and CWSO launched a peer-reviewed book series, *Research in Creative Writing*. These developments, along with AWP's gradual warming to creative writing scholarship, has led to the international growth of Creative Writing Studies.

Toward Programatic Change

In addition to re-envisioning creative writing scholarship, the reform movement also contributed to the creation of innovative academic programs. For several decades now the University at Buffalo, State University of New York, has been offering graduate students an alternative to the traditional MFA workshop model. Its expansive Poetics Program attempts to overcome the historic rift between fine art and philosophy by combining cultural theory with poetic practice. In a holistic approach that echoes Iowa's early PhD offering, the program investigates the way creative writing "scrutinizes and activates language as a medium that materializes history and power and forms the very frames of perception and consciousness" ("Poetics"). The university's current certificate program in Innovative Writing provides students an opportunity to "reflect on the ethical and political implications of creative writing within the matrix of global citizenship; tease out evident and obscured connections between contemporary and historical texts; consider how aesthetic concerns are inflected by various systems of power" ("Innovative"). Other programs have followed Buffalo's lead. On the undergraduate level, Cal State Monterey Bay has been offering students a concentration in Creative Writing and Social Action since 2004. The program "brings together the study of creative expression, culture, communication, and community involvement" ("Creative")—an echo of June Jordan's Poetry for the People and a far cry from the insularity of "the text itself" or the prohibitions offered by New Critics and their fellow "craftsmen."

In addition to these academic alternatives are two summer programs run by nonprofit literary service organizations and designed specifically for writers of color. Cave Canem's annual retreat offers a weeklong series of workshops to "black poets of African decent, ages 21 and over." The founding mission of Cave Canem, which was established by Toi Derricotte and Cornelius Eady, was to "remedy the under-representation and isolation of African American poets in the literary landscape" (*Cave Canem*). Indeed, the summer retreat provides a strong and supportive alternative to the limited perspective of the traditionally white MFA workshop, offering a unique space for African American poets to build community while "writing without fear of censure or the need to defend subject matter or language—an intellectual and physical site where they validate their own and their peers' voices" (*Cave Canem*). The Voices of Our Nation Arts Foundation (VONA) was founded in 1999 with a somewhat similar goal for a more expansive population. The organization's mission is to "change the landscape of the literary world by supporting writers-of-color through workshops, mentorship, community building, and information sharing." VONA continues to bill its summer workshop program as "the only multi-genre workshop for writers of color in the nation" (*Voices*). Of course, this billing reveals a significant problem in the broader culture. While reformers attempt to make their universities' creative writing programs more inclusive and welcoming to diverse populations of writers, VONA remains the *only* multi-genre workshop designed specifically for writers of color.

If you're interested in alternatives to mainstream notions of creative writing (and we think you probably are if you've picked up this book), we suggest that you familiarize yourself with some of the texts and programs mentioned above. Taken collectively, they have effectively worked to bust the myth that emerging writers should be interested only in a limited understanding of craft. Although still somewhat on the fringes, they have opened up a space for us and others to start treating students of creative writing more respectfully, and more like actual authors: i.e., living, breathing people who write for a tremendous variety of reasons that extend well beyond the ambition to make something beautiful and mute. In other words, they remind us to acknowledge the complications of life and career and subject position and survival that motivate writers to create and enable them to produce their art. As the example of just two contemporary authors suggests, these motives tend to involve a vast amalgam of personal, professional, economic, and cultural issues. Mary Karr has stated the following about her authorial ambition: "I write to dream; to connect with other human beings; to record; to clarify; to visit the dead. I have a kind of primitive need to leave a mark on the world. Also, I have a need for money." (qtd. in Maran 107). In contrast, Armistead Maupin has suggested "Sometimes I write to explain myself to others. Thirty-four years ago I told my folks I was gay through the 'Tales of the City' character Michael Tolliver . . . When Michael came out in a letter to his parents, my own parents were the ones who got the message" (qtd. in Maran 130).

Can you imagine "convicting" these authors as "propagandists" for being "preoccupied" with worldly issues like financial security and sexual identity? Can you imagine being condemned in a similar fashion because of your own motives for writing? Neither can we. And, despite what many conventional handbooks might suggest, neither can many creative writers of our generation.

As we move away from our inheritance of the New Critical/Iowa paradigm and toward more diversified and inclusive approaches to creative writing, we continually look for ways to free ourselves from the strangleholds of aestheticism so that we may move beyond the artistry of "the text itself" and reach outward to examine other myths and truths and topics for debate. In fact, now that we've examined how the academy has shaped our ideological understanding of craft, we'd like to put this whole topic behind us, or at least put it to bed for a while. To this end, we'd like to personify Craft, give it its own king-sized mattress, luxurious 1000-thread-count sheets, and a whole bottle of Ambien, so we can move on to other, perhaps more interesting topics—most immediately the question of where authors' personal creativity comes from. We'll take up this subject in our next chapter while Craft sleeps so soundly we're not able to tell whether it's living or dead.

Discussion Questions

1. How has creative writing been presented to you during your history as a student—as an art, a craft, something else entirely? According to your current university or community of writers, what is creative writing? How and why do people do it?

2. Why do *you* write? We're not necessarily looking for confession or drama or the profundity of an ultimate answer here; rather, we are asking for a sincere and critical exploration of your motives. What are some reasons that might include but also extend beyond the act of creating something beautiful?

3. In the introduction and again in this chapter, we've taken issue with DeMaria's suggestion that writers are not "special interest readers," because we think that issues of race, class, and gender affect all writers. How has your race, class, or gender affected your relationship to writing? How has it shaped your feelings about what it means to be a writer? What sort of "special interest" writer are you?

4. What was your understanding of creative writing's history before reading this chapter? Why do you think it might be important (or not important) for emerging authors to be exposed to this history?

Your Turn: Questions, Concerns & Creative-Critical Comments

1. ______________________________

____

____

____

2. ______________________________

____

____

____

3. ______________________________

____

____

____

Writing Experiments

1. We've referred to Archibald MacLeish's "Arts Poetica" a number of times in this chapter. Please read the poem in its entirety—it's brief and available for free online. Then, ask yourself how your ideas about the function of creative writing support, intersect, or contradict MacLeish's argument. Write a brief "Arts Poetica" of your own in response to MacLeish's work. If you don't feel like remaining in the genre of poetry, take the liberty of considering MacLeish's argument as relevant to the field of creative writing as a whole and apply this exercise to the genre of your choice. Whatever form your writing takes, you should respond to and argue with MacLeish's work in language that is critical, precise, and creative. In short, your work should "be" *and* "mean."

2. We grappled with a serious problem while writing this chapter. Although it was not our intention, when we discussed the foundational influence of Iowa and the New Critics on the development of creative writing, we may have

silenced alternative histories. We didn't want to present the Iowa/New Critical alliance as a monolithic affair; at the same time, however, we didn't want to underplay its overwhelming impact on creative writing's dominant form of pedagogy. Further, the histories available for us to draw upon were severely limited. Only within the last several years have scholars called for more expansive representations of creative writing's past. In her 2016 article in the *Journal of Creative Writing Studies*, "Inclusion and Diversity: A Manifesto and Interview," Tonya Hegamin articulates a need to reexamine the contemporary creative writing classroom as "a direct product of grassroots community activism" with precedents in "The Harlem Renaissance, the Black Arts Movement, Beat Poetry, Spoken Word, Feminist, Queer and Disability Studies" (3). Unfortunately for us, this history has yet to be written and, hence, we could not rely on it. Fortunately for you, this history has yet to be written, and you have an incredible opportunity to write a version of it! We invite you to do so through the following method. First, select a creative writing program to examine—maybe the one in which you are enrolled? Then, instead of tracking the Iowa influence, look into how one of the grassroots movements Hegamin mentions (or doesn't mention) has influenced it. How has queer studies or spoken word played a role in shaping this program? What influence from Disability Studies or the Black Arts Movement might you reveal? To conduct this research, you may need to interview faculty members and cull texts from institutional archives. Whatever your methods, tell this program's untold story.

Deep Reading

In "The Affective Fallacy," New Critics W K Wimsatt and M C Beardsley argue against the notion that the meaning of literature lies outside of the printed page. In Chapter 5 of his book, *Literature and Revolution*, Leon Trotsky argues against Formalism (a school of thought with sensibilities similar to those of New Criticism) and in favor of the "social dependence and social utility of art." In "Africa and Her Writers," Chinua Achebe argues that art exists neither for its own sake nor for the sake of the State; instead, art exists as a feature of community. Hunt down these sources, read them and consider their arguments. How is each author responding to the claims of the others? Find and articulate your own position in this debate. You might also consider how each author's perspective would direct your own creative process. How would your writing practice be different if you agreed wholeheartedly with Wimsatt and Beardsley, or with Trotsky, or with Achebe?

2

Smoke Dispersed in the Ether: Authors' Creation Myths and the Problem with Genius

Have you ever seen the movie *Wonder Boys*? It's a film based on Michael Chabon's novel of the same title. We suggest you take a look. In the meantime, we'll fill you in on the important parts, or at least the aspects of the film relevant to our work in this chapter. The story centers on the character of Grady Tripp, a novelist and creative writing teacher who is struggling to complete his second book. Despite the exigency of this task—his editor has just flown into town expecting to receive a completed manuscript—he spends the vast majority of his time getting high. In fact, he dedicates so much more of his energy to smoking pot than he does to actually writing that he has trouble producing a fluid, comprehensible text, let alone a finished, saleable manuscript. As we get to know Grady's backstory, we come to understand that if the activity of smoking pot may have served as inspiration for writing his first novel (THC functioning, perhaps, as his chemical muse), it has since turned into a debilitating habit. Through a comedic focus on Grady's struggles, failures, and farcical escapades, the film lampoons popular notions about artistic temperament, authorship, and inspiration, poking fun at aphorisms like "the book will write itself" and "genius can't be rushed." Much to Grady's chagrin, the former statement turns out to be decidedly false, and the notion of a *bona fide* genius is proven to be an antiquated delusion.

At the source of the film's parody is a problematical but widely circulated myth about how literature gets written, one that downplays the actual activity of writing and favors the mystique of inspiration over the hard work of what writing scholars call "invention," the means by which writers discover and refine their ideas. By "myth" we mean the notion that good writers, by definition, are so at ease with the process of writing that their acts of creation are nearly effortless, a notion that dates at least to the European Romantic legacy of the late eighteenth and early nineteenth centuries. Since that time, it has—despite its problems—shaped popular perceptions of the ways writers work and how their texts come into being. In this chapter, we offer a brief examination of this myth through three case studies of famous authors and explore its implications for contemporary students of creative writing.

Who Cares about Genius? A Necessary Disclaimer

Before we get into our case studies, we have to admit that we've made a big assumption in writing this chapter: namely, that the myth of genius would be one worth debunking for you. We figured that most of you would have been exposed to this myth at some point and that many of you grew up within a culture that supports it. But we acknowledge that, for many writers around the world, the idea of a literary genius—a solitary author independently and effortlessly producing literature in a fit of inspiration—is both strange and foreign. The Anglophone literary tradition to which our case studies belong is only one of many global possibilities; other traditions offer radically different ideas about creativity. For example, in "Language and Literature from a Pueblo Indian Perspective," Leslie Marmon Silko describes a notion of invention that is far removed from the legacy of Romanticism. Instead of thinking of poems and stories as the result of an exotic source of inspiration or having come from the exceptional mind of a gifted individual, the Pueblo treat literature as one of the ordinary collective forces that holds their culture together. The stories the Lagunas tell—from their Creation story to that of a veteran's red Volkswagen falling into a ravine—all root the people of their Pueblo together in a shared, common history. Literary work in this tradition is not the work of solitary, spontaneous "genius," but a customary practice emerging from and within the long, collective narrative of the Laguna Pueblo's life.

The Mbari Club—a collective of writers, artists, and musicians—offers an historical and distinctively Nigerian perspective equally removed from Romantic constructions of genius. Here, Wole Soyinka, Chinua Achebe, and other authors who came to international attention in the latter half of the twentieth century pursued an Igbo-inspired approach to arts and arts-education that aimed to reflect "the total life of the community" (Achebe 33). In many senses, these authors modeled their approach to literary production on the Igbo tradition of *mbari*, a cultural/religious festival of art and architectural production that draws participants from various sectors of Igbo society in an effort to reflect the culture's "startling power and diversity" (Achebe 33). In this model, no single, special soul suddenly burps forth artistic gems; rather, a whole society comes together, drawing on its rich variety of life experiences, and labors to build something together.

Perspectives like those of the Pueblo and Igbo provide welcome antidotes to the kind of thinking we critique in this chapter, which is entangled in all the cultural baggage of the Euro-US tradition. Writers like Leslie Marmon Silko and Chinua Achebe did not grow up in literary traditions that supported this myth, and maybe you didn't either. If so, you may find that we spend a lot of time in this chapter arguing for something that you already find obvious. Please bear with us. Even if the myth of genius is not entirely pervasive, we nonetheless find value in debunking it for a number of reasons, including its continued (read *frustrating*) presence in many literary scenes, its use to preserve power for established authors (at the expense of others), and its potential for perpetuating problems like writer's block, self-doubt, and drug abuse—particularly among emerging writers. With that disclaimer out of the way, let's turn to a legacy of magic and lies.

Drug-Addled Daydreams and Literary Marketing Schemes

When Samuel Taylor Coleridge published "Kubla Khan" in 1816, he attached a preface that explained its composition, claiming that he offered the poem "rather as a psychological curiosity, than on the ground of any supposed *poetic* merits." Coleridge tells us (in the third person) that "the Author, then in ill health, had retired to a lonely farmhouse" and imbibed an "anodyne," or medicinal tincture, for his "slight indisposition." Coleridge reports then falling into a deep sleep while reading "Purchas's Pilgrimage," a volume of travel writing he'd brought with him. Dreaming for three hours about the foreign places he'd read about, "all the images rose up before him as *things*," he tells us, "with a parallel production of the correspondent expressions, without any sensation or consciousness of effort" ("Of the Fragment" 52, his emphasis). According to this account, a poem of some 200 lines appeared to him in his dream. It came to him fully formed, as a sublime vision. He didn't need to struggle with ideas or engage in multiple brainstorming sessions; he didn't need to arrange or outline the components of his project; he didn't need to bounce his ideas off an audience or solicit feedback from colleagues or mentors; he didn't even need to make conscious choices. He merely had to expend the energy to pick up his pen and drag it across the page as the poem wrote itself almost automatically.

Coleridge reports that he began "instantly and eagerly" transcribing the poem from memory on awakening from his dream. However, he was soon interrupted by a caller, who detained him on business. When he returned to write, Coleridge found that the poem had vanished irretrievably from his mind "like the images on the surface of a stream into which a stone has been cast" ("Of the Fragment" 53). And so all that remains of "Kubla Khan," one of Coleridge's most famous works, is a fragment of 54 lines, a small piece of the poem that initially came to him whole and unadulterated. The complete work, the *real* "Kubla Khan," known only once to the poet during his moment of extraordinary psychic clarity—before the mundane tasks of the ordinary world interrupted him—has been lost forever.

For creative writers, the value of this "psychological curiosity" should be evident. In describing his fantastical process, Coleridge suggests that poems—even what might become famous, canonical ones—can be written without any effort on the poet's part. The normal work of invention, drafting, and revision, of forming and reforming language, of configuring and reconfiguring ideas, of struggling with the labor of writerly and editorial decision-making, is altogether unnecessary. Good, authentic, true poems (sort of like telepathic messages) simply show up ready-made when the author is in the right frame of mind to receive them. If we were to extend Coleridge's logic to contemporary reality, we might advise aspiring writers not to study the craft of poetry or dedicate themselves diligently to MFA programs, but rather to imbibe strange medicinal tinctures and perhaps join the Psychic Friends Network. Through this combination, they might learn to engage in whatever sort of New Age psychic brain exercises might prepare their minds for the reception of fully-formed literary texts.

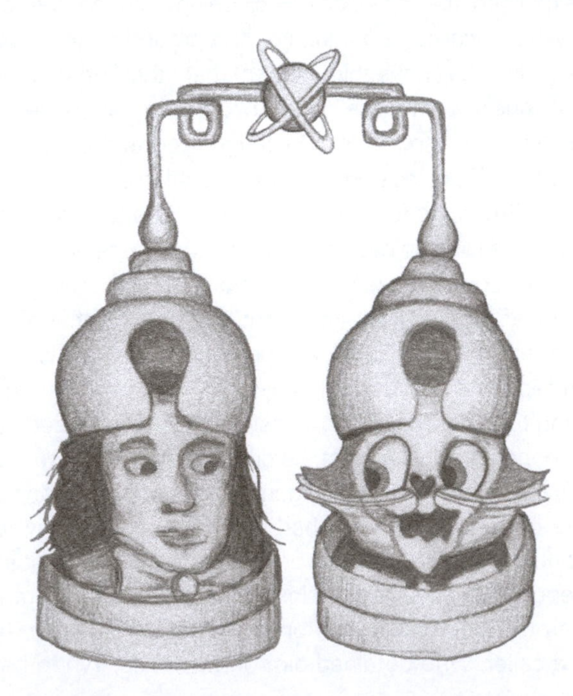

Frivolity aside, the idea of spontaneous, subconscious composition is a compelling one, as it captures the aspect of creativity that is not wholly volitional. In fact, Coleridge's explanation of his work's mystical origin functioned as a means of promoting the poem. The sense of mystery the preface cultivated gave the poem a certain cultural cachet, elevating it from an ordinary product of social and literary discourse to a sublime, authentic creation, one that tapped into the poet's natural, unconscious psychic abilities. As critic Raymond Wilson suggests, this is, in fact, what "led to the poem's being highly valued . . . Just *because* the poem was 'A Vision in a Dream' and not at all the product of conscious composition, it came to be regarded as an example of indisputably authentic inspiration" (xxxviii, his emphasis). In a sense, this characterization of the poem functioned as an enticing marketing vehicle. If you'll permit us to apply a contemporary advertising slogan anachronistically, we might say "Kubla Khan" was the Coca Cola of early nineteenth-century literature: The Real Thing™. Or at least, its preface enabled it to be sold as such—if not as a kind of hyper-authentic flavor, then as a kind of hyper-authentic literary voice—a tactic that would appeal not only to literary circles of the era, but also to readers and writers of generations to come. As Wilson notes, "Its prestige rose when, in the second half of the nineteenth century, a cult of 'Art for Art's sake' prevailed" and this prestige continued to rise further into the twentieth-century when "theories of psychology, with their emphasis on the unconscious and the value of dreams captured the popular imagination" (xxxviii). As Wilson suggests, Coleridge's description of his visit to the lonely farmhouse has inspired many twentieth and twenty-first century writers to carry his proverbial torch (or bottle of tincture, as it were) and keep his notions of creativity alive—however Real™, surreal, or unreal these notions might, in fact, be.

Benes and Magic Scrolls: the Romantic Creation Myth meets the Beats

A young, aspiring Jack Kerouac could well have been channeling Coleridge when he sat in his apartment in Chelsea in April of 1951 with a long, assembled scroll of paper loaded into his typewriter. In three short weeks, he composed a novel of 125,000 words, which is a pace of roughly 6,000 words per day. (Good luck trying to top that during NaNoWriMo.) As the story goes, Kerouac made use not of a mysterious anodyne but of Benzedrine, one of the more popular stimulants of his era, to stay glued to his task. Each line of *On the Road*, the novel that would transform him from an aspiring writer to a household name, was composed on the spot, in an act of pure spontaneity.

Writing about the novel later for *The Village Voice*, Kerouac's friend, the poet Alan Ginsberg, called this act of writing "a flash of inspiration on a new approach to prose, an attempt to tell completely, all at once, everything on his mind . . . spill it all out at once and follow the convolutions of the active mind." In Ginsberg's thinking, and in the hearts of the novel's many fans, the work was made especially authentic by its spontaneous production. Its literary value was a result of its raw, unfiltered expression of the author's mind. In other words, it, too, was marketed and perceived as The Real Thing™.

Capitalizing on this notion of authenticity—one remarkably similar to that found in Coleridge's preface—Kerouac later released guidelines for his fabled writing process. He promoted these guidelines under the name "Belief and Technique for Modern Prose," which included pointers like "Something that you feel will find its own form" and "Struggle to sketch the flow that already exists intact in your mind" and "You're a Genius all the time" (59). These statements are, of course, just the kind of affirmations that, looking backward, would have been welcome among the Romantic poets of Coleridge's time, and, looking forward, would provide fodder for parody in the film *Wonder Boys*.

Coleridge's Wake-up Call and Kerouac's Long, Slow *Road*

While these descriptions of subconscious, spontaneous composition may be alluring, they do not hold too closely to the facts, for *neither Coleridge nor Kerouac actually wrote their work in the manner described*. The stories they tell about their process of literary creation are, in a word, *bullshit*. In Coleridge's case, we know that his writing process was different from that stated in his preface because in 1934, the Marquis of Crewe loaned an early manuscript of the poem to the National Portrait gallery in London. This version of "Kubla Khan," known now as the "Crewe manuscript," offered a different, more succinct description of the poem's composition: "This fragment with a good deal more, not recoverable, composed, in a sort of Reverie brought on by two grains of Opium taken to check a dysentery, at a Farm House between Porlock & Linton, a quarter of a mile from Culbone Church, in the fall of the year, 1797" (Shelton).

You may have already suspected that the "anodyne" and "dream" of Coleridge's 1816 preface were euphemisms; here, Coleridge makes it evident that the anodyne was opium and the dream was the "reverie" brought on by that drug. Far more important than the accurate identification of the drug is the following revelation: the Crewe manuscript includes variants of several lines and shows clearly that Coleridge revised his poem. For example, line 6, which in the Crewe Manuscript reads "So twice six miles of fertile ground," becomes "So twice five miles of fertile ground" in the published version, a change that adds a touch of consonance to the line. Line 7 of the Crewe Manuscript reads "With Walls and Towers were compass'd round." In the published version, Coleridge changed "compass'd" to "girdled," a tighter, more intimate choice. In line 41, the name of a mountain changes from "Amara," a location also referenced in Milton, to "Abora," which exists nowhere else in literature. Line 17 of the Crewe Manuscript is particularly interesting, because it contains an edit in progress. The line reads "And from this chasm with hideous Turmoil seething," but the words "And from" have been crossed out and the words "From forth" written in their stead. The published version undoes this change and makes another, swapping "ceaseless turmoil" for "hideous."

These may not seem like earth-shaking changes. In fact, the general structure and narrative of the poem remain similar from Crewe to publication. Our point is not that there is a huge difference between these manuscripts but that there is *any difference at all*. This poem was supposed to have been delivered in a dream state, perfect and fully formed, but if that were the case, Coleridge would not have needed to tinker with the meaning and music of his lines. From our own efforts at poetry, we know all too well how much work goes into the process of reworking verse. We know what it means to decide we don't like the sound of a line or the general look of a poem on the page. We might decide in such a moment, for example, that a poem needs to be split into more stanzas (the published version contains one more stanza break than the Crewe Manuscript), or that we've simply used too many apostrophes, or that "Kubla" looks much better next to "Khan" than "Cubla" does (the latter is the spelling of the Crewe Manuscript). These choices represent the mind of an author in the process of revision, an author who wanted to refine his work to make sure it was presented in its best form—not in its first draft or initial articulation. "Kubla Kahn," then, was not formed whole and perfectly in Coleridge's subconscious mind; rather, the poet was inebriated, produced some sort of draft, and then sobered up and went about the actual work of writing poetry. He reconsidered the meaning, sound, and meter of his lines and revised them. If the date listed on the manuscript is not mistaken, nineteen years passed between his first draft at the farmhouse in 1797 and the poem's publication in 1816, and while we don't know for certain at what point during this window Coleridge produced the Crewe Manuscript, we think it's fair to assume that this was not his only other draft.

Coleridge was no stranger to fabricating stories about his writing process. In his biography of Coleridge, scholar Norman Fruman enumerates a host of lies the poet told about his work. Coleridge included stanzas of already-written poems in letters to friends, stating that he composed them during the act of writing the letter. He claimed that his poem "To a Friend" had "flowed from

[his] Pen extemporaneously," even though its lines are "almost identical with passages in a letter he had written a few months before." In a letter to his friend Sotheby, Coleridge says "I involuntarily poured forth a Hymn," meaning his poem "Hymn Before Sun-Rise," which Fruman identifies as *a different author's work*: "a poem derived from an obscure continental poetess." Other poems that Coleridge translated from German were passed off as his own, "offered to intimates as compositions written on the spur of the moment," a practice that would be called plagiarism today. Further, "the dates he gave to his compositions were often very wrong, and surely sometimes deliberately affixed so as to give the impression of his having possessed amazingly precocious poetic powers" (336).

Apparently, Coleridge cared a great deal about the public perception of his writing process. He worked at presenting himself in the image of a poet who was close to his muse, easily entering into states of inspiration. We think it no coincidence that this image closely aligns with Coleridge's published writings on the nature of creative genius. In his *Bibliographia Literaria*, Coleridge works out a model of the creative process, arguing for the notion that poets are a special class of people, set apart from normal humans. He states, "The man that hath not music in his soul can indeed never be a genuine poet." Poetry is a "gift of imagination," and the abilities required to produce it "may be cultivated and improved, but can never be learned. It is in these [gifted few] that '*poeta nascitur non fit*,'" which translates to "A poet is born, not made" (Ch XV para 3). For Coleridge, then, there was not only a rather pretentious penchant for dropping Latin phrases to establish his ethos but, more significantly, a great deal of pressure associated with being a poet. He had to prove that he was born with special gifts, and what better proof was there than the spontaneous production of well-wrought verse? Therefore, Coleridge labored to invent himself as a genius by fabricating tales of his writing process (and, in some cases, fraudulently presenting others' work as his own). He wrote not only poetry, but also a myth of The Poet, and he did what he could to write himself into that myth.

In Kerouac's case, we have even more evidence to debunk popular notions of how the author wrote his novel, for Kerouac's notebooks and many drafts have been archived and made available to scholars. Critic Howard Cunnell reviews the evidence and concludes that "*On the Road* does not appear out of clear blue air" (3). Instead, it was developed from Kerouac's travel journals as he journeyed through the US and Mexico from 1947 to 1950. As Kerouac journaled, "he collected material for a road novel he first mentions by name in an entry dated August 23, 1948" (3). So Kerouac began work on his novel not in 1951 with a scroll of paper but three to four years earlier with a notebook. The volume of prose produced in those years is significant. Cunnell notes that "it would take a full-length book to do justice properly to the amount of writing Kerouac produced between 1948 and 1951 as he worked on his second novel . . . [filling] notebooks, journals, hundreds of manuscript pages, and letters, as well as conversations, with ideas for it" (4). To be clear, Kerouac's activities were not limited to note-taking; over this period, he drafted substantial portions of what would slowly evolve into his most famous book, going so far as to produce what Cunnell has deemed three "proto-versions of the novel" (4).

Far from consistently spontaneous and inspired, Kerouac hit many occasions of roadblock and writer's block along the way. He once complained in a letter to a friend that, "I've got to admit I'm stuck with *On the Road.* For the first time in years I DON'T KNOW WHAT TO DO. I SIMPLY DO NOT HAVE A SINGLE REAL IDEA WHAT TO DO" (Cunnell 14, Kerouac's emphasis). By the time he had his scroll assembled, Kerouac had a pile of material to work with, all of which he kept at hand during those three weeks of furious typing. His process was not so much spontaneous composition, but quick drafting based on copious notes and previous drafts. Nor was the scroll seen by Kerouac as an authoritative version of his text, for he began revising it immediately. He wrote to his friend Neil Cassady a month later, stating that he'd spent the last 30 days "typing and revising" since his publisher was "'waiting to see' the novel" (Cunnell 26). Two full drafts followed the "scroll" version, each edited in collaboration with Kerouac's publishers. In total, writing *On the Road* consumed nearly a decade of Kerouac's life.

I Wrote Your Autobiography and It's Genius: Gertrude Stein Revises the Myth

The myth of genius perpetuated by authors like Coleridge and Kerouac is not without its consequences, particularly for writers who, by virtue of one or more identity markers, are read by their contemporaries as incapable of producing great work. Historically, 'genius' has been a label applied by white men to other white men, while white women and writers of color—however brilliant their work—have often been overlooked. Some theorists have been more explicit than others in their racism and sexism when discussing the notion of genius. For example, the early twentieth century Austrian philosopher Otto Weininger argued that Jews and women "were the negation of the ideal and universal type of 'genius'" (qtd. in Doyle 44). In the same year that Weininger published his sexist, anti-Semitic work, Gertrude Stein moved to Paris, where she wrote and collected art and became well known among artists and writers for hosting a salon frequented by people like Henri Matisse, Ezra Pound, Ernest Hemingway, and Pablo Picasso. In other words, Stein's place in Paris became a hub of activity for male artists and writers who many viewed as geniuses. While her own writing was indeed brilliant, Stein knew well that the same critics who recognized genius in Hemingway and Pound were not likely to see it in her. Stein was a woman. She was Jewish. And she was a lesbian. At best, she would be seen as a hostess to famous men, a literary socialite who sometimes wrote strange books on the side.

Stein's response to this predicament was to write a witty and best-selling book, *The Autobiography of Alice B. Toklas*. In *The Autobiography*, Stein takes on the persona of her life partner, who, in the fashion of women's autobiographies of the time, speaks glowingly of her mate. "I may say," says Stein's Toklas, "that only three times in my life have I met a genius and each time a bell within me rang and I was not mistaken . . . Gertrude Stein, Pablo Picasso, and Alfred Whitehead" (5–6). By labeling herself a genius through the voice of her partner, Stein makes a claim for her membership in this particular 'boys club.' In doing so, she opens that club to other writers like herself and so also changes the nature of the club (i.e., if Stein can be a genius, then other women, Jews, and lesbians can too). As Stein claims a place for herself among the artistic 'Greats' of her time and tradition, she remakes genius in a way that never would have occurred to authors like Kerouac or Coleridge. Stein's genius is not solitary—her work does not arise spontaneously in a vacuum. Rather, Stein's is a collaborative genius.

Literary scholar Nora Doyle argues that, by viewing her own salon from the eyes of Toklas, Stein is able to observe that "the only certain thing about these 'geniuses, near geniuses, and might be geniuses' is that they all have wives . . . a point that makes it difficult to take seriously the notion of the autonomous male genius as a unique and superior specimen of humanity" (60). For Stein, genius is a "shared identity rather than a singular category" (64), one defined "by the shared rhythms of eating, socializing, housekeeping, and writing." In short, "Stein executes a radical re-gendering of the category of genius, associating it with notions of collaboration, dependence, and domesticity that have historically been linked to femininity" (66). Stein resists traditional notions of genius by reimagining hers as the common property of Gertrude Stein and Alice B. Toklas, life partners for whom writing is one of their shared activities, supported and enabled by their mutual love, attention, and labor. Stein's notion of genius does not allow for an autonomous writer or instantaneous revelation. Unlike Kerouac and Coleridge, Stein's Toklas is under no illusions about the nature of creative work. Creative work is *work*, just like cooking and hosting and housekeeping. Further, the work of the creative writer does not exist in a separate sphere from that of the cook or the hostess or the housekeeper. Instead, all these forms of labor are normal, natural aspects of a shared life. No laudanum-inspired visions are necessary. No magical scrolls of spontaneous prose are anywhere in sight. Just two women in love living in Paris, cooking and writing and eating and hosting parties, and all of it—their whole life together and all the books it produces—is a singular work of genius.

Romanticism Reversed: A Gratifying Loss of Inspiration

Despite the work of Stein, the myth of spontaneous literary production perpetuated by the creation stories of Coleridge and Kerouac too often reaches into the present (especially in the US and UK), coloring many emerging writers' notions of how they should expect "authentic" literary work to come into being: i.e., quickly, with little effort, and somewhat mystically—sometimes as a result of falling into a drug-altered psychological state. As we've suggested, it is a variation of this myth that is parodied in *Wonder Boys*. The film not only satirizes the sort of advice found in Kerouac's "Essentials for Spontaneous Prose"; it also references Coleridge's loss of his fully formed psychic poem. *Wonder Boys* transforms this internal loss into a material loss through an external event more suitable for the visual genre of film.

In a scene toward the end of the movie, Grady Tripp places the only typewritten copy of his manuscript (which he has finally completed), on the passenger's seat of a car that his editor, Crabtree, is driving. After exiting the vehicle and engaging in a conflict with two other characters, Grady watches as Crabtree (a notoriously terrible driver) proceeds to mishandle the gearshift and steering wheel, skid through the street, and somehow push open the passenger's door while the car is in motion. In a stunning instance of cinematography, the pages of Grady's manuscript then fly out of the open door, soar through the air, skirt along the pavement, and vanish into a nearby river. Unlike Coleridge's loss, which supposedly consisted of about 75 percent of his fully-formed psychic poem, Grady's loss consists of roughly 99 percent of his physical manuscript. This loss may, at first, seem tragic; the character's immediate reaction is to suggest that his editor be shot dead. However, it functions ultimately more as a boon than a burden. As the film progresses, we learn that this loss leads to an epiphany for Grady, who shortly thereafter makes major lifestyle changes and, as a result, not only returns to better physical health but also matures quite rapidly as a writer and person. The loss of a manuscript in this particular instance reverses the Romantic paradigm to function more as a positive reality check than a regrettable departure from a mystical state of inspiration.

In some ways, the disappearance of Grady's manuscript isn't really a loss at all. We learn in different scenes that the manuscript was an outrageously long and laborious text so devoid of smart—or even conscious—writerly decisions that it read as a muddled mishmash of terrible prose. When Grady is asked what the now-vanished manuscript was about, he replies in all seriousness, "I don't know." The work was perceived by the few characters who had read it as an utter disappointment. In fact, in an earlier scene of the film, one of Grady's young female students, who managed to stealthily read through the novel, tries to offer some advice to Grady based on his own teachings about creative writing. Hannah states, "You know how in class you're always telling us that writers make choices . . . It sort of reads in places like you didn't really make any choices. At all. And I was just wondering if it might not be different if, maybe, when you wrote, you weren't always . . . under the influence."

Upon hearing Hannah's feedback, Grady becomes defensive and in a mocking voice suggests that plenty of famous writers have written while high. However, after the loss of his manuscript, he not only accepts the validity of Hannah's criticism, but goes so far as to give away his last dime bag. This symbolic gesture signifies his decision to finally reject the myth of drug-addled, spontaneous genius that had defined his attitude toward the writing life and ultimately failed him as a writer. Shortly after his purging of pot and near the very end of the movie, Grady is shown—for the first time—thoroughly engaged in the ordinary, conscious labor of inventing text: he is sitting at a desk in his home office, typing several sentences and finishing up his work session for the day—this time on a computer that, unlike his previous typewriter, has a "Save" function. We are to understand that this piece of writing-in-progress will not be lost. In fact, it turns out to be the story that was being told throughout the film: a successful, completed piece of writing.

Not coincidentally, Grady's transformation from immature to mature writer, from scatterbrained pothead to deliberate crafter of prose, coincides with his new status of fatherhood. We learn that after Grady lost his manuscript, he not only began engaging in regular, sober writing sessions, producing more comprehensible text at a faster rate than he had previously, but he also married the woman with whom he was having an affair, and the two had a child together. The transition to fatherhood clearly represents a symbolic rite of passage. Grady can no longer be a seemingly eternal adolescent who has a penchant for wandering rather aimlessly into trouble or an *artiste* with his head in the clouds, whom other people wind up taking care of (his roles throughout most of the film). Rather, he begins to behave as a person grounded in the daily domestic realities of work and family who is responsible for the welfare of others. By the end of the movie, the main character is able to grow up (however belatedly), reinvent himself and his writing, and create a more meaningful book and a more meaningful life precisely because he gave up the idealization of Romantic mythology. In this sense, he transitions from the legacy of genius as defined by Coleridge and Kerouac to that revised by

Stein. Although certainly a male figure in a heterosexual relationship, he matures artistically precisely because he relocates to the domestic sphere and adopts the daily responsibilities of collaborating with his partner and nurturing a family.

If We Hath Not Music in Our Souls Are We Incapable of Learning?

We include this lesson from *Wonder Boys* in relation to our commentary on Coleridge, Kerouac, and Stein not because we bear some bitter grudge against wonderment or want to somehow "uninspire" people. We do not wish to suggest that we can somehow unlock or explain away *all* of the mystery of inspiration or come to a complete and total understanding of its relation to the early stages of the writing process, which often represent, in part at least, productive subconscious activity. In short, we value inspiration and we find it almost everywhere (and we're sure you do too). That said, we do mean to illuminate some of the problems associated with taking writers like Kerouac and Coleridge too much at their word, especially when their word has proven decidedly not to correspond to their actual practice. To trust in the myth of Romantic literary genius (i.e., to put *excessive* faith in inspiration and believe that poems and stories will somehow spontaneously write themselves) is not only to engage in delusional thinking, but also to risk setting oneself up for failure in a variety of ways, three of which we discuss here.

First, we have found that if you insist on doing nothing but waiting for inspiration—in the form of a telepathic message from your muse, or some other kind of quasi-divine intervention—you risk waiting for an exceedingly long period of time. Or perhaps more accurately: an exceedingly long, boring and potentially anxiety-inducing period of time, in which very little of anything—especially writing—actually happens. The kind of monotonous, nervous waiting we're talking about here, while unique to its own circumstances, is akin to that portrayed in Beckett's "Waiting for Godot": it involves doing a torturous amount of nothing for a potentially infinite period of time, or at least until your life ends—hopefully not because of a suicide attempt (like the one the characters Vladimir and Estragon seem to persistently botch). In short, the act of waiting for inspiration, while perhaps conducive to absurdist suicide attempts, is not exactly conducive to successfully completing writing projects.

Second, comes the issue of drug use. As *Wonder Boys* suggests, relying on certain drugs for inspiration carries with it the risk of obstructing rather than enhancing the writing process. While in his famous preface, Coleridge may have exaggerated his poetic prowess and glorified his experiences on opium, elsewhere he was much more regretful about his relationship with the drug and its effect on his consciousness. In intimate, private letters to friends, he admitted that his use of opium went far beyond occasional experimentation. In a letter to Joseph Cottle, he calls what was really an addiction that would follow him to his deathbed an "ACCURSED habit" (*Collected* 476, his emphasis). In other letters, he expresses the sorrow and regret he felt because of his addiction. He claims his repeated use of opium, in various forms, led to "the barbarous neglect" of his family (*Collected* 489) and caused him to exhibit "unnatural cruelty" to his children (*Collected* 511). In correspondence with his friend, John Morgan, he goes into further detail about his disdain for the drug and the penchant for lying brought about by his addiction:

> I have in this one dirty business of Laudanum [a tincture of opium] an hundred times deceived, tricked, nay, actually and consciously *lied*. And yet *all* these vices are so opposite to my nature, that but for the *free-agency-annihilating* Poison, I verily believe that I should have suffered myself to have been cut to pieces rather than have committed any one of them . . . From the Sole of my foot to the Crown of my head there was not an Inch in which I was not continually in torture.
>
> *Collected* 489–491

Far from providing value to his writing practice, his opioid addiction had a detrimental effect on his personal and professional life. In fact, there was a period of his later career, shortly after Thomas De Quincey published *Confessions of an English Opium-Eater*, in which his authorial reputation suffered dramatically.

In the wake of Kerouac, and since the emergence of the genre of so-called "junkie literature" in the late twentieth century, many contemporary writers have acknowledged that they, like Coleridge, were able to write successful literary texts not because of, but in spite of, their drug use. Jerry Stahl, author of the memoir *Permanent Midnight,* reveals that his use of heroin never enabled him to achieve any sort of elevated state of poetic inspiration or close connection with the muse. Rather, it simply allowed him to remain relatively functional. In his words, it "made the [desk] chair a lot more comfortable. That's about it" (qtd. in O'Neill). Now clean, Stahl expresses an extreme distrust of Romantic notions of drug use and writers' sublime states of consciousness, stating with deliberate candor, "I don't know that opiates have a hold on anybody's imagination—except for opiate addicts . . . Only civilians [i.e., non-users] romanticize this shit" (qtd. in O'Neill). Extending this line of thought and drawing on his own experience as a former drug addict, Stahl's contemporary and fellow novelist, Tony O'Neill, puts things this way: "So many writers have openly talked about their romance with drugs of various kinds that there's a skewed perception out there that drugs are somehow a shortcut to creativity. Anyone who has either done drugs for any length of time or worked in the arts will certainly attest to the fact that this is a ridiculous idea."

The third problem associated with the Romantic myth of spontaneous genius is perhaps the most prevalent. While it may not be as immediately risky or permanently damaging as the problem of drug abuse, it is at least (in its own way) as debilitating. We're talking about the issue of self-doubt. Emerging writers who are, by definition, early in their studies or careers—those who have not yet established themselves in literary circles or publishing networks and, hence, have not yet received the kind of recognition that might boost their confidence—are already vulnerable to questioning or mistrusting their abilities and identities as writers. They are especially prone to do so when confronted with inherited Romantic lore about who *real* writers are. Let us explain what we mean by returning to the ideology of Coleridge's preface and *Bibliographia Literaria*.

Here, two Romantic ideas work in conjunction to promote an unobtainable model of "authentic" authorship: first, the notion that real writers have an easy time composing works of literature quickly, almost effortlessly; second, the notion that real writers are born, not made. By the way, we realize that Coleridge referred most immediately to "poets," when he made these proclamations, but we also recognize that the Romantic lore handed down from his generation to ours tends to get garbled in a giant, historical game of telephone. (We imagine, at this point, the voice at the other end of the line sounds a bit like Charlie Brown's teacher.)

We feel that our present culture—in the era of Jerry Stahl, Tony O'Neill, and any number of post-Beat early twenty-first century novelists—tends to apply its version of these ideas to all creative writers. So, we'll stick with the extended application.

Here is the problem: Say we—James and Steve—are emerging writers who, quite naturally, have some insecurities about our level of talent. Again, if we could go back in time and show you our recent past, you'd see that we don't exactly have to stretch our imaginations to envision ourselves in this role. We've lived it. Actually, we're still living it. (Although we may be a bit more enfranchised within literary communities than we were several years ago, we still struggle—as every author we know does—with issues of writerly confidence.) Now, say, in the context we've asked you to imagine, we find ourselves suffering from writer's block, struggling to articulate our ideas, maybe producing text that we dislike, or perhaps simply taking what seems like an eternity to get through a paragraph. If years of experience have not yet taught us the inherent difficulty of writing, and if Romantic lore has predisposed us to believe that these sorts of activities should come easily to us, we are apt to amplify our insecurities. Even though the circumstances described above represent perfectly ordinary challenges that all writers struggle with, whether novice or veteran, we might wonder why we are having such a difficult time with what should be, in Coleridge's words, "effortless" tasks. If Kerouac and other writers are capable of being "geniuses all the time" and if we fail to articulate ourselves the way we would like in what we might consider rather pedestrian writing exercises, then perhaps the problem is, indeed, *us*.

In other words, if we are not aware of the fraudulence of Coleridge's and Kerouac's claims about authorship, then we may internalize the myth they've perpetuated and, in an ironic turn, consider *ourselves* frauds. Maybe we are not *real* writers. This kind of thinking is debilitating when further complicated by Coleridge's notion of authors' biological determinism. Instead of characterizing writing as a social activity or understanding that writers develop their abilities through a longitudinal process of growth that involves experiential learning, ritualized behaviors, linguistic missteps and recoveries, and, above all, repeated practice (as contemporary composition researchers now know), the inherited logic of Romanticism tells us that if we are not *real* writers now, or—more accurately, if we were not predisposed to be real writers at birth—then we never will be. What, then, can we do? Should we abandon our ambition if we lack not only the right opioids but also the right DNA running through our bloodline? Should we give up if we hear only the songs that issue from the ear buds of our iPads and not the music of our souls?

Rather than pursue this determinist trajectory, a mode of thinking that should have gone the way of social Darwinism or been as discredited as Eugenics nearly a century ago, we find it imperative that emerging writers understand the productivity of their own and other writers' shared struggle to create works of literature. If nothing else, the perpetuation of the myth of spontaneous genius should remind us just how important it is for creative writers to work through the mythology they inherit and attempt as earnestly as possible to understand the sources of their creativity. In other words, in order for writers to enable their own growth and move beyond empty lore that begins and ends with a combination of inspiration and genealogical coding, they should spend some time figuring out where their ideas for literature really come from and how their invention of text genuinely happens, a subject we take up in the next chapter.

Discussion Questions

1. As this chapter reveals, Coleridge often deliberately lied about his writing process. Kerouac, too, may have intentionally misled the public, perhaps in some capacity to sell books. Have you ever lied about your creative process? For what purposes?

2. Why do you think the myth of spontaneous genius has survived for so long? And why do you think some writers work to sustain it?

3. Why do you think the myth of drug-induced inspiration is so often affiliated with writers? What does this say about cultural perceptions of who writers are?

Your Turn: Questions, Concerns & Creative-Critical Comments

1. ______________________________

____

____

____

2. ______________________________

____

____

____

3. ____

____

____

____

Writing Experiments

1. Write two narrative vignettes. In the first one, try to represent your process of writing as accurately as possible without glamorizing or romanticizing any of the activities in which you engage. Aim for naturalistic description and develop a portrait of what exactly you do when you sit down to write. In the second vignette, lie through your teeth in order to make your writing process seem sexy as hell, otherworldly, exciting, or dangerous. Use hyperbole. Embellish. Do whatever you have to do to make your process seem enticing, to "sell" it to others, or to market it as The Real Thing™. After you've completed both drafts, share them with your peers and eventually discuss the following questions: Which vignette did you enjoy writing more? Which would you want a novice writer or an established author to read and why? What are the ethics involved in this decision?

2. Do what Kerouac pretended to do, and write spontaneously. Take up a pencil and paper and write as quickly as you can about whatever comes to mind. Don't doubt yourself. Don't stop to think. Put as much language on the page as possible as quickly as possible and for as long as you can. As soon as you catch yourself editing, or at a loss for words, put the pencil down. Put the paper away. Wait a day or two. Then, take the paper out again and examine it from a critical distance to see if you have created a fully formed work of spontaneous literary genius. If so, call the Psychic Friends Network and arrange for another visit from your telepathic muse. If not, see if there is anything useful or salvageable to be pulled from your text; then, revise, rework, and extend whatever you find into a text you might share with your peers. When you get together to discuss your work, share both drafts and consider which of these processes made you feel more like a "real" writer.

3. Watch a movie that represents a writer's life: e.g., *Her, Stranger Than Fiction, The Royal Tenenbaums, Barton Fink*. Regardless of your choice, pay close attention to what sort of myths are perpetuated by this representation. Does the film recycle lore about spontaneous genius or about writers being a genetically gifted breed of people? Is the writer's lifestyle portrayed as glamorous, dreadful, eccentric, ordinary? Does the writer struggle with the

act of writing, or does s/he have an easy time of it? How is the actual activity of writing represented? After you've finished watching, gather your ideas and develop a piece of creative writing that addresses one or several of the issues mentioned above. You might write an essay. You might work with movie-editing software to make a mash-up that reveals something about representations of writers. You might write a dramatic monologue from the point of view of a particular character in the film you watch. Perhaps this character is talking back to the film's director, suggesting how she'd prefer to be portrayed? Take liberties and feel free to experiment boldly. Report back to your class or writers' group with the work you generate.

Deep Reading

1. In the first chapter of her book *The Midnight Disease*, Alice Flaherty describes a type of temporal lobe epilepsy known as "hypergraphia," which causes a person to write compulsively. In "Belief and Technique for Modern Prose," Jack Kerouac outlines his guidelines for spontaneous writing. Read both and compare. Is spontaneous production of writing desirable? Is it valuable? Is it essential to good writing?

2. David Mura's book *A Stranger's Journey: Race, Identity, and Narrative Craft in Writing* collects essays that examine the nexus of culture and writing. His chapters "The Student of Color in the Typical MFA Program" (available online at *Gulf Coast*) and "Writing Teachers—Or David Foster Wallace Versus James Baldwin" (available online in Vol. 1. Issue 1. Of *Journal of Creative Writing Studies*), demonstrate the ways that many white writers and writing instructors continue to "gatekeep" the role of "genius author" in ways that exclude writers of color. Read these essays. In what ways could creative writing instruction be made more inclusive? In what ways could you make your own workshop more welcoming to diverse voices? Are there any benefits to retaining a revised, inclusive notion of "genius," or should the idea be eliminated altogether?

3

Repurposing Spontaneity: From Inspiration to Invention

A number of creative writing scholars have begun to examine where ideas for poems and stories come from by moving beyond authors' radically embellished narratives about inspiration and toward more nuanced understandings of invention. In their work, they often rely less on tinctures of opium or the fine art of bullshitting and more on scholarship from the field of composition-rhetoric. Dianne Donnelly makes note of the novelty of this trend in her book, *Establishing Creative Writing Studies as an Academic Discipline*: "While the field of composition studies yields many useful taxonomies and axiologies on the teaching of writing, the field of creative writing studies is just beginning to emerge in this area of research" (15). In her work, Donnelly indeed acknowledges drawing from a range of compositionists including James Berlin, Wendy Bishop, Peter Elbow, Tim Mayers, Patrick Bizzaro and others as she transfers a systematic way of understanding how writing gets produced from composition-rhetoric to creative writing. Here, we'd like to acknowledge our debt to Donnelly and the scholars mentioned above. We'd also like to admit that we don't completely see eye to eye with Donnelly's vision, and while the taxonomy we present below may overlap with hers to a significant degree, it varies considerably from the model she articulates. With that disclaimer out of the way, we would like to use this chapter to build upon the work she and others within the field of creative writing have begun, specifically by introducing you to several theories of creative writing's epistemological origins: that is, we ask you to examine, question, and contend with four different understandings of where, indeed, the literature that writers produce actually comes from.

New Critical Craft Criticism

We'd be amiss if we didn't start with the pedagogical orientation that has dominated creative writing throughout its history (even though, as you'll see in a moment, it may not be the most relevant here). As we've suggested, the New Critics tended to isolate texts from their social contexts of production and distribution. In fact, they were sometimes so preoccupied with examining the formal relations within completed works of literature that they tended to forget about the issue of how authors actually bring texts into being—a rather ironic problem for a group that sought to treat literature as if writers were, indeed, going to write more of it. As Donnelly suggests, this preoccupation led them to treat texts more as finished products than experiments-in-process (30–32). While such an orientation might be practically useful for going over penultimate drafts during the later stage of a workshop (so that an author might receive feedback for a final revision, say), it doesn't do much good for writers trying to invent text in the earliest stages of composition when the blank page is at its blankest: its most gleaming and intimidating shade of white. In short, the New Critical approach to craft doesn't particularly care how creative writing originates. This might explain why the field of creative writing as a whole has refrained from substantially discussing theories of invention for so long. Thankfully, other schools of thought have taken on the issue more readily.

Expressivism

The second perspective we'd like to examine has come to be called alternately "expressivism" or "expressionism" since its emergence in composition circles around the 1960s. Of the four pedagogies we examine here, it is the most closely linked to Romantic thought, although it distinguishes itself through prominent differences. Like Romanticism, expressivist thought tends to treat writing foremost as "an art, the original expression of a unique vision" (Berlin *Reality* 147). Consequently, expressivism locates the source of creativity within the mind of an individual writer and suggests that this is the place where literature comes into being: i.e., creative writing emerges from an author's subjective consciousness. Compared to Romanticism, it is concerned less with the sublime and more with modern cognitive psychology. In other words, rather than value inexplicable, fleeting psychic or hallucinatory visitations from the muse, expressivism suggests that successful writers nurture their ability to express themselves by attempting to bridge subconscious and conscious thinking within their psychological selves—largely through various writing activities. Indeed, expressivists have designed invention exercises and oriented their advice to writers specifically with this goal in mind.

Natalie Goldberg's *Writing Down the Bones*, a popular creative writing handbook, presents a shining example of this sort of orientation. In various instances, Goldberg insists that emerging writers' top priority should be getting in touch with "the essential, awake speech of their minds" (4). Although her use of the word "awake" would seem to suggest a desire for "conscious" speech or thinking, in the context of her work, it more accurately signifies an ability to move beyond what Freud would call the superego (the realm of self-consciousness and social etiquette: i.e., interference) and toward the place where the ego meets the id (the realm of survivalist need and primal desire: i.e., authenticity). Speaking directly to readers, she offers the following advice: "burn through to . . . the place where you are writing what your mind actually sees and feels, not what it thinks it should see or feel" (8). She further instructs her readers to "capture the oddities of your mind" (8). The tensions between conscious and subconscious activity exemplified here—the attempt to access unconscious oddities through the highly deliberate activity of writing, the attempt to capture the "awake" speech of the dreaming reptilian mind—are important to expressivists like Goldberg precisely because this is where they believe a writer's authentic voice comes from. True expression results not from the inspiration of an external vision, but from repeated engagement in exercises that link or conflate conscious and subconscious activity within the deeper self. If Romanticism is concerned with the music of our souls, then expressivism is concerned with the music of our psyches.

While the expressivists' emphasis on developing voice through repeated practice does not altogether dismiss Romantic notions of spontaneity, it certainly reconsiders and reconfigures these notions. In her handbook, Goldberg suggests that developing one's authentic voice requires less of an uprooted "spontaneous overflow" and more of a grounded process of what might be deemed a wee bit less romantically as "slow decay" (a term we think would make a great name for a retro-nineties goth band, by the way). In one of her chapters, she compares authors' practices of writing to gardeners' practices of enriching soil through composting. She writes, out of the "fertile soil" of our minds "bloom our poems and stories. But this does not come all at once. It takes time" (14). Paradoxically, according to Goldberg, writers must first understand how to facilitate gradual and lengthy processes of decomposition before they can invent new compositions, for, here, the soil is made fertile by the nutrients of the compost, the organic matter that must be tended to achieve a certain state of decay before it can be used to enable growth. As Goldberg extends her metaphor, she emphasizes not only patience and time but also deliberate acts of repetition. She claims that writers need to engage in "raking their minds and taking their shallow thinking and turning it over" through consistent practice and multiple drafts (15). For Goldberg, conditioning is key.

When she describes her own activity of journaling as "composting" she echoes Kerouac's actual—not mythical—writing process (albeit on a much smaller scale):

> [Y]ou can look at my notebooks from August through December 1983 and see that I attempted several times a month to write about my father dying. I was exploring and composting this material. Then suddenly, and I can't say how, in December . . . a long poem about that subject poured out of me. All the disparate things I had to say were suddenly fused with energy and unity".
>
> 15

Here, a certain level of mystery still accompanies the writing process. Goldberg cannot entirely explain the reasons her poem finally came together during the particular writing session she describes. She can suggest only that it was the result of a culmination of conscious and unconscious activity that had been enabled by repeated journaling activities. The text she produced does not necessarily represent a finished product—the poem did not come to her ultimately whole and complete like the one that supposedly came to Coleridge—but, according to her story, it did allow her to produce a long, useful, and surprising draft, one that she could continue working on.

The very idea of using journaling as a means toward eventually crafting a poem represents expressivists' attempt to democratize the invention of literature through "prewriting" activities: informal invention exercises designed to provide specific entryways into the larger process of writing. You have probably come across these sorts of activities in composition classes or in your own writing practice. They include not only journaling, but also freewriting (timed journaling sessions on a particular topic), clustering or mapping (the creation of a "word map" of associated ideas), outlining (a more linear approach to the organization of your thoughts), listing ideas, or simply engaging in conversation about potential writing projects. Through concrete exercises like these, expressivists effectively remove the shroud of mystery surrounding Romantic notions of authorship and reinvent the production of literature as, in the words of James Berlin, "an art of which all are capable" ("Ideology" 675). Under this treatment, "writer" is no longer a title limited to an inherently gifted breed of people who triumph in the musicality of their souls because they were born with the mythical writing gene; rather, it becomes an expansive identity open to anyone who can engage in the activity of putting words on paper (or characters on a computer screen) in order to discover what they are thinking. The reversal in this latter notion is key to understanding expressivist thought. Here (unlike in Romantic ideology), inspiration, or the discovery of an idea, does not precede acts of prewriting. It is not a complete or manifest idea—much less a fully formed text—that comes into the brain of a writer and then gets transcribed; rather, it is the act of engaging in invention exercises (putting pen to paper or fingertip to keyboard) that gives rise to inspiration, to the discovery of an idea. In turn, this discovery-through-prewriting gives birth to drafting, and eventually, to a completed essay or story or poem. Ultimately, according to the genealogy of expressivism, it is not a writer that gives birth to another writer, but prewriting that gives birth to writing. Perhaps the expressivist paradigm is a bit less exotic than Coleridge's creation story, but it is certainly more egalitarian. And significantly more honest.

Social-Epistemic Rhetoric

Social-epistemic rhetoric (sometimes called "social constructionism," a term that sounds only slightly less clunky to our ears) has a long and diverse history. It came into prominence in writing instruction in the 1980s and 1990s, thanks in part to the work Patricia Bizzell, David Bartholomae, and especially James Berlin. If Romanticism is concerned with the music of the soul and expressivism the music of our psyches, then social-epistemic rhetoric is concerned with the music of the streets. In some ways, it reacts to expressivism (at least in Berlin's articulation), suggesting that expressivists' ideas about invention focus too narrowly on individuals' cognitive processes at the expense of larger social contexts and communities. In fact, social-epistemic rhetoric suggests that writing develops from much more of a transactional than a personal process, or in Berlin's words, "out of a dialectic, out of the interaction of individuals within discourse communities" (*Reality* 17). Here, Berlin deploys a term common to contemporary rhetoricians, "discourse communities," to signify social groups that have established agreed-upon conventions for using language in particular ways. Examples of these communities might include avant-garde writers who deploy neo-surrealist poetics, speakers of Creole English who reside in particular regions of the southern US, physics professors who speak in the specialized jargon of their academic discipline, or young teens who communicate largely in the coded acronyms of text-speak so their parents won't understand the messages they send to each other. Regardless of the particulars at play, each of these groups provides their members specific ways of communicating through a shared understanding of language.

To explain how this works on a minor, concrete level, we might use the example of our very deployment of the term "discourse communities" in the paragraph above. This term did not emerge from the depths of Steve's or James's own interior world or psychological self; it was not something residing within us that we then expressed. Nor was it something that came to us in an inexplicable vision. Rather, it was made available for use by a community of scholars within the field of composition-rhetoric. Our interactions with them or, at least, their scholarship, enabled us to articulate the term and introduce it to you. According to this way of understanding where texts emerge, writing does not come from the brain of an isolated or autonomous writer—in social epistemic parlance, a "transcendent consciousness"—that is somehow unaffected by discourse communities and, perhaps even more importantly, the material conditions and cultural contexts in which these communities are grounded. As Berlin suggests, the locus of writing "is never simply 'in here' in a private and personal world. It emerges only as the three—the material, the social, and the personal—interact" (*Reality* 17).

According to the more radical advocates of social-epistemic rhetoric, it is not merely the "interaction" of individuals or of the three terms listed above that enables the production of literature. Rather, the "material" and "social" conditions of existence actually construct the "personal" thinking of an individual writer. At the risk of being a bit reductionist and twisting a few tongues, we might say that *culture writes a writer's consciousness*. Let's think of this problem through examples of limitation. In late eighteenth-century England, while Coleridge may have composed lyrical ballads praising the glory of the middle classes and the natural world—a form and subject culturally available to him at the time—he could not possibly have offered a fictional vignette involving an American woman putting gasoline in her Toyota Prius at a Chevron station near a movie theater in Los Angeles. Nor could his conscious or unconscious mind (however sober or high) have even dreamed of witnessing such an activity. The cultural vocabulary that would enable such a projection into the future had not been invented yet. Presently, when we think of our own attempts to project into the future, we realize that the source and language of our projection come from outside ourselves. Permit us to get a little weirder and use the example of imagining the discovery of alien life, say in the year 2045. When you think of what an alien might look like or where it might live, where does the vocabulary of your thoughts come from? Does it emerge from the unique vision of your core self or does it come from an amalgamation of the discourses of popular culture with which you are familiar: TV episodes, astronomy textbooks, films, science fiction novels, NASA photos, postcards from Roswell?

In many ways, discourses outside of ourselves write and structure our consciousness of the future. According to this way of thinking, suggests Berlin, each writer "is regarded as the construction of the various signifying practices, the uses of language and cultural codes, of a given historical

moment. In other words, the subject [or writer] is not the source and origin of these practices but is finally their product" (*Rhetorics* 62). Put a little more simply, this paradigm might be seen as a reversal of Romantic and expressivist notions of authorship.

Let us further explain what we mean by returning to passages from *Writing Down the Bones*. When Goldberg instructs writers to express "what your mind actually sees and feels" or "capture the oddities of your mind," she assumes the existence of an autonomous consciousness: a core self. Further, she suggests that writers can find their authentic, individual voices if they can tap into this self. In contrast, social-epistemic rhetoricians would suggest that "what your mind sees and feels" has already been provided and structured by culture. Your way of thinking about the world has been created by what they would call your "subject position," your social and cultural vantage point within different discourse communities, and might include considerations like how this position—in terms of economic, gender, and ethnic relations—shapes your view of the world. According to social constructionism, if your mind does have "oddities" or unique qualities, they are more a result of your cultural positioning than any core identity that can somehow transcend its social and material conditions of existence. Social-epistemic rhetoricians would be less concerned, say, with how Richard Wright's *The Outsider* may have emerged from the author's subjective unconscious and more interested in how the work reflects the social experience or "subject position" of an African-American man working within communities of writers in New York and Paris near the middle of the twentieth century. Similarly, they would be less concerned with how the individual, Jack Kerouac wrote *On The Road* and more concerned with how America wrote Jack Kerouac, examining the cultural and political explanations for why a middle-class Catholic man from New England should come to be credited with representing the voice of a generation and inventing what many consider one of the great American novels.

In this way, social-epistemic perspectives not only challenge notions of original authorship; they also implicate writing in contestations for social power. According to Berlin's logic, if the source of invention is not a "transcendent consciousness" but, rather, a transaction of material, cultural, and personal circumstances, and, further, if an author's creativity is, in some ways, prewritten by culture, then writers are inevitably "engaged in the play of power and politics, regardless of their intentions" (*Rhetorics* 77). Phrased differently, in what has become a pithy aphorism from social-epistemic rhetoricians, "the political is always in one sense aesthetic, and the aesthetic is always political" (*Rhetorics* 55). As a text comes into being, it carries with it not only internalized formal and artistic structures but also biases and representations that may or may not favor different populations; the text may validate one group's identity or agenda while oppressing another's—regardless of its author's deliberate purposes or conscious goals. This problem has become, perhaps, the central focus for social epistemic rhetoric, a problem that its advocates continually investigate.

But where does this mode of thinking leave creative writers? It is one thing to understand social-epistemic rhetoric's chief concern theoretically, but quite another thing to apply it to the process of inventing a poem or short story. If "the play of power and politics" occurs inevitably and even unconsciously, what should creative writers actually do with this information? While advocates of social-epistemic rhetoric have tended not to address this question head on, they have suggested at least two possible answers. First, their work implies that writers should strive to develop more of an awareness of the power dynamics at play during their process of creation and, in turn, investigate how their own emerging representations of characters and voices may or may not promote social justice. In this sense, they advocate increasing consciousness, or more particularly developing a kind of meta-social-consciousness, in which writers become as self-reflective and self-aware as they can about how their inventions may stabilize or challenge distributions of power. Second, they often advocate collaborative approaches to authorship. This tactic not only disrupts the perceived isolation of individual writers, contesting quasi-Romantic notions of subjective genius by allowing for a multiplicity of voices, but it also addresses the problem of critical awareness. By offering variations in perspective, collaboration may increase the capacity for critical self-reflection that might otherwise not be possible for an individual working alone. Authoring with others—the act of engaging in transactional dialogue with people who occupy different subject positions—might bring to consciousness issues that would otherwise be overlooked. What sort of political realities might emerge, for example, if Richard Wright and Jack Kerouac, two authors who lived very different lives during roughly the same era of history, worked on a novel collaboratively? What sort of representative tensions might define their story?

Despite these two gestures, social-epistemic rhetoric continues to come under criticism for a number of issues, including oversimplifying the importance of the individual imagination within larger social and political arenas and (despite its claims of increasing agency) not offering enough of a practical application for writers to be of immediate use. In short, it is sometimes perceived by writers to begin and end with the problem of political entanglement.

Process Paradigms

To this point, whether discussing invention under expressivist or social-epistemic theories of composition, we have characterized writing largely as a "process," and we have taken for granted our casual use of this term. It seems perfectly ordinary to deploy the term to describe writing—whether defined most immediately as a personal or social practice—as an ongoing activity that involves multiple stages of thinking and drafting and occurs not instantaneously but develops over a significant period of time. However, the use of "process" to characterize writing did not become commonplace in education until the last third of the twentieth century, when composition specialists like Janet Emig, Linda Flower, Nancy Sommers, and Maxine Hairston shifted their focus of research from completed written products to writers' methods of composing. They engaged in this research primarily in an effort to better understand how writers create texts so that they might subsequently use this knowledge to inform their teaching practices. As Hairston writes, "[W]e cannot teach students by looking only at what they have written. We must also understand how that product came into being, and why it assumed the form that it did. We have to try to understand what goes on during the . . . act of writing" (446). In attempting to achieve this understanding, Hairston and others contributed to what is probably the most revolutionary change in the history of writing studies. As one composition scholar notes, "no development has been more influential than the emphasis on writing as a process" (Faigley 652). Certainly, this very chapter—one that examines the myths and realities of how creative writing comes into being—could not have been possible without the precedent established by scholars' investigations into process.

Process paradigms address the subject of invention much more directly than social-epistemic rhetoric. While in their earliest manifestations, they may have overlooked questions of social power, they offered a scientific approach to studying how texts are invented with useful implications for emerging writers. In the late 1970s and early 1980s, Linda Flower and John Hayes, a composition specialist and psychologist, respectively, conducted a number of empirical studies, in which they treated writing "as a problem-solving, cognitive process" through what they deemed "protocol analysis" ("Cognition" 468). They describe their method as follows:

> To collect a protocol, we give writers a problem, such as 'Write an article on your job for the readers of Seventeen magazine,' and then ask them to compose out loud near an unobtrusive tape recorder. We ask them to work on the task as they normally would—thinking, jotting notes, and writing—except that they must think out loud. They are asked to verbalize everything that goes on in their minds as they write . . . The transcript of this session . . . is called a protocol".
>
> "Cognitive" 255

Collecting protocols allowed Flower and Hayes to describe and analyze "what writers actually do" in the moment of their composition as opposed to relying on inherited mythology, theorists' arguments, or authors' own retroactive accounts of the writing process, all of which the two researchers deem "notoriously inaccurate" ("Cognitive" 469–470). Kerouac's and Coleridge's creation stories would tend to validate their assertion on this matter.

Their findings challenged inherited ideas about invention and reconfigured certain expressivist understandings of discovery. In fact, Flower and Hayes deem "discovery" as much a myth as the Romantic notion of spontaneous genius, suggesting that even when writers engage in successful prewriting activities like those advocated by expressivists, they are *not* doing so to suddenly access preformed ideas that had been latent in their psyche. In other words, they are not experiencing "Eureka" moments in which they find "hidden stores of insight and ready-made ideas . . . buried in the mind" ("Cognition" 467) like a prospector might find gold glinting in the water of a stream. Instead, they are creating meaning. If we have to belabor what is not a terribly good metaphor, we might characterize them less as prospectors and more accurately as alchemists (or the very geological processes involved in the actual formation of gold). Regardless, Flower and Hayes redefine the term "discovery" more constructively to reflect this problem, stating specifically that "discovery is an act of making meaning, not finding it, in response to a *self-defined* problem or goal" ("Cognition" 469, their emphasis). This "self-defined problem" is key to their notion of invention. They found through their analysis of protocols that writers begin inventing text by constructing a situated rhetorical problem in need of thorough examination and address. Further, they discovered that the more fluent or advanced writers constructed this problem in multidimensional ways. While inexperienced writers tended to conceptualize their problem as a relatively straightforward task—something that might be tackled quickly, dare we say *spontaneously*—experienced writers paid more than superficial attention to issues like their own particular goals in relation to the larger project, their desired effect on their audience, their use of an appropriate persona, as well as their use of formal conventions of style and genre. Successful invention was a result of their "exploring the entire problem before them and building for themselves a unique image of the problem they want to solve" ("Cognition" 477). Here, extended rational thought, however unglamorous, takes precedence over spontaneous genius, deliberate mental imaging over haphazard hallucinatory episodes.

Of crucial importance is what Flower and Hayes discovered about the temporality of how writers construct their self-defined problems. In the theoretical model they had inherited (largely from the work of Rohman and Welke), the process of writing was divided into three rather neat stages—prewriting, writing, and rewriting. Within this model, not only were the stages conceptualized as discrete and successive (separate activities progressing along a linear path), but thinking was often perceived to be "different from writing and antecedent to writing" (Faigley 654). In other words, prewriting was believed to occur before actual composition (which in turn was believed to occur before revision). Flower and Hayes found this notion entirely fallacious when tested against writers' actual practices. Protocol analyzes revealed that "writers are constantly planning (prewriting) and revising (rewriting) as they compose (write), not in clean-cut stages" ("Cognitive" 253). In other words, according to Flower and Hayes writers "continued to develop and alter" the representation of their self-defined problem "throughout the writing process"; this activity did not occur simply at the beginning of their writing session ("Cognition" 476). Indeed, for Kerouac, it occurred on and off for between seven and eight years. With this in mind, we might borrow a term from Janet Emig and say that writers' problem-solving processes were found to be not separate or linear but "recursive": that is, they cycle and overlap rather messily through various rhythms and repetitions.

Although this understanding of the writing process may seem relatively obvious to us today, it still maintains extraordinary implications for invention. It is one thing to suggest that ideas develop throughout the process of writing, it is another thing to really understand what this reveals about how writers invent texts. Writing begins to come into being not when an author first confronts a blank page but when an author confronts a blank page *and* when an author confronts a partially written page *and* when an author confronts a fully completed page *and* when an author confronts a fully completed page with handwritten notes from a reviewer in the margin *and* when an author confronts a second page, and so on. As Nancy Sommers reminds us, invention happens all the time—even and especially during revision. If prewriting is not limited to the initial stage of the writing process, and if revision is not treated as an afterthought, a finalizing activity adjunct to the regular writing process, then both contribute to facilitating processes of invention. Relying on Flower and Hayes's redefinition of discovery as an act of making rather than finding meaning, Sommers writes, "revision strategies are a process of more than communication; they are part of the process of *discovering* meaning altogether" (325 her emphasis). Elsewhere, she describes these strategies as "a repeated process of beginning over again, starting out new" (331): i.e., a means of creating, or "inventing" new material.

One of the key figures in recognizing the potential of this sort of insight for creative writing students was Wendy Bishop. Uniquely trained as a qualitative researcher and poet, Bishop transferred findings from cognitive studies in the field of composition-rhetoric to the creative writing classroom, applying the work of Flower, Hayes, Emig, Hairston, Sommers and others to pedagogical practice. In her earliest book on the subject, *Released into Language*, she describes a transactional workshop designed to facilitate recursive processes of invention, drafting, and revision in ways that help creative writers better understand their own composing processes. She not only includes protocol templates within her appendices of teaching materials, but she also advocates a looser portfolio approach to instruction that emphasizes metacognitive reflection through a variety of writing exercises that prompt students to articulate why and how they make particular choices as they compose their poems, stories, and other texts. The influence of Bishop's work on creative writing's understanding of process paradigms is too extensive to attempt to cover here; let us simply say that she challenged and changed the status quo of the workshop, upending rather restrictive ideas of who creative writers could be and how creative writing comes into being.

If we return to our genealogical terms, we might say that according to advocates of process pedagogy (like Bishop and others), it is not talented writers who give birth to talented writers within predetermined bloodlines. Nor is it a separate stage of prewriting that enables real writing to occur. Rather, it is the activity of writing that enables the production of more writing. Maybe the image of an ouroboros rolling around on a keyboard is appropriate? Or, to return to our other metaphor: if Romanticism is the music of the soul, expressivism the music of the psyche, and social-epistemic rhetoric the music of the street, then process paradigms are a song that never ends, a melody that reinvents itself ceaselessly through combinations of rhythm and harmony and noise. But what does all this really mean?

How the Beat Goes On: Repurposed Spontaneity and the Implications of Process Theory

It might be tempting to align ourselves with one of the particular schools of thought we've described above and advocate for its particular convictions. And it's safe to admit we (and many scholars of our generation) tend to have a bias toward social-epistemic rhetoric. That said, we find it more productive to see all four of these ways of understanding writing—craft criticism, expressivism, social-epistemic rhetoric, and process paradigms—as more strangely compatible than they may at first seem. We think that the most innovative work comes from writers and scholars who treat these schools of thought less as oppositional and more as co-influential. And we, ourselves, tend to look for compatibilities, hoping to consider perceived borders more porous than solid, and drawing our own ideas about invention from an amalgamation of sources.

Regardless of how we might or might not align ourselves, we can't help but follow Bishop's lead in recognizing the value of process paradigms to contemporary literary production. Whether they affiliate themselves more with, say, expressivism or social construction, if emerging writers overlook the importance of invention as it occurs and reoccurs throughout continually recursive processes of drafting, they will likely miss out on the very thing that makes writers successful. When we revisit the actual practices of Coleridge and Kerouac, we find that they spent much less time courting their mystical muses and much more time inventing, reinventing, drafting and redrafting material almost obsessively: Coleridge by revisiting poems and altering them within the contexts of different manuscripts and letters to friends, Kerouac by revisiting his notebooks over a span of several years and reinventing his loosely-connected musings into a series of "proto-novels," and, then, in turn, reinventing proto-novels into different versions of the *On The Road* manuscript. The findings of Flower and Hayes, Sommers, and other advocates of process pedagogy reveal that veteran writers engage in multiple, recursive drafting activities more extensively than novice writers and, furthermore, that as writers grow in their art, their appreciation of drafting multiple layers of text deepens. This is especially true of their ideas about revision: during their processes of drafting, experienced writers tend to be less concerned with grammar, word choice, or sentence-level correctness—the stuff of copyediting—and more concerned with larger, conceptual, problem-solving issues that enable them to transform and reinvent their texts as they write and rewrite.

On a more practical level, the work of these scholars suggests that if we do attempt to write spontaneously, to compose what we might call quick "first-drafts," we should do so without the expectation of getting things right the first go-around, or somehow pulling a complete, fully-formed text out of the ether. Instead, as Anne Lamott suggests in *Bird by Bird*, we will find ourselves much less debilitated if we give ourselves permission to write "shitty first drafts," which is exactly what Lamott insists many good writers do—before they return to their texts-in-the-making and rework material (21). It's what Coleridge did. It's what Kerouac did. It's what Stein and Toklas did together. It's what writers of countless generations have done and continue to do—over and over and over again.

To be clear, as we conclude this chapter, we want to acknowledge our recognition that spontaneity, indeed, has a place in the writing process; we simply need to know how to make good and realistic use of it. Purposeful spontaneity—sudden drafting with the intent of further drafting and further revision and further invention and reinvention—may result in wildly productive writing sessions. It may also maintain the possibility of writers surprising themselves as they draft to reinvent ideas in ways that may not have initially occurred to them. If we drop the trappings of the Romantic myth and commit to revisiting the methods actually employed by writers, we may find ourselves making use of an entirely different kind of inspiration, one so integral to the process of text-making itself that it can't be described neatly in the stuff of legend or myth.

Discussion Questions

1. Now that you've been given several perspectives on invention, where would you say your creative writing comes from? Is it a means of psychological expression, a response to your place in history and culture, or a cognitive process of working toward a goal that you designed for yourself? Is it some combination of these, or something else entirely?

2. In our section on social-epistemic rhetoric, we suggest that scholars from this school of thought are interested in examining how a writer's distinct voice might be the result of his or her subject position within specific contexts of culture. How would you describe your own subject position, and how do you think it affects your writing practice?

3. How important is inspiration or invention to your larger process of writing? Is there anything you would like to change about your writing process? How might you go about doing so?

Your Turn: Questions, Concerns & Creative-Critical Comments

Writing Experiments

1. Take a moment to further consider not just your writing process but more particularly the kind of impediments that sometimes prevent you from drafting as fluidly or prolifically as you'd like. With these thoughts in mind, write a satirical instruction manual on "How Not to Get Writing Done" or some variation to this effect. Your work might take the form of a numbered list, or it might consist of a series of diagrams, illustrations, or charts. You might consider parodying one of those little instruction booklets that come with furniture that is supposed to be easy to assemble but somehow always seems more difficult to build than an elevator to the moon.

2. In his essay "Toward a Phenomenology of Freewriting," Peter Elbow states that he often begins workshops with two periods of freewriting, one private and one public, in order to draw attention to the difference between writing for others and writing for ourselves. We suggest you try this. Time yourself for

ten minutes and write freely about anything you like, knowing that you will share this piece. When you're done, read your text aloud to someone, and listen to theirs. Time ten more minutes of freewriting, this time knowing that you will not ever have to share the writing with anyone. At the end of ten minutes, compare the two drafts. What is different between them? Which do you like better? Do you consider one a more honest or genuine example of "self-expression" than the other? Why or why not?

3. Earlier we asked what might happen if Richard Wright and Jack Kerouac worked on a novel collaboratively. In the spirit of this question, we'd like you to develop a piece of creative writing based on an imaginary conversation that could have taken place—but didn't—between two authors or cultural figures who occupied dissimilar subject positions during roughly the same historical era. You might ask, for instance, what would Sun Tzu say to Siddhartha Gautama, or Sojourner Truth to Edgar Allan Poe, or Anna Akhmatova to Marcel Duchamp, or Fred Rogers to Che Guevara? Regardless of your choice, write a dialogue that reveals the world-changing potential of their meeting. As you write, consider not only the subject positions of your interlocutors, but also their distinct voices. Would John Milton speak to Matsuo Basho in blank verse? Would Basho respond in haiku? After you've taken the issues described above into consideration and completed a draft of your work, share it with your peers and request their feedback on whatever issues you find most important.

Deep Reading

1. In "Writing Freely," the second chapter of *Telling Writing*, Ken Macrorie describes the process and value of freewriting, a staple exercise of expressivist writing pedagogy. In "The Composing Process: A Review of the Literature," from her book *The Composing Process of Twelfth Graders*, Janet Emig speaks of writing as a process and examines available sources on that process. In her article "Professing Multiculturalism: The Politics of Style in the Contact Zone," Min-Zhan Lu examines the treatment of cultural difference in the writing classroom. These three sources represent expressivist, process, and social-epistemic views of writing respectively. Read all three and compare and contrast their approaches. Find value in each essay, and also find the limitations of each.

2. In the second chapter of *Tiger Writing*, "Art, Culture, and Self," novelist Gish Jen explores how "independent" and "interdependent" modes of self-construction are influenced by culture and history. She then suggests that

these modes influence the kinds of art and narratives that different cultures produce and appreciate. In his chapter "Zora Neale Hurston and the Speakerly Text" from *The Signifying Monkey: A Theory of African-American Literary Criticism*, Henry Louis Gates, Jr. explores the cultural and linguistic pressures that presented themselves to Hurston as she composed her novel *Their Eyes Were Watching God*. Read these sources and reflect on the ways in which history, culture, and language influence writers (including you).

SECTION TWO

Who Creative Writers Are (In Relation to Others)

4

Beyond A Room of One's Own: Toward Collaborative Understandings of Authorship

The psychoanalyst and object-relations theorist Donald Winnicott once said, "There is no such thing as a baby." He later explained: "if you set out to describe a baby, you will find you are describing a baby and someone. A baby cannot exist alone, but is essentially a part of a relationship" (88). We contend that when we substitute "author" for "baby" in the statements above, the result is equally true. There is no such thing as an author, for if you set out to describe an author, you will find you are describing an author and someone. All writers, in some form or another, collaborate as they write, so an author is best understood as essentially part of a relationship. Or, rather, a whole bunch of relationships. Unlike a baby, an author is not literally tied to one primary caregiver, but more expansively attached to an entire social matrix. We might say s/he comes into the world with a network of umbilical cords.

We concluded our last chapter by describing the importance of understanding creative writing less as a burst of inspiration and more as a recursive process; in this chapter, we examine who engages in, or contributes to, this process both literally and symbolically. That is, we investigate the mysterious "and someone" of an author's network to discover who exactly the others at the ends of all these cords might be.

Visualizing The Image of Authors

Two of the premises we start with here—the image of the networked author wrangling his or her way through a tangle of relationships, and the very idea that writing is a social activity—may seem counter-intuitive to some readers. After all, we tend to sit alone when we write: to escape our mundane lives, to

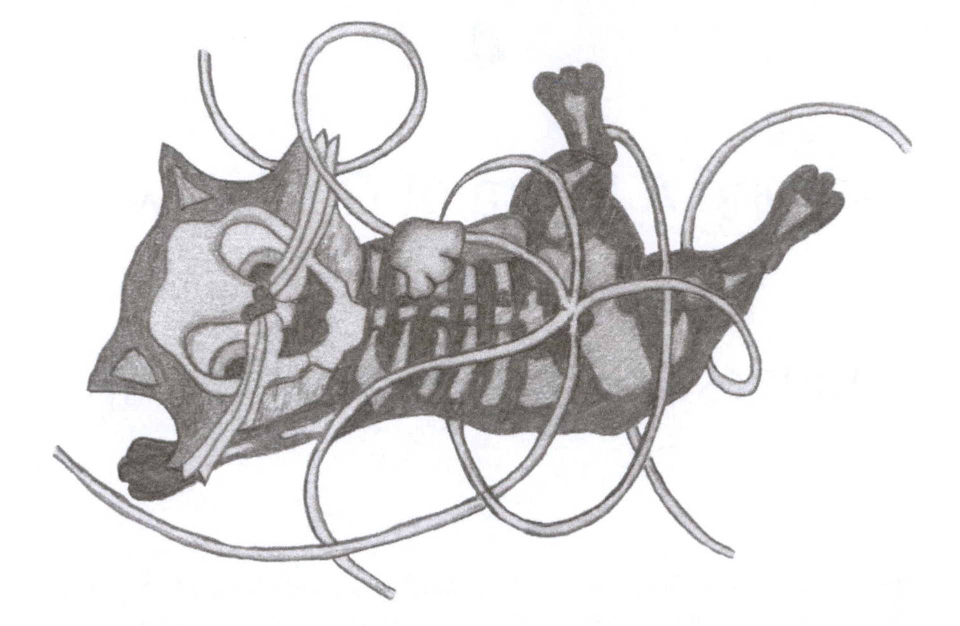

be with our thoughts, and to avoid the distraction of others. No one else's voice whispers in our ears as we type. No one else's hands do our typing for us. We write our own name on our bylines—and not anyone else's—because we invent our writing by ourselves. Or so we think. And to a certain extent, we have been taught to think this way. There is an entire legacy of images within modernist literature and visual art that influences our understanding of who writers are and how they work. This legacy depicts authors isolating themselves in discrete physical spaces in order to engage in their process of composing.

Take for instance, the portrait of Sir Humphry Davy, which was painted by Thomas Phillips in the early nineteenth century. (Figure 1)

Davy was a poet, writer, and chemist, as well as a friend and contemporary of the Romantics. You may know him less for his literary works and more for his famous contributions to experimental science; he was one of the first people to recommend the use of nitrous oxide as a surgical anesthetic. The subtle smile on his face may seem rather inexpressive for a man who experimented on himself regularly with laughing gas—frankly, we expected more of a maniacal, Cheshire grin.

Regardless, we are less concerned here with how Phillips's representation may or may not meet our expectations, and more concerned with how Phillips's artistic decisions reflect his era's larger cultural and ideological understandings of authorship. Take a look at the other choices the artist made when developing this portrait. Davy is seated alone next to his writing quill in

FIGURE 1 *Phillips, Thomas.* Sir Humphry Davy, *1821. Public Domain Image.*

front of an opaque black background that is so dark almost no light is allowed to penetrate through it. Here, the background functions much like a blackout curtain does in a twenty-first century hotel room: that is, it keeps the light of the world at bay so that the room's occupant will not be disturbed. In this sense, it provides a kind of illusory and peaceful isolation from the bustle of society, the presence of others, and the passing of time. The combination of Davy's pensive pose and Phillips's manipulation of light—the only illuminated objects are the face, hands, blouse, writing quill, paper, lamp, and desk—suggest that the thoughts of the writer depicted here have nowhere else to develop other than from the immediacy of a single consciousness working alone. They are quarantined, in this sense, to the boundaries of the illuminated space, which hardly extends beyond the author's physical body and not at all beyond the requisite tools of his craft. Using the taxonomy we presented in the last chapter, we might say that this author looks like a parody of a lone, exaggerated expressivist. Attached to no one, he is part of no social matrix whatsoever, and his creativity would appear to develop exclusively from within.

The portrait of Davy represents a norm that would last well into the twentieth century and remain in place as the popular medium of portraiture shifted from painting to photography. Artists and photographers continued to depict authors in literal isolation with, at best, only symbolic hints toward acknowledging others' participation in the writing process. As Karen Burke

LeFevre states, "our standard images of writers reflect their solitary modes: the poet in the garret, the novelist in the cabin at the writers' colony, the scholar alone in the library carrel" (12). As we've suggested, our repeated exposure to such images even today (in fine art, in popular movies, on the internet, or on the back covers of books) tends to shape our expectations, whether or not we are entirely conscious of this effect. On closer critical inspection, however, it becomes evident that writing involves much more than sitting alone in a room of one's own, especially in our contemporary networked universe.

Implicit Collaboration Part I: Invoking Others

As we stated in the previous chapter, Berlin and other social constructionists have suggested that writers' consciousness is prewritten by a culture's discourse communities. In *Invention as a Social Act*, Karen Burke LeFevre builds on Berlin's work to make a study of the ways in which even the most seemingly isolated writers inevitably engage in collaboration (of one form or another) as they invent their texts. LeFevre claims that authors are always writing in relation to others, both implicitly and explicitly.

On the most basic level, LeFevre suggests, authors cannot avoid implicit collaboration, for their very medium—language itself—is a symbolic system that is "socially created and shared" (2). In this sense, the very term "invention" is a misnomer: apart from rare cases of neologisms, authors are not inventing new words but rearranging units of linguistic material that have been provided by millions of humans communicating with each other over a span of millennia—in the case of the English language, around 16,000 years. And, like the medium of language, the genres in which authors write have social and collaborative histories. An author writing a short story, for example, makes use of a form that was crafted by other writers and carries with it certain cultural expectations (as does a poem or a play or a text message). When examined this way, an author of a contemporary short story is taking part in an implicit dialogue with all of the authors of short stories that have preceded their act of writing. Because language and genre are really the inventions of history and culture—not an individual typing furiously behind closed doors or the opaque shield of a blackout curtain—writers cannot claim that their words are entirely their own. In fact, critic Roland Barthes has famously called literature a "tissue of quotations" that consists of "multiple writings, drawn from many cultures and entering into mutual relations of dialogue" (146, 148). As etymology attests, language tends to work this way; it is a vast collage of the world's conversations that is continually being reinvented. This does not mean that authors lack a capacity for innovation, or eccentric brilliance even, but rather suggests that because they use language as their medium, they realize this capacity through real or imagined discussions with innumerable others.

Of course, as they experiment with the shared social system of language, writers engage in implicit collaboration not only with other writers but also with readers. Our use of the term "readers" here is a bit complicated, for we mean not only the living breathing people who might buy an author's book—we'll get to them a bit later—but, more immediately, the idea of readers that authors imagine when they engage in the writing process, or what composition scholars Lunsford and Ede have deemed the "invoked audience" (see "Audience Addressed/Audience Invoked"). To be clear, when we're talking about invoking an audience, we're not talking about conjuring the ghost of a reader as one might invoke an elusive muse—there is no supernatural vision or sublime Coleridgean bullshit here. But we are talking about ordinary and yet fascinating conscious and unconscious mental projections that happen all the time when writers sit down to work. As Walter Ong suggests in his landmark essay, "The Writer's Audience is Always a Fiction," in order to write successfully, an author must "construct in his [or her] imagination, clearly or vaguely, an audience cast in some sort of role—entertainment seekers, reflective sharers of experience . . . and so on" (60). For instance, as we draft the section of the book before you, we find ourselves constructing an image of you—our invoked audience—that guides our choices about what exactly we should do with this chapter. We have assumed that you are a student who is experienced in creative writing and curious about its larger histories and social functions. That said, we're not sure how much knowledge you may have or not have about philosophies of composition. As we write, we wonder what we should do to achieve a balance between providing too much and too little information on this subject. If we overload you with academic theories of audience, will you grow bored and resentful? We're tempted to apologize for being so "meta," but if we offer such an apology, will you know what we mean? Should we clarify that in writing-geek slang being "meta" means writing self-consciously about the very process of writing in which one is engaged, as we are doing right now? If we offer this definition and maybe allude to famous meta-fiction writers like Donald Barthelme and John Barth, will we make you think we are talking down to you (by providing info you clearly already know) or maybe that we are intolerably pretentious? Would the word *pedantic* resonate more in your ears?

Clearly, we've made the choice of continuing this line of thought for too long. The point here is not to expose our neuroses (although we tend to do a great job of that inadvertently all the time) but to reveal the extent of an invoked reader's influence on everything from diction to content. As Ede and Lunsford suggest, we "analyze" and "invent" you in this manner almost constantly as we make our decisions about what roles are appropriate for us in our relationship to you. Of course, the other you—the person made of flesh and blood—can't literally affect us while we are drafting the text you now hold in your hands; temporally, this embodied you tends to encounter our book after we've written it (unless we had the foresight to plan alternative arrangements in advance by, say, asking you to review drafts as we wrote, or perhaps more simply, giving you a time-travel machine).

There are exceptions, of course, but for now, we'd like to simply reemphasize that the you of our mental projection—however "real" or "fictional"—is nothing less than a vital collaborator who has a profound influence on our work and shares in its production. As Le Fevre states, the ability to invent a text is "enabled by an internal dialogue with an imagined other or a construct of audience that supplies premises or structures of belief guiding the inventor" (34). In other words, the process that brings a piece of writing into being is "made possible by an 'otherness' that is dynamically present in each I" (54). In this case, our other is you, and you are tremendously important to us. (Have we flattered you enough to make you stay with us? We certainly hope so because this next section gets crazy.)

Implicit Collaboration Part II: Writers, Readers, and Role-Play

As we've suggested, relationships between writers and readers tend to be complicated, especially since one has to always imagine or invent the other. In early audience theory this imagining was a rather one-way affair, with more attention devoted to writers invoking their readers, and significantly less attention devoted to exploring readers' own consciousness. For instance, in Ong's seminal work, it is assumed that readers always remain complicit with writers' constructions of their identity. After a writer invents the fiction of his or her audience, states Ong, "the audience must correspondingly fictionalize itself. A reader has to play the role in which the author has cast him [or her], which seldom coincides with the role in the rest of his [or her] actual life" (60 our emphasis). Ong assumes that for successful communication to occur, readers are left no choice but to take on this role; they have almost no agency in the matter. What Ong neglects to discuss is the diversity of readers, the multiplicity of their ways of thinking, and their potential to resist the very roles that authors create for them. What happens when readers are more feisty than the yes men Ong envisions? What if they refuse to be typecast? Does the kind of implicit collaboration we've been discussing suddenly stop?

In the late twentieth century, a number of critics looked into this problem and effectively reversed the paradigm we've been examining. In other words, instead of investigating the ways authors invoked readers, they began to investigate the ways readers invoked authors. In fact, some critics sought to radically reinvent the dynamics of implicit collaboration by crediting readers instead of writers with actually inventing texts. Roland Barthes supported this revolution more dramatically than any other critic. In an essay not-so-subtly entitled "The Death of the Author," Barthes more or less invited authors to their own funerals, which he graciously organized. Well, not exactly. He was concerned less with living, breathing authors and more concerned with readers' and critics' philosophical construction of what we might call the "invoked author," especially its use to control or delimit the range of meanings possible in a text. In other words, Barthes was not ultimately a sadist who hoped the breath of all writers would suddenly cease, but a philosopher hoping to change the theoretical orientation of French literary criticism, which was entrenched in a form of biographical explication. We can't entirely blame him for that motivation.

In his work, Barthes presents a complicated argument that is difficult to explain briefly. We suggest you read his essay, with one caveat. If you consider yourself an author, you may find yourself suddenly becoming a resistant reader—unwilling to fit into the role Barthes constructs for you, as, well, it resembles a coffin. Many authors responded this way when Barthes' work began to be applied to the enterprise of creative writing. That said, we assure you that reading through his essay will not be the death of you. We'd like to remind you that in his work, Barthes is discussing the *idea* of an Author (he often uses a capital A), and not recommending that actual authors jump off the Golden Gate Bridge or walk into a river with stones in their pockets.

He starts by asserting that the concept of the Author has held too much power for too long. He is upset with the way readers imagine Authors as omnipotent by attributing them too much of an ability to determine the ultimate meaning of a text. He claims that "the image of literature to be found in ordinary culture is tyrannically centered on the author, his person, his life, his tastes, his passions . . . The explanation of a work [of literature] is always sought in the man or woman who produced it" (143). This quotation reflects what we mean when we say the criticism of the era had a rather myopic fascination with authors' biographies. Barthes is reacting to a literary establishment that invoked the concept of the Author to serve as the supreme authority of what a text should be and mean. While most theorists today acknowledge that at least four key concepts contribute actively to the creation of texts—writers, readers, language itself, and contexts for language use—the critics to whom Barthes was reacting afforded the Author a disproportionate amount of control over this process. What was understood or imagined of an author's intention, background, or experience took precedence over not only readers' own subjectivities but more significantly readers' roles in inventing and understanding the actual text in front of them.

After clarifying this problem, Barthes questions—and by questions, we mean argues dogmatically against—a fundamental assumption about the order in which both authors and texts come into being. Common sense tells us that an author who already exists in the world works on her novel or collection of poems and thereby brings it into being, gives birth to it, if you will. If we press this idea a little further, however, our thinking might change. On a practical level, we can probably agree that a science fiction author is not a science fiction author before she writes a science fiction book. The notion that readers will imagine her identity as an author is contingent upon the existence of this novel. This is not to deny that a person in the world labors to create a book but, rather, to suggest that, in a sense, it is the book that gives birth to its Author, or at least makes this role possible. This may not be the cleanest of reversals in terms of temporality. But at the very least, if the book doesn't precede its author, it must exist in order for its author to exist *as an author*. According to Barthes, "the modern scriptor is born simultaneously with the text, is in no way equipped with a being preceding or exceeding the writing, is not the subject with the book as predicate; there is no other time than that of the enunciation, and every text is eternally written here and now" (145).

If we are readers, rather than invoke what we imagine to be the Author's intention, or try to interpret a text's supposedly "true" meaning by invoking what we imagine to have been the Author's past experience, we should remain within the present linguistic play of the language on the page before us and assert our own agency to determine its multiple meanings and implications, which, because of the nature of language, tend to be more indeterminate than definitively settled. At least, this is what Barthes suggests. In order to shift the locus of power from the Author to the reader in this manner, Barthes prioritizes language above everything else, stating that "it is language which speaks, not the author," for "language knows a [grammatical] 'subject,' not a 'person'" (143, 145). In other words, in the here and now of you reading this book, the Author does not exist, except as a rather anonymous construction of language. The flesh-and-blood people, Steve and James, are not speaking to you right at this very moment in time; rather, the "we" on the page is speaking to you. If this is the case, according to Barthes, you have the ultimate power and responsibility of constructing the identity of this "we," as well as creating any ostensible meanings or messages the words on the page might contain.

Let's return to our initial image to explore this issue further. According to Barthes, the author does not have the power to express an original idea from someplace outside of language—she is not the figure alone in the darkness of Phillips's thick black oil paint—but rather her "only power is to mix writings, to counter the ones with the others" already in existence in the tissue of quotations to which we alluded earlier: a pastiche and palimpsest of combinations of words, or what Barthes calls "a ready-formed dictionary, its words only explainable through other words, and so on indefinitely" (146). There is no ultimate Author-driven meaning behind or beyond the text, for in the present there is only the text: a ceaseless performance of signification that "has no other origin than language itself" and therefore may be infinitely "ranged over" but not "pierced" or penetrated (146–147). If the Author, as a controlling concept, is done away with, then language is free to play without constraint, and readers are afforded more willpower, freedom, and agency to actively construct meanings while inventing the text before them. As Barthes famously concludes, "the reader is the space on which all the quotations that make up a writing are inscribed, without any of them being lost; a text's unity lies not in its origin, but in its destination" (148).

Every time we quote Barthes, we feel like we should be hearing Wagner's Ride of the Valkyries or John Williams's Imperial Death March in the background. His stylistic flair is so pronounced, his tone so dramatic, that we might expect Darth Vader to appear at any moment. In fact, Barthes has been criticized for being so caught up in his own histrionics that he offers too exaggerated and violent a reversal of power between writers and readers. In his effort to overturn an existing paradigm, he turns perhaps too far to the other side, simply reversing an entrenched binary by valorizing the Reader, imbuing the idea of this figure with just the sort of authority he seeks to strip from the Author. Why should the Reader have any more ability than the Author to ultimately unify or control the play of language and signification that collides all over a page? Perhaps at the time of Barthes' writing, it may have seemed necessary to perform this reversal before offering a more evenhanded arrangement. Maybe his elevation of the Reader's status was the necessary antithesis within a larger and longer dialectical process. Perhaps the world wasn't yet prepared for synthesis.

From our current position in history, it seems weird to treat writers and readers less as collaborators who construct texts collectively from their different subject positions and more as aggressors involved in a duel or death match. In fact, we find it a little hard to stomach Barthes's final contention that "the birth of the reader must be at the cost of the death of the Author" (148), and, as we've suggested, we certainly aren't the only ones to take issue with this sentiment: William Irwin's *The Death and Resurrection of the Author*, Sean Burke's *The Death and Return of the Author*, Michelene Wandor's *The Author Isn't Dead, Merely Somewhere Else* and many articles concerned with the theoretical rebirth of the (variously-termed) "author" or "writer" or "composer" seek to develop a more generous and holistic understanding of readers' and writers' collaborative relationships.

While we may have our issues with Barthes, we nonetheless value his contribution to what would come to be called reader-response theory, a body of criticism concerned with readers' part in the meaning-making process. In many ways, Barthes's work enabled scholars like Michel Foucault, Stanley Fish, and others to offer more nuanced explorations of the ways in which readers participate collaboratively in creating literature. As reader-response criticism evolved, it perhaps began to move more in the direction of dialectical synthesis, positioning readers and writers more as tentative allies—or at least shifty co-conspirators—than archenemies. It disrupted the perceived opposition between these roles as it overcame some of the trappings of Barthes's initial foray into this subject.

For instance, in *Is There a Text in this Class?*, Fish moves beyond Barthes's supposition that there is nothing outside of language and takes issue with his rather abstract construction of the Reader to examine how specific interpretive communities within specific social and institutional contexts collaborate to invent the meaning of texts. In the chapter "How to Recognize a Poem When You See One," Fish describes an experiment he performed in a class on English religious poetry of the seventeenth century. According to his account, Fish taught two classes in the same room, back to back. Just prior to his poetry class, he taught a linguistics course. One day, when his poetry students arrived, the assignment for this linguistics course—a list of names of authors they needed to read for next week—was still on the board. It looked like this:

Jacobs-Rosenbaum
Levin
Thorne
Hayes
Ohman (?)

323

As his poetry students took their seats, Fish drew a frame around the assignment and wrote "p.43" at the top. He then told his class that what they saw on the board was an English religious poem from the seventeenth century, and he asked them to interpret it. His class did so, and uncovered a surprising amount of religious meaning in the text. Students applied their understandings of visual and symbolic interpretive schemes to the words, suggesting that the marks on the board comprised a "hieroglyph" of sorts "in the shape of a cross or an altar." They further made sense of the words by suggesting that "Jacobs" was "a reference to Jacob's ladder," an obvious symbol of "the Christian ascent into heaven." However, in this case, they believed the ladder was replaced specifically by a "rosenbaum," a term of

German-Jewish origin that translates to "rose tree." Taken in conjunction with the word "Thorne," this "rose tree" was then perceived to be symbolically associated with the Virgin Mary, "who was often characterized as a rose without thorns." Pursuing the language of the "poem" in this manner, Fish's students ultimately determined that the text before them was "an iconographic riddle" that "at once posed the question, 'How is it that a man can climb to heaven by means of a rose tree?' and directed the reader to the inevitable answer: by the fruit of that tree, the fruit of Mary's womb, Jesus." (324). When they finished their reading, Fish revealed the nature of his experiment, telling them that the list of surnames was not supposed to have been as immediately significant to religion as it was to linguistics.

Fish could have easily concluded that poetry students are a gullible lot who should really develop a more critical stance toward their professors, but instead he offered a surprising reading of the experiment: the words on the board really were a poem, so long as his students were willing to read them as poetic. As a collective of readers trained in a particular kind of interpretation, Fish's students transformed the text into a poem by imbuing it with meaning in the way they were trained to do in his class. This, says Fish, is how all reading works. Groups of readers accustomed to particular styles of meaning-making form interpretive communities. When these communities recognize a text as valuable literature, they actually *turn that text into literature* through their interpretation. In Fish's words, "interpretation is not the art of construing but the art of constructing. Interpreters do not decode poems; they make them" (327).

For Fish, then, all reading is productive and collaborative. A group of readers can make meaning out of almost anything, without requiring any understanding of an author's intentions. What enables them to do so is not the death of the author, per se, but their position within specific social and institutional contexts. In fact, the interpretive communities that form within these contexts are really what interest Fish above all else. He is less concerned with how an individual reader might subjectively make meaning from a text in the absence of an author figure and more concerned with how that reader's thinking is collectively and collaboratively structured by "interpretive strategies" that "have their source in publicly available systems of intelligibility" (332). A lone reader does not invent a Christian allegory out of thin air but borrows strategies, schema, and ways of knowing from the interpretive communities to which she belongs. Fish's obsession is less a battle of readers vs. writers and more a meditation on the question of how "the publicly available system of intelligibility" makes readers' constructive acts possible. Unlike Barthes, he doesn't assassinate authors, he just makes them rather irrelevant to his main subject of inquiry, or confines their identities to his interpretive frameworks so that all readers are writers in the sense that they actively construct the meaning of the texts they encounter. He just doesn't care so much about individuals trying to make careers writing fiction or poetry.

Nonetheless, we feel there is a healthy role for authors to play in the work Fish describes. After all, writers are readers too, and writers generate texts in the hopes of participating in ongoing conversations in one or more interpretive communities. For example, when a new mystery author publishes her first novel, she hopes that mystery readers will recognize her work as a valuable contribution to the genre and will interpret it as such. Similarly, we (Steve and James) hope this book will enter conversations among creative writing teachers and students in a way that is productive and useful for that interpretive community (a community to which we both belong).

There is much more to say about reader response criticism, however we don't have the time or space to survey the subject in all its varieties; instead, we'd merely like to suggest we find this body of criticism a useful reminder that the implicit collaboration between writers and readers is not a one way monologue in which the former creates the identity of the latter. Rather, it is a two-way conversation, in which both parties share the tasks of inventing, imagining, and invoking the other from variant material, social, historical, institutional, and cultural contexts that *do*, in fact, exist outside of language. At this point, we have grown weary of all the dramatically proclaimed deaths and resurrections of writers and readers and literary figures. Rather than populate the world of creative writing with yet more authorial zombies and ghosts, we'd like to return, in the next chapter at least, to the living. Or, more accurately, to flesh-and-blood people—collaborators who have worked with each other in the material world—whether they currently happen to be living or dead.

Discussion Questions

1. How conscious are you of your invoked audience while you are writing? In what ways does this sort of consciousness facilitate or disrupt your writing process?

2. Think of a specific time when you were a resistant reader. What were you reading and why did you find yourself resisting the role in which an author had cast you? How exactly did you react?

3. Based on your response to the question above, how important do you think it is to research your audience and try to meet what you imagine to be their expectations? Are there moments when you would like to subvert their expectations or encourage their resistance purposefully? When, how, why?

Your Turn: Questions, Concerns & Creative-Critical Comments

1. ______________________________

____

____

____

2. ______________________________

____

____

____

3. ______________________________

____

____

____

Writing Experiments

1. Read Barthes's essay—you can find it online—and write a reply to his work. Adopt whatever persona and use whatever genre you'd like to experiment with. Get creative here! Perhaps you will play the role of Balzac and write a letter to Barthes, describing the ways he has misrepresented your work. Alternatively, you might wear the mask of an author who was buried alive but somehow managed to scratch and crawl her way out of the grave and is now looking to reap vengeance on Barthes—think Uma Thurman's character in Tarantino's *Kill Bill*. Maybe, from this perspective, you will write an open letter to Barthes, explaining why you have come back to haunt him and detailing all of the tortuous ways, in which you will exact your revenge. Whatever choice you make and however crazy you get, please engage carefully and closely with Barthes's ideas.

2. Find a portrait of an author (other than Sir Humphry Davy). You could pick a painting like Winold Reiss's portrait of Langston Hughes, or Pablo Picasso's portrait of Gertrude Stein. Alternatively, you could pick a photograph like

Robert Giard's picture of Tony Kushner reclining on his couch, or John Bryson's shot of Ernest Hemingway kicking a beer can. Once you've chosen a portrait, write an artist's statement as if *you* were the painter or photographer who produced the piece. Why did you pose your subject in a particular way? Why did you choose a particular setting or particular props? What was the rationale underlying your use of colors, lines, angles, or the overall composition? Most importantly, *what did you hope to say about your subject, their relationship to the rest of the world, and the sources of their creativity?*

3. Imagine that an artist wants to paint a portrait of you as a writer. Be a control freak and compose a set of instructions for this artist about what objects to include and how to stage or frame them so that they capture your authorial identity and influences on your work. What will be foregrounded in this picture, and what will sit in the background? From where will the light emanate? How would a viewer be able to tell that it represents you and not another writer? If you'd like to assert even more control and develop this project further, create a multimedia portrait of yourself based on the questions above.

Deep Reading

1. In chapters 16 and 17 of *The Author Isn't Dead, Merely Somewhere Else*, Michelene Wandor tackles the notion of the "Death of the Author" from the perspective of a creative writer. Read Barthes's essay, and then these chapters from Wandor. Evaluate the argument of each writer from the perspective of the other. Does Wandor do a decent job of responding to Barthes? Would you have argued differently? Does Barthes's position have some value for creative writers that Wandor overlooks?

2. Read Lundsford and Ede's "Audience Addressed/Audience Invoked: The Role of Audience in Composition Theory and Pedagogy" and Walter Ong's "The Writer's Audience is Always a Fiction." Next, see what you can glean of Reader Response theorist Wolfgang Iser's notion of the "Implied Reader" from his book of the same name. What do these three conceptions of audience and reader have in common? How do they differ? What can you gain from each that is useful in your own writing?

3. We recommend Jane Tompkins's *Reader Response Criticism: From Formalism to Poststructuralism* as a good place to start exploring the various theories of reader response. For a reworking specifically of Barthes's ideas, see Michel Foucault's "What is an Author?"

5

Making Collaboration Explicit: Co-Creating With Actual Others

As much as we inevitably engage in implicit collaboration all the time, we also find ourselves more deliberately working with others to co-create texts. As writers, we often require not only the *idea* of each other to guide our thinking through internal dialogues but also the material presence of each other to contribute more than theoretically to the construction of literature. That is, we need flesh-and-blood people to work with us—in actual practice—whether this means sharing ideas, providing feedback, editing passages of text, or writing and rewriting alongside us. In fact, we would suggest that, despite the dominant mythology of so-called single-authorship, models of explicit collaboration tend to be more the norm than the exception.

There are many ways of understanding this kind of collaboration. LeFevre offers at least three predominant roles that collaborators play; we suggest that these roles not be understood as entirely separate but rather overlapping and interconnected. She claims that writing becomes "explicitly social when writers involve other people as *collaborators*, or as *reviewers* whose comments aid invention, or as '*resonators*' who nourish the development of ideas" (2, our emphasis). For our purposes, we might say that *collaborators proper* are writers who actively produce literature together (as your actual flesh-and-blood authors, Steve and James, have done here). They work toward developing a project with one another's input, perhaps sometimes assigning sections for one or the other individual to begin initially drafting, perhaps sometimes co-writing together from the earliest stages, perhaps sending drafts back and forth through email or drafting together on platforms like Google Docs. *Reviewers* are those whose comments and criticism offer writers valuable feedback to apply to the development of their work. You might consider writing teachers a formal, institutional manifestation of *reviewers*, as they evaluate drafts and provide guiding commentary to student-writers. In other contexts, you might imagine workshop peers, writing group members, or editors fulfilling this role. *Resonators* are sympathetic people who listen to writers, serving as proverbial sounding boards for their ideas; talk over subjects of interest from which writers might draw inspiration; or help writers in other ways by providing environments that are conducive to their development. Examples of *resonators* might range from a writer's friends and relatives who offer friendly ears, to patrons of the arts who offer psychological or financial support, to bookstore owners who provide venues for readings.

Although we tend to think of authorship as a singular affair, collaboration happens all the time, and collaborative relationships appear in most writers' lives. Because these relationships are essential to a productive writing process and a successful writing career, we thought we'd examine a few of the more famous canonical collaborations in modern literary history. As you read through the case studies below, we recommend that you think about the *collaborators, resonators*, and *reviewers* in your own life and how their contributions to your writing compare or contrast with the relationships of the authors under study.

Case Study I: Eliot and His Other

After moving from the United States to London in 1914, T S Eliot anticipated our good advice and looked for like-minded writers to work with. It wasn't too long before he made the acquaintance of Ezra Pound, a fellow ex-patriot and poet. Pound was more established than Eliot and had a keen interest in developing the careers of younger poets. Eliot's poetry showed promise, and Pound found Eliot venues for publication. A collaborative friendship evolved between the two, and Eliot entrusted Pound to comment on early drafts of his work; in this sense, he welcomed Pound, at the very least, into the roles of *resonator* and *reviewer*. The relationship between the two poets, defined in this manner, proved crucial to the production of what would become Eliot's best known and most influential poem, "The Waste Land."

Eliot began work on a collection of poems in 1919, which he deposited before Pound in 1921 as a 1000-line collection of texts called "He Do the Police in Different Voices." It began like this:

> First we had a couple of feelers down at Tom's place
> There was old Tom, boiled to the eyes, blind
> (Don't you remember that time after a dance,
> Top hats and all, we and Silk Hat Harry,
> And old Tom took us behind, brought out a bottle of fizz,
> With old Jane, Tom's wife; and we got Joe to sing
> "I'm proud of all the Irish blood that's in me . . ."
>
> *FACSIMILE* 3

When Pound was through with his edits, the collection was reduced to a single poem of 434 lines—over half of the lines were deleted, including the first several pages, so that the poem then began with these now famous lines:

> April is the cruelest month, breeding
> Lilacs out of the dead land, mixing
> Memory and desire, stirring
> Dull roots with spring rain.
> Winter kept us warm, covering
> Earth in forgetful snow, feeding
> A little life with dried tubers.
>
> "The Waste Land" 10

The difference in tone is striking, and representative of the edits Pound made throughout. Summarizing these edits, Peter Ackroyd states that Pound "curbed the tendency of the poem toward dramatic and fictional exposition. . . . [He] heard the music, and cut away what was for him the extraneous material which was attached to it" (119–120).

Eliot was grateful for Pound's contribution, though he was unsure how to recognize it publicly. When the poem was published in his first collection, *Poems 1909–1925* he added the dedication "For Ezra Pound / *il miglior fabbro*" which translates to "the better poet" (Stillinger, 131). But was a mere dedication really enough credit? In a 1946 Essay in *Poetry*, Eliot was more forthcoming about his collaboration with Pound, calling his original manuscript "a sprawling, chaotic poem" that Pound thankfully "reduced to about half its size." He then goes on to state, "I should like to think that the manuscript, with the suppressed passages, had disappeared irrecoverably: yet on the other hand, I should wish the blue penciling on it to be preserved as irrefutable evidence of Pound's critical genius" (qtd. in Stillinger, 132).

This is no small compliment from Eliot. Of course, the suggestion that one is a "critical genius" might always be flattering (however fallacious a term), especially when it comes from a Nobel Laureate. But from Eliot, the compliment was still more profound, for in Eliot's mind, the critical activity of a writer is the most important part of the creative act. In his essay "The Function of Criticism," Eliot suggests that "the larger part of the labour of an author in composing his work is critical labour; the labour of sifting, combining, constructing, expunging, correcting, testing: this frightful toil is as much critical as creative" ("Function" 73). Although he appears to subscribe to the notion of "genius," Eliot offers a rather anti-Romantic idea: he opposes the notion that great literature is produced in a single, sudden, inspired draft, and he is far more honest than Coleridge and Kerouac about the necessity of revision. But for Eliot, revision, or criticism of one's own work, is not just necessary; *it is the most important part of the writing process*. In fact, for Eliot, "some creative writers are better than others," not because they are closer to the muse, but "solely because their critical faculty is superior," or, in other words, because they are better at reviewing, editing, and revising ("Function" 73). Eliot's statements here remind us of Nancy Sommers's suggestion (discussed in Chapter 3) that more accomplished writers revise more often and more completely than novice writers.

Now, it was Pound, not Eliot, who revised "The Waste Land," and who therefore did "the larger part of the labour of an author" on that poem. The extent of Pound's revisions, the fact that they radically reshaped the poem, and the way in which Eliot simply accepted Pound's notes without hesitation suggest that Pound was more than just a *resonator*, and still more than a *reviewer*. Pound was a full and proper *collaborator*. We might even say he was a *co-author*. This is literary scholar Jack Stillinger's opinion. He calls "The Waste Land" a "notable instance of multiple authorship" (122), for the poem could not have come into being without both parties. Stillinger claims that it took one poet "to create those 434 lines in the first place, and another to get rid of the several hundred inferior lines surrounding and obscuring them" (128). Again, in its final version, less than half of the poem consisted of Eliot's original invention and more than half of the poem consisted of Pound's edits (a kind of invention through deletion and rearrangement). This being the case, we arrive at an interesting problem. If Pound fulfilled all three of the collaborative roles LeFevre explores—serving as *resonator* by mentoring Eliot; acting as *reviewer* by offering developmental commentary on early drafts of Eliot's poetry; and ultimately serving as *collaborator* and even *co-author* by utterly transforming "He Do the Police in Different Voices" into "The Waste Land" through what Eliot himself calls the critical "labour of an *author*" (our emphasis)—why was he not given authorial credit for his contributions? Why didn't the poem's byline read "by T S Eliot and Ezra Pound"?

This question is not easy to answer. Clearly Eliot felt indebted to Pound, and eventually publicly acknowledged his support; there is no reason to believe that Eliot had some particular motive for denying Pound his due. So why did he? We might say rather simply that we don't usually put two names on a poem. We prefer one, and so collaborators, no matter how significant their contribution to a literary text, are generally not credited in the work, except perhaps in an "Acknowledgments" section or dedication. In short, Pound didn't receive credit because co-authors rarely do. We might think that's just the way it is. But if we probe a little deeper into the matter, we find ourselves faced with a more troubling question: *Why* don't we usually put two (or more) names on a poem? In other words, if single authorship is "normal," where does this norm come from?

To answer this question, we have to look back in time to 1710 when the Statute of Anne offered the first legal basis for authors (rather than publishers) to claim copyright of their work. According to literary scholar Martha Woodmansee, prior to the Statute of Anne, "it was not generally thought that the author of a poem or any other piece of writing possessed rights with regard to these products" because writing was "considered a mere vehicle of received ideas which were already in the public domain, and, as such a vehicle, it too, by extension or analogy, was considered part of the public domain" (434). This neo-classical attitude toward writing might seem odd to contemporary writers, but it was commonplace then, and reflected the practices of English authors. Literary critic Northrop Frye notes that famous English authors up to that point included "Chaucer, much of whose poetry is translated or paraphrased from others; Shakespeare, whose plays sometimes follow their sources almost verbatim; and Milton, who asked for nothing better than to steal as much as possible out of the Bible" (96). Where there is no copyright, there is also no plagiarism, and authors of all kinds were expected to borrow from whatever sources were available to them.

At that time, authors relied on patronage, or family wealth, for their support, rather than book sales. But the eighteenth century, with its growing literate middle-class and its proliferation of capable presses, hinted at the possibility that authors might earn their living through the sale of their work. The Statute of Anne provided a first suggestion that the law would defend authors' ability to support themselves in this way. With this shift in economic and legal conditions came a shift in attitudes toward writing that moved away from the neo-classical and toward the Romantic. According to scholar Jacqueline Rhodes,

> [T]he closely connected ideas of text-as-capital and author-as-owner emerged from the specific cultural conditions of the European Enlightenment, new conditions that demonised plagiarism and valorised *individuality*, especially as an economic construct . . . The new conceptions of writing and reading entailed seeing the writer as an originator, one who no longer produced texts as a cog in a publication machine, but instead created them as an *author.*
>
> 4

With the promise of economic independence to inspire them, writers began to think of themselves as the kind of Capital "A" Authors whose death Barthes would announce centuries later. Instead of the folks who produced page filler for printing presses, they were now originators and sole proprietary owners of the work they produced.

The Romantic notion of authorship drove further legislation protecting the newfound rights of authors, and these new laws, which extended an author's copyright beyond the protections of the Statue of Anne, further reinforced the Romantic notion of authorship. In fact, US copyright law today is based on this idea of Romantic originality and sole authorship. In a pivotal 1991 decision, Supreme Court Justice Sandra Day O'Connor wrote that "the *sin qua non* of copyright is originality" (Feist v. Rural). In other words, when single authors produce wholly original work, they are entitled to legal protection.

From the Statue of Anne to the Romantic attitude toward authorship to more recent legal decisions, history has arrived at a situation in which legal, economic, and cultural forces all seem to require that an author be the sole originator of his or her writing. Clearly, Eliot and Pound could not have anticipated the state of copyright in our cultural present. Regardless, similar legal and ideological forces that treated single authors as originators and owners of their texts defined the culture of publishing in 1922. Thus, although T S Eliot may have co-written "The Waste Land" with his *reviewer, resonator,* and *collaborator*, Ezra Pound, he perhaps could not have readily understood that relationship as one of co-authorship, and neither could his readers. The appearance of two names on a poem seemed odd then, and perhaps seems odd now, not because it is inherently odd—it is no more inherently odd than the notion of single authorship—but because over the last 300 years we have all gotten used to the idea that writers write alone and have exclusive legal rights to their work. This situation is not a simple one. It is complex and problematic, for it insists on a performance of solitary authorship even while the writing process, by nature, involves collaboration. So while authors must reach out to others in order to produce creative writing, they may simultaneously feel (perhaps like Eliot did) that they must take credit for the contributions of others or even deny the involvement of other writers who essentially served as co-authors.

In a previous chapter we saw how the myth of spontaneous genius led to a situation where creative writers could feel that they are not up to the task if their writing process does not live up to the false model promoted by writers like Coleridge and Kerouac. In that case, a lie about the nature of writing led to problems. The myth of solitary authorship can create similar problems. As we shall see in our next case study, when authors feel that they must suppress the details of their collaboration in order to pretend that they wrote their work alone, they can create anxiety for themselves as well as a potential for scandal.

Case Study II: Carver's Signature Style

Raymond Carver, the iconic American short-story writer, won fame and critical praise for a spare, minimalist style that offered a counterpoint to the brainy, labyrinthine stories of the early Postmodernists. What has come to be known as Carver's signature style (sometimes called "Kmart realism" for its presentation of the lives of middle-class Americans in the 1970s) has exerted a strong influence over the short story and much realistic fiction. One could argue that in many creative writing workshops, the injunctions to "cut dead weight" and "show don't tell" are really hints that the novice writer ought to produce prose more like Carver's. But Carver's style is not his own. It is not his at all. Instead, the "Carver" signature short story style really belongs not to Carver but to his editor and collaborator, Gordon Lish—or, rather, *to the collaboration between* Carver and Lish.

Lish became fiction editor for *Esquire* in 1969, promising to introduce innovative new voices to the magazine. He called on his friend, Carver, who was unknown at the time, to send in some stories. Carver sent him three, and, according to D T Max, who studied the Carver manuscripts, Lish edited them heavily, cutting out all traces of introspection and sentimentality, leaving only the bare essentials of the narrative. In "Fat," Carver told the story of a waitress who becomes obsessed with her memory of an overweight customer to whom she served a large meal. Lish essentially rewrote the story. According to Max, he "moves the story into the present tense . . . And he eliminates the waitress's self-reflectiveness, so we seem more involved than she does in what she is feeling. (Critics would later declare such touches to be trademark techniques of Carver)." Lish also added several lines that pick up on the sexuality latent in Carver's description of the fat man's "long, thick, creamy fingers." Lish adds a line in which the waitress says "My God . . . those were fingers," and another in which she describes her lover as "a tiny thing and hardly there at all." These lines introduce a new thematic layer to the story, which elevated heaviness into an emblem of "sexual potency, fullness, presence," and emphasized "the connection between longing and sexuality" (Max).

Lish published "Fat," and Carver's other stories with his own edits, and then talked them up to his literary friends and associates. Critics soon buzzed about the arrival of a new minimalist literary voice. This initial success energized the pair: Carver and Lish began a collaboration that would span the next decade, with Carver submitting drafts, and Lish paring them down and reworking them. In 1976, Lish secured publication with McGraw-Hill of Carver's first story collection, *Would You Please Be Quiet, Please?*. Carver was ecstatic, and he wrote Lish in gratitude for their collaboration, asking for his continued direction on future stories: "Tell me which ones and I'll go after it, or them . . . Or I will leave it up to you and you tell me what you think needs done or doing" (qtd. in Armitage). As in the relationship between Eliot and Pound, the one between Carver and Lish involved a kind of collaboration that moved well beyond *review* and *resonance* to encompass co-authorship.

Despite this reality, when critics praised *Would You Please Be Quiet, Please?*, they unanimously attributed the final work with its spare style, to

Carver alone. *The New York Times Book Review* described "Carver's collection as 'carefully shaped' and 'shorn of ornamentation,' marked by 'spells of quiet and tensed apprehension,' and suggested that Carver's prose 'carries his mark everywhere: I would like to believe that having read the stories I could identify him on the evidence of a paragraph' " (Max). The success of this initial collection more or less launched Carver's career, facilitating his transformation from a writer toiling in relative obscurity to an internationally recognized name: the collection was nominated for a National Book Award; two years later, Carver was given a Guggenheim Fellowship; and in 1979, Syracuse University hired Carver as a professor of English.

With this mounting success, Lish's edits became increasingly drastic. By the time of Carver's 1981 collection, *What We Talk About When We Talk About Love*, Lish was freely cutting out half or more of the content of Carver's stories, and of those stories, he rewrote 10 out of 13 endings. Having been rewarded for a style not his own, Carver became anxious at the possibility of exposure. He had a new circle of literary friends, and he had shown them his early drafts of the stories in this new collection. If they saw the stories in their final form, they would know that the work was not his own. If they made their discovery public, Carver's reputation might crumble in the resulting scandal. Carver wrote a long letter to Lish, begging Lish not to publish the collection with his severe edits. The tone of Carver's letter is one of desperation: "Please, Gordon, for God's sake help me in this and try to understand," he writes, "I'll say it again, if I have any standing or reputation . . . I owe it to you. I owe you this more-or-less pretty interesting life I have [but] I can't take the risk as to what might happen to me . . . [M]y very sanity is on the line here." Carver concludes by stating "if the book were to be published as it is in its present edited form, I may never write another story" (qtd. in Max).

In spite of Carver's pleas, Lish published the collection as he had edited it. Critics praised its style, which they again attributed solely to Carver, and Carver's reputation as a literary minimalist was secured. Carver subsequently separated himself from his collaboration with Lish, and his later work shows the difference. No longer spare or "shorn of ornamentation," the narratives contain introspective characters who feel feelings and talk about them at length. Even so, and to this day, the "Kmart realism" label is firmly affixed to Carver's name. The irony here is, of course, overwhelming. As time has passed, the work that Carver co-developed with Lish has come to be considered the "original" Carver style, and the work that he developed without Lish has come to be dismissed as the anomalous, largely forgettable work of a celebrity writer past his prime.

The dynamic between Carver and Lish could only exist in a culture out of touch with the collaborative nature of the creative process. In an environment dominated by the ideal of solitary authorship, Lish's role was suppressed so that Carver could be understood as the sole originator of his stories. This suppression gave rise to the potential of exposure and also to Carver's anxiety. If Carver and Lish had lived in a time and place where collaboration was understood to be a normal part of writing, the relationship between this author and editor could have been made public without anyone so much as flinching.

As we've been suggesting, the relationships between Eliot and Pound and that between Carver and Lish are not at all abnormal. If anything, they are the rule, rather than the exception. The appendix to Jack Stillinger's *Multiple Authorship and the Myth of Solitary Genius* lists 97 canonical British and American authors who collaborated to the extent of what Stillinger calls "multiple authorship." He deems his appendix a list of "pared-down results," since he has only included those cases in which there is "some kind of extrinsic (biographical or other documentary) evidence" for explicit collaboration (204). On his list are authors like Austen, Dickens, Trollope, Conrad, Joyce, Lawrence, Orwell, Beckett, Emerson, Melville, Dickinson, Twain, Fitzgerald, Faulkner, Hemingway, Hurston, Wright, Vonnegut, Barth, and Plath. And these are only the most obvious cases of collaboration. Not on Stillinger's list are all those historical collaborations that were successfully suppressed, all those that fall outside the confines of the British-American tradition, and all those that fit less neatly into LeFevre's *reviewer* or *resonator* categories.

Revisualizing The Image of Authors

The climate of our current literary culture may be moving away (however sluggishly) from the myth of single authorship. And while we don't necessarily care to yet again proclaim the second or third or fourth death of the resurrected Author—could this figure possibly have more than nine lives?—we certainly welcome the move toward acknowledging the inherent multiplicity of all authorship. We don't want our next generation of authors to suffer the kind of anxiety Carver experienced while trying desperately to maintain the fiction of his own singular voice. We also don't want emerging writers to think they are in this career all by themselves—isolated, without a support network—and imagine their successes and failures rest entirely on their own shoulders. Frankly, as our following chapters on publishing suggest, we think anyone who would like to make a career out of writing in twenty-first century America cannot afford to isolate themselves.

As we envision the future of creative writing, we envision one that treats collaboration less as a dirty little secret and more as an accepted and normal part of the writing process. From what we've noticed, the contemporary images associated with writing and writers' lives may finally be beginning to reflect this change as they are becoming more attuned to the reality of collaborative processes. Take for instance, the following picture, which the LA Writers' Group has used to promote itself on its website (Figure 2).

Here, we have an image not of solitary authorship, but of writers working together. This snapshot may not fall within a fine arts tradition of portraiture like the image we presented earlier of Sir Humphry Davy, but it is the picture this particular group of writers chose to publicize itself. In other words, the group considers it valuable and representative of their collective identity. Furthermore, it contains many of the common motifs found in traditional portraits of writers; they simply happen to be rearranged and redefined. For instance, a bookshelf representing the symbolic presence and influence of other authors appears in the background, placing the writers in relation to larger, diverse traditions of authorship. Although the door and windows in the photograph appear to be closed, they nonetheless suggest openings to the world outside the room depicted. Clearly, this room is no garret or isolation chamber. Perhaps the most telling transformation of common motifs—other than the presence of six rather than one author-figure—involves the sources of illumination. Light emerges not from a lamp on a sole author's desk; it is literally found between writers, suggesting that ideas and inspiration emerge

FIGURE 2 Los Angeles Writers' Group, *2014. © Nicole Criona, Los Angeles Writers' Group http://www.lawritersgroup.com*

from the very relations between collaborators. In fact, the most prominent area of luminescence—the lamp on the left hand side of the picture—is located between two writers' brains, for it is level with the head of the writer wearing a headband and the head of the writer dressed in a striped tank top. This picture offers a vision of writers that is not only more attuned to our contemporary culture but also to our genuine processes of composition. Instead of relegating collaborators to an area outside the picture frame or to merely a symbolic presence in the background, it offers the "and someone" of writers' lives center stage.

Many contemporary examples of literary collaboration value the sort of luminescence or clarity depicted here: i.e., made possible by co-authorship. In this sense, they reject the ego-driven secrecy, awkwardness, or shame that defined the work of canonical twentieth-century predecessors like Carver and Lish. While recognizing their individual limitations, they very publicly celebrate the advantages of working with one another. For instance, several years ago, Matthea Harvey and Amy Jean Porter began developing a collaborative project entitled *Of Lamb* (now available from McSweeney's) that evolved into an innovative text perhaps best described as part erasure poem and part picture book. Harvey began the project by selectively whiting out sections of text from the pages from David Cecil's biography, *A Portrait of Charles Lamb*, so that the remaining words formed short lyric poems vaguely related to the nursery rhyme "Mary Had a Little Lamb." Then, she recruited Porter to bring these poems to life through illustrations. The results are marvelous, childlike, and peculiar. Discussing the collaborative process underlying the book's creation, Harvey explains the value of working with someone whose aesthetic vision was unlike her own: "I wanted to see the poems through someone else's lens—to have someone do visually to my words what I had done to Lord David Cecil's text and I couldn't have been luckier in Amy Jean . . . [S]he made things even stranger!" (Interview). In this particular case, Harvey and Porter had the advantage not only of working with one another but also implicitly collaborating with another "and someone": the biography's original author, David Cecil. And, yes, all three authors receive credit (even if Cecil's unwitting contribution isn't celebrated until the end of the book in a section entitled, "A Note About the Process").

Two other recent cases attest to the importance of using collaborative practices to move beyond one's individual aesthetic routines and biases. In the sixth chapter of *Citizen*, a book of hybrid poetics, Claudia Rankine includes scripts for "situation videos," which her husband, John Lucas, produced as "short video essays." This genre-bending collaboration combines the sensibilities of a poet and videographer to address problems of racism in contemporary US culture. Rankine describes the advantages of their collaborative approach:

> The use of video manipulation by John Lucas allowed me to slow down . . . as if I were there in real time rather than as a spectator considering it in retrospect. As a writer working with someone with a different skill set, I was given access to a kind of seeing that is highly developed in the visual arts, and that I don't rely on as intuitively.

Lucas's contribution provided a visual immediacy to the acts of micro-aggression Rankine sought to capture—a quality that may not have made its way into the work if Rankine had taken on the project alone. You can find links to the situation videos on YouTube; we suggest you take a look.

A similar advantage is described by poets Dolores Dorantes and Rodrigo Flores Sánchez, who recently collaborated on a book entitled *Intervene/ Intervenir,* which centers on the theme of intervention through, alternatively, violence and love within postcolonial contexts. On the *Best American Poetry* Blog, Sánchez describes their collaboration this way: "This process was a radical questioning of what identity means and of the 'style' of a piece of writing. The process is the inverse of Ariadne's thread. The intention wasn't to leave the labyrinth but rather to go further in, to get lost in the questions, recurrences and stylistic marks of the other" (Interview). With the help of the "other," each author celebrates the advantages of getting lost, of having their habitual writing practices productively disrupted, of freeing themselves from what they (and millions of Buddhists and social constructionists alike) consider the illusion of an autonomous self. Through occasions of metacommentary, the book further contests the myth of single authorship by inviting readers to "INTERVENE IN ME," suggesting in some lines that the very processes of collaborative influence is inescapable: "The world / never closed to you. The world / COLLABORATES." (From 28).

As these examples suggest, we see contemporary writers and artists treating collaboration less as a shameful secret and more as an honest, ordinary, and valuable means of producing literature. When authors are more focused on the interconnectedness of their practices and less concerned with egocentric or individualized constructions of "genius," they can move beyond the trappings of the Carver/Lish case to better understand the worth and wonderment of alternative viewpoints and perspectives. Dorantes and Sánchez's work particularly resonates with us because it leads one step further toward understanding the social and cultural value of getting out of ourselves, specifically for a larger, defined purpose (rather than the production of literature in the abstract). When we meditate on the implications of *Intervene/Intervenir*, we appreciate not only the *inevitability* but also the *strategic utility* of collaboratively authored literature as applied to specific cultural projects. Let us explain what we mean with two more examples.

Strategic Collaboration: On Human Rights and the Future of Space Exploration

Our first example, "A Collaborative Poem for the Hazara," combines the work of 23 poets from 16 different countries, ranging from Iceland to Zimbabwe. The poem was developed to raise global awareness for the plight of the Hazara people (originally of Afghanistan), who in recent history have been subject to displacement, genocide, and innumerable human rights violations. The multiplicity of voices and tones that define the multi-authored work juxtapose haunting images with hopeful defiance. For instance, in the following passage, the horror of the first two lines by Jessie Kleeman are subsequently tempered by a resolution offered by Siki Dlanga:

> Ameer your name sounds like Amee'q which means,
> Your skin has been taken off of you
> . . .
> Hazara
> Your name cannot be erased
> Now it is in the prayers of every language
> . . .
> The hatred of your enemies
> Has won you the love of the world.
>
> Hazar 522–524

Throughout the work, contributing poets engage in this sort of contrasting dialogue. They also use different strategies to reconcile their own subject positions with those of the people they are writing to and about. Indian poet K Satchidanandan attempts to encourage cross-cultural identification and empathic connection by assuming the persona of the persecuted. He writes, "I am the hunted Hazara, / I am the fallen Buddha of Bamiyan, / the innocent's blood on the nascent snow" (Hazar 532). In contrast, Swedish poet Boel Schenlaer writes from an outsider's identity, juxtaposing his position of relative privilege and stability in relation to a population that has been forced out of their homeland by government factions and terrorist organizations:

> I dedicate the future
> and all the collected
> bowls of water
> . . .
> and the benefits of social security

the forests of tomorrow

. . .

to the Hazara people.

Hazar 527

With lines like these, the collaborative poem reads as a risky but useful text full of emotional resonance that not only invokes compassion among readers but also offers a more direct, tactical purpose: to lobby for real-world political change on behalf of the Hazara.

The context in which the poem originally appeared reveals the tangible nature of this purpose. Published in *Poems for the Hazara: An Anthology and Collaborative Poem* in 2014, the work is followed by a document entitled, "An Open Letter from World-Wide Poets Addressed to World Political Leaders." Indeed, this open letter reads as a petition signed by 354 poets from 96 countries, which formally requests government officials to take immediate political action. After outlining several recent atrocities committed against the Hazara, the authors introduce a list of requests addressed directly to world leaders. It begins with the following four items:

1. Declare a state of emergency regarding the Hazara state of affairs, as authorized by the Convention on the Prevention and Punishment of the Crime of Genocide.
2. Apply diplomatic pressure on both the Afghan and Pakistani governments to immediately cease acts of discrimination against the Hazara and to stop supporting terrorist groups who commit violent acts against them.
3. Ask the Refugee Convention's state parties to protect Hazara asylum seekers and grant them asylum.
4. Establish an international truth Commission to investigate crimes against the Hazara. (Rendon 545)

The seemingly unorthodox combination of the collaborative poem and the open letter works to effectively move readers toward activism. The refiguring of poetry and diplomacy into this shared enterprise is made possible precisely because of the collaborative activity of writers from radically different cultural contexts coming together for a shared humanitarian goal—one larger than themselves. Indeed, the defining purpose of petitioning government leaders drives the work from its inception, making the idea of writing to achieve some sort of individual literary stardom a moot point, if not a narcissistic undertaking.

Our second example of utilitarian collaboration comes from Japan. While it is radically different from the Hazara project, it shares a foundational goal: i.e., using collaborative writing for a precisely defined cultural purpose. Since 2006, the Japan Aerospace Exploration Agency (JAXA) has been organizing an annual poetic collaboration through its *Ucyu Renshi* program. Loosely translated as "The Space Poem Chain," *Ucyu Renshi* is essentially a series of linked poems that explores the nature of the universe and reflects "an awe for the infinite" (JAXA). Each year, JAXA has been creating the poem chain by soliciting work from established poets, astronauts, and scientists; accepting unsolicited submissions from an international public; and inviting Japanese school children to contribute to the project. Contributors range in age from 8 to 98. Some are experienced writers; many are not. From this diverse pool of material, pieces are selected and combined into a collaborative work of roughly twenty-four alternating 3–5-line poems. The form itself (*renshi*) has a history steeped in collaborative practice. Largely popularized in the late twentieth century by Makoto Ooka and others, it modernizes medieval traditions of *renku* and *renga*, linked verse composed within the context of a group activity. Essentially, individuals would display their wit as they took turns spontaneously composing verses in response to one another. Under JAXA's treatment of the form, an invited poet usually composes a poem of five lines; then, people from Japan and across the globe submit three-line responses, and the most appropriate is selected for inclusion.

The following excerpt from the first "Space Poem Chain" reveals the workings of the form and its diverse approach to co-authorship:

On a package tour to the Moon
our guide turns to us with a warm smile
How are the old bamboo cutter and his wife these days?
The oceans so blue the sparkling green the kind people
How I miss your star!

A star that is our cradle
our heart—from where we took our leap
but why?

Riding in a cradle
I'm headed for the other shore so far away . . .

JAXA

The first five-line poem reproduced above was written by Keiko Nakamura, a molecular biologist; the three line response is the work of Frank Hogan, a writer from Ireland; and the beginning of next poem was penned by the late Yoshio Fujita, former astronomer, astrophysicist, and professor emeritus at the University of Tokyo. As exemplified by this excerpt, the different poems are connected by the reproduction of an exact word or phrase—in this case "star" and "cradle" serve as hinges. In other instances, the poems are more loosely connected through indirect reference.

More important than the formal design of the "Space Poem Chain" are its cultural functions. JAXA uses it for two main purposes. First, the poem is transported by an astronaut to the International Space Station, where it is uploaded to the Japanese Experiment Module, or "Kibo." Here it is used to represent citizens of earth and "connect people, including crew members in space" in ways that are "unfettered by barriers of nation, culture, generation, profession, and position or rank" (Koyama). On a grand scale, the democratic ideal of this collaborative project seeks to engender empathic human connection; more immediately, it might be used to soothe the loneliness of an astronaut serving a tour of duty at the space station, which can be an isolating endeavor, to say the least.

Second, the "Space Poem Chain" is integrated into educational curricula, where it is used (1) to teach cooperation among school children and (2) to

generate interest in the science of space exploration. Within the contexts of elementary school language classes, visiting poets offer *Ucyu Renshi* as a lesson in cooperative composition and representation. Here, students work together to collectively compose linked poetry (Koyama). One can imagine the excitement elementary school children must feel at the prospect of having their verse potentially make its way into outer space!

Post Script: Play Nice, Say "Please" and "Thank You"?

And speaking of cooperation . . . We suspect it is obvious by now that *Poems for the Hazara* and *Ucyu Renshi* offer more ideal approaches toward collaboration than the Carver/Lish model. In fact, we recommend that as you forge your own working relationships with collaborators, you aim for transparency, cooperation, kindness, and respect. To this end, you may find it beneficial to create a set of ground rules—even if it is only a loose set of principles like the ones drafted by poets Denise Duhamel and Maureen Seaton whose "Ten Commandments of Collaboration" includes useful edicts that range from "Thou shalt trust thy collaborator's art with thy whole heart" and "Thou shalt trust thy collaborator's judgment with thy whole mind" to, perhaps most importantly, "Do not be an egotistical asshole" (Duhamel). Whether or not you formalize a set of guidelines, we hope that you allow your collaborative relationships to be informed by principles of fair play and mutual goodwill.

Discussion Questions

1. Think about the people who affect your creative writing. Who are your reviewers, resonators, and collaborators proper? How exactly have they helped you develop your work?

2. Why would you want to credit or not credit these contributors as co-authors? Does anything in particular—say economic, legal, pedagogical, or ideological pressure—prevent you from doing so?

3. Think more specifically about your workshop or writing group. In what specific ways do the activities you engage in here encourage or discourage collaboration? In what ways does this environment sustain or challenge the ideal of single-authorship? Why do or don't you credit your workshop or writing group partners as co-authors in your work?

4. Within other contexts, co-authorship is a norm rather than an exception. In academic publishing (particularly the sciences) it happens all the time. Here, it doesn't carry the sense of shame or fear of discovery that it did for Carver and other creative writers. Why do you think the field of creative writing, in particular, has retained a stigma against co-authorship for so long?

Your Turn: Questions, Concerns & Creative-Critical Comments

1. ____

____

____

____

2. ____

____

____

____

3. ____

____

____

____

Writing Experiments

1. To ease into collaboration, you can first engage in a bit of meta-collaboration: that is, in small groups spend some time inventing all the ways you can think of for individuals to act as co-authors of a work. Write down as many ideas as possible, however far-fetched. Think of different technologies that might be employed and different ways to employ them. Imagine methods for groups of two, three, twelve, fifty, a thousand. If you're looking for inspiration for this

challenge, consider taking a look at Eric Whitacre's Ted Talk, in which he discusses using YouTube to enable a virtual choir of over 2,000 singers to collaborate on a song from distant points all over the globe. You can find his talk on the Ted website or YouTube. You might also check out the film *Life in a Day*, a crowd-sourced documentary that was compiled from over 80,000 different video submissions. Whether you find yourself leaning toward large- or small-scale collaborative activities, make sure you engage in a robust brainstorming session that covers a range of possibilities. Then, after this session, come together as a class or writers' collective so you can share ideas. Keep a personal list of methods you might consider using later, should you choose to develop a collaborative writing project.

2. For this exercise, we will relax our earlier suggestion that you play nice with your collaborators. Pick a published book and then be a Lish. Gut the work. Cut it by 40–70 percent. Keep in mind that if you choose to gut a contemporary text, the work you produce for this exercise will be acceptable for our immediate purposes but may not be publishable elsewhere. If you want to use this exercise to create a publishable/saleable product, you might want to look into local copyright law, especially the sections related to "fair use" and "derivative works." If in doubt about whether you can use a particular source text, consider selecting a piece of literature that is in the public domain. (This will allow you to dodge the issue of copyright, for the most part.) If you're looking for examples of authors who have reinvented literature in the manner we are suggesting, take a peek at Mary Reufle's *Little White Shadow*, Jonathan Safran Foer's *Tree of Codes*, Janet Holmes's *The Ms of my Kin*, Ronald Johnson's *Radios*, or Tom Phillips's *A Humument*. All of these models reinvent inherited public domain texts entirely through processes of editorial deletion. Reufle, for instance, uses white out to convert an obscure nineteenth century booklet into avant-garde poetry, Johnson excises words from Milton's *Paradise Lost*, and Foer literally cuts out sentences from a public domain novel to invent a new narrative.

Deep Reading

While explicit collaboration may seem unusual or even contrary to our received notions of authorship, the practice is far more common than you might suspect. For a solid introduction to the phenomenon, you might consult Jack Stillinger's *Multiple Authorship and the Myth of Solitary Genius*, which includes case studies of the collaborative production of Wordsworth's *Prelude*, Keats's *Isabella*, and, interestingly, John Stewart Mill's *Autobiography*. For an adventure in collaborative poetry, consider Soft Skull Press's *Saints of Hysteria:*

A Half-Century of Collaborative American Poetry. If you're more interested in fiction, you might pick up *The Floating Admiral*, a novel collaboratively written by The Detection Club, a group of British mystery authors including Dorothy Sayers, Agatha Christie, and G K Chesterton. You might also read *Caverns*, a novel Ken Kesey wrote collaboratively with his fiction class at the University of Oregon. If you'd really like to go down a rabbit hole, consider researching the phenomenon of *A Million Penguins*, the first ever collaborative wiki-novel, which Penguin Books launched in 2017 and then abruptly closed after it was targeted by internet trolls.

SECTION THREE

How Creative Writers Find Their Audiences, or How Publishing Works

6

What Your Creative Writing Teacher May Not Have Told You: On The Problem of "Greatness" in the Literary Marketplace

So far, we have discussed the false Romantic notion that literature arrives in the world in sudden bursts of inspiration, leaping from the mind of an author directly onto the page. In debunking this myth, we've tried to reveal how all authors, even so-called "great" ones, rely more on continual activities of drafting, rewriting, and revising—the labor of the writing process, if you will—than any spontaneous psychic visitation from the muse. We've also challenged the popular assumption that authors work in isolation by revealing how all writing involves some form of implicit or explicit collaboration. We've offered our alternative perspective on these issues not because we want to cultivate an image of ourselves as writing rebels in the academic equivalent of trashing a hotel room or setting a textbook on fire—i.e., defiance for the sake of defiance—but because we find the promotion of these myths genuinely damaging, and we'd like to change them. At present, they offer a distorted perspective on the field of creative writing and, in the process, mislead emerging authors.

By the way, we probably should have made something clear long ago: we assume that if you're reading this book, you are indeed an emerging author. Further, we assume that as an emerging author, you are interested in disseminating your work to a reading public of some sort or another. If our assumption isn't too far off, then we need to discuss the issue of publishing and revisit at least three more of the myths that continue to promote ill-informed ideas about creative writing: the myth of the absent marketplace, the legend of inherent greatness, and the fallacy of an egalitarian publishing industry.

Against Greatness: On Content, Context, and the Reality of Rejection

Most creative writing programs focus so exclusively on the crafts of fiction and poetry that they offer limited opportunity to critically investigate how creative writers actually get their work into the hands of readers. While they dedicate an abundance of time and energy to offering students advice on the form and content of their writing, they dedicate significantly less time and energy to helping students successfully navigate the contexts of journal and book publishing. Certainly, *Poets and Writers' Magazine*'s regular column "The Practical Writer" and occasional articles in AWP's *Writer's Chronicle* offer useful guidance to this end. However, the industry conversations begun in journals like these rarely transfer or extend into substantial classroom dialogue, for in a typical workshop setting—a place where aesthetics reign—it may seem crass, awkward, or corrupting to bring up issues related to placing or "selling" literature. Suggesting that writing is not only an art but also a commodity might seem to threaten the supposedly safe space of the atelier or the integrity of the artistic process. As a result, conversations about how to find or create publishing venues rarely occur with enough regularity or depth. We have frequently heard creative writing teachers suggest that students wait until after they've polished their work to worry about publishing it, or defer questions about publishing by simply suggesting they'll talk about the subject later, perhaps at the end of the semester. These are perfectly reasonable reactions. The problem is that all too often *later* never arrives. Questions get postponed indefinitely, and the perpetually deferred literary marketplace becomes all the more obscure and enigmatic in its absence, transforming into the stuff of mystery, like a scene from an Agatha Christie novel. We imagine Hercule Poirot sniffing around the writer's workshop, twitching his mustache, and looking troubled. "Where have the publishing opportunities gone?" he asks himself, and "Why is no one talking about their disappearance?"

The very lack of these conversations promotes the myth that great literary works somehow move suddenly and brilliantly from an author's desk into the world. By perpetually delaying an examination of the ins-and-outs of the marketplace and focusing instead solely on craft, writing programs can give their students the impression that publication simply happens when writers produce work at a certain level of quality. Of course, the path to publication is never so simple; nor is it easy for creative work to find friendly critics and a large audience of readers. In fact, the careers of most creative writers start, in a word, with *rejection*.

We realize that rejection may seem like a strange place to begin our discussion of publishing, but if you're going into this profession, it's likely to be precisely where you find yourself (early on, at least). And if you do wind up here, you'll be in good company. Initial rejection is more the norm than the exception for even—and especially—the world's most successful authors. Several years ago, Richard Oram spoke to NPR's Weekend Edition about rejection letters from the Knopf archive. Among Knopf's rejects are some of the biggest names in twentieth-century literature: Sylvia Plath, Vladimir Nabokov, Jack Kerouac, George Orwell, and many others. Orwell's *Animal Farm* was rejected by an editor who said "It is impossible to sell animal stories in the USA." Kerouac's *On the Road* drew harsh commentary from one editor, who suggested that "this huge sprawling and inconclusive novel would probably have small sales and sardonic, indignant reviews from every side." Of course, Knopf is far from the only publisher to reject what would become renowned works of literature. Alice Walker, Agatha Christie, C S Lewis, J D Salinger, Yann Martel, H G Wells, Herman Melville, Louisa May Alcott, Mary Shelley, Joseph Heller, Norman Mailer, Catherine O'Flynn, Jorge Luis Borges, Madeline L'Engle, and D H Lawrence are only several celebrity authors who had what would become their most famous works rejected ("Best-Sellers"). Irving Stone's *Lust For Life* was rejected sixteen times; Richard Adams's *Watership Down* was rejected seventeen times; William Golding's *Lord of the Flies* was rejected twenty times, James Joyce's *Dubliners* was rejected twenty-two times; Margaret Mitchell's *Gone with the Wind* was rejected thirty-eight times; and Katheryn Stockett's *The Help* was rejected sixty times ("Best-Sellers," Vincent).

These rejection numbers might strike some readers as humorous because we all know that those works went on to popular success or critical acclaim. Since *Animal Farm* and *Dubliners* are considered modern classics, it is easy to assume that the editors who rejected them made a laughably big mistake: they overlooked greatness when it was right there in front of them. However, to say that the editors somehow missed out on inherently eminent literature is to assume that a given work of literature can somehow be inherently eminent. The idea of the "great books" myth is that some writing is so amazing that it will find its way to publication, success, and canonization of its own accord. Great books make their own way in the world. They're just that great.

But this is not how the literary marketplace works AT ALL. *Lord of the Flies* and other titles were not great books until after they were published. Before publication, they were merely manuscripts being shopped around, which may or may not have had a chance at success. They were potential investments upon which publishers had to decide whether to take calculated business risks. Likewise, Kerouac was not a "great author" until after his book was published, well-reviewed, and frequently purchased. That is to say, a nexus of contributing factors and entities, including the promotion of Kerouac by colleagues like Ginsberg, the marketing and publicity team at Viking Press (his publisher), the cultural buzz of the Beat Generation, the advent of youth culture, and the subsequent decision of university professors to adopt *On The Road* for classroom use (to name only a few factors), effectively built the reputation of Kerouac and his novel after the work had been released into the world. Perhaps our point is most readily demonstrated in the plainest of economic terms. In 1957, the first hardcover edition of *On the Road* (whether signed or unsigned) cost around $3.95—a rather average, unexceptional price equivalent to comparable books at the time. In 2002, an inscribed copy of the first edition sold at auction for $185,000 ("Sold"). In 2019, a signed first edition copy was listed on AbeBooks for $89,509 ("On"); in the same year, unsigned first editions varied from $2,000 to $6,000. This change suggests that the value of Kerouac's book is not and was never inherent. It couldn't be, for in different contexts, the same product—even when adjusted for inflation—was worth vastly different sums of money. Rather, the book's dramatic increase and subsequent fluctuation was made possible by history (the passing of time) and culture (the prioritizing of worth).

The book's literal change in economic value sheds light on its symbolic value as a piece of literature. Unlike the many first editions of other titles that now sell for less-than cover price in online markets or used bookstores, *On The Road*'s first edition is so expensive because historical circumstances have aligned in such a way that it has become a prized piece of literature. In the imagination of many, it has become "the defining work of the beat generation" ("On"). Literary greatness is not an inherent quality that dwells inside a novel or a poem or a play. Rather, it is a quality bestowed upon writers and their writing by the cultures they inhabit and the cultures that inherit their work. In this sense, it is somewhat akin to Stanley Fish's ideas about meaning in a poem, which we touched on in the last chapter: i.e., greatness is not intrinsic to a work but created and imposed upon that work by interpretive and collaborative communities occupying specific cultural and historical contexts. These contexts draw a figurative frame around works like *On The Road* in a manner analogous to the way Fish drew a literal, chalk frame around his linguistics assignment. Both frames shape the way readers perceive the chosen texts in the same manner: they enable us to recognize those texts as creative and important work. This is not to say that there are no differences in the quality of poems, novels, or plays—that would be an absurdly reductive position—but rather that these differences are constructed and contextual. Let's take a brief look at a case study of another of America's supposed great authors to further explain what we mean.

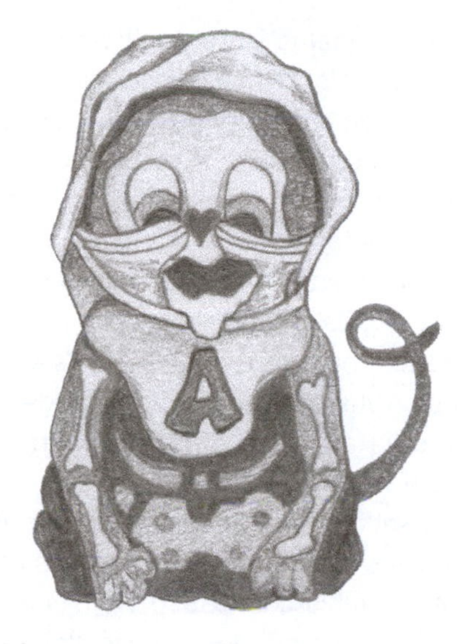

Nathaniel What's-His-Name and His Unremarkable Little Tales

At present, Nathaniel Hawthorne is arguably considered one of America's greatest writers. That wasn't always the case. In *Sensational Designs: The Cultural Work of American Fiction, 1790–1860*, Jane Tompkins reveals how exactly Hawthorne gained his literary reputation—his greatness, if you will—through specific historical and cultural circumstances. She reverses the notion that greatness transcends circumstance to reveal how circumstance creates greatness.

As a first case-in-point, Tompkins observes that all of Hawthorne's early stories—his work published from 1828 to 1836, which are now considered among his best pieces—went unnoticed by the critics of his time. "Indifference" is the word Tompkins uses: critics ignored the stories completely. But why is it that no one noticed Hawthorne's supposedly greatest works when they first came out? The answer is that readers in Hawthorne's time encountered those stories in a very different context than we do. At the time of publication, Hawthorne's stories were released in collections known as "gift book annuals," books that featured an editor's name but kept the authors' names anonymous. Tompkins notes that the "annuals were rather lightly regarded at the time, critics had no expectation of finding anything of merit in them" (6). Further, there was nothing remarkable about Hawthorne's stories that would have led a reader to think they were anything special. "Hawthorne" was an unknown name, the stories he published, unexceptional.

In our time, Hawthorne's status is quite different. Usually readers today cannot help but read his novels and stories in light of his reputation as an important, canonical American author. In fact, most of us encounter his work in the context of a classroom where we are studying classic American literature, and Hawthorne's fiction, often *The Scarlet Letter* and "Young Goodman Brown," are presented to us as significant to our study. We are not in the position of a gift book reader, who has been given no reason to believe the stories are anything special. Quite the reverse: we have a context for reading that is devoted to singling out Hawthorne's work and assuming or explaining its value to us. Whereas the gift book reader would have to work hard to find a reason to call Hawthorne's stories important, we would have to work hard to make a case that they are not.

The story of this reversal further demonstrates how greatness is awarded to literary work. As Tompkins describes it, Hawthorne's career was defined by the progressively more favorable contexts in which he was able to publish. The first improvement in Hawthorne's lot came in 1836—eight years after his first publication—when one of his stories was accepted by *The Token*, a more prominent gift book annual, and its editor, Samuel Goodrich, began talking up Hawthorne's work to other editors. The following year, due to the buzz created by Goodrich, Hawthorne was able to publish the first volume of *Twice-told Tales*, which reprinted his stories from the annuals in a new context. He received one "extremely laudatory" review from the editor of the *Salem Gazette* and another, equally laudatory review from an old classmate of his from Bowdoin College, Henry Wadsworth Longfellow. Longfellow was now a professor at Harvard with significant cultural cachet; he wrote for the *North American*, an elite journal popular with the New England literati (10). Longfellow's hype spread Hawthorne's reputation as a rising literary figure up and down the Eastern seaboard. By 1848, when Hawthorne lost his job as surveyor at the customs house in Salem due to a change in administration, he was famous enough that his firing caused a scandal. Newspapers around the country ran the story of an American author getting discharged from his job for political reasons. All of this press served to bolster Hawthorne's reputation. In fact, the scandal drew the attention of publisher James T Fields, "who until then had not printed a word of Hawthorne's, but whose business instincts now prompted him to Salem on the off-chance that Hawthorne might have something ready for the press" (24). Field's instincts—his decision to capitalize on an existing public scandal and take a calculated risk on a manuscript—proved astute, and "Hawthorne's first book to appear after the customs house fiasco sold remarkably well: the advance publicity had guaranteed that *The Scarlet Letter* would be a success" (24). Interestingly, it was not the novel so much as Hawthorne's preface to it that drove early sales of the book. Written at Field's suggestion, the preface insinuated that the novel was actually a manuscript Hawthorne had discovered while working at the customs house, thus tying the work directly to the scandal that had made him famous nationwide. It was the act of cashing in on a public scandal—not inherent greatness—that established Hawthorne's first book as a good read.

It wasn't until well after the popularity of *The Scarlet Letter* that Hawthorne was established as an important writer. In fact, most of his literary reputation was established after he died. Among the factors contributing to this reputation, Tompkins cites publishing giant Houghton Mifflin's acquiring of publication rights, repeated promotion of new book editions, and the entrance of Hawthorne's writing into the academic establishment. Houghton Mifflin published his work in its American Classics for the Schools series, and Yale included junior class essay questions regarding the relevance of his work to debates over realism that were occurring at the time (29). It was because of these collective circumstances—especially colleges' and universities' adoption of the texts—that Hawthorne's work was enabled to reach the status of (apparently) essential reading.

Hawthorne's story is not unique. The factors that led to his publishing success and subsequent "greatness" are similar to those of other well-published, well-regarded authors. He wrote stories and published them without any fanfare. A break-through publication combined with the help of some well-connected friends allowed his star to rise. Then a combination of historical accident and savvy promotion cemented Hawthorne's name in the canon of American literature. Importantly, most of the work to transition Hawthorne from writer of unexceptional "gift book" stories to "great American author" was not performed by Hawthorne himself but by an assortment of friends, publishers, editors, reviewers, and academics largely after his death. Nathaniel Hawthorne wrote stories, but it was others who converted those stories into supposed "great literature."

Back to the Future: Collaboration and Context Then and Now

Forgive us for belaboring our point about Hawthorne. We do so because the details of his success story reveal at least three important implications for contemporary writers. First, they reveal another limitation of the "craft only" approach to creative writing. By focusing exclusively on the formal features of well-regarded stories and poems, writers tend to overlook the ways in which the craft of those works *have very little to do with their cultural success*. "Well-craftedness," we might say, is a necessary but not sufficient condition for great literature. For every Hawthorne, there are many thousands of writers whose work remains "unexceptional" not because it isn't well wrought, but because, for whatever reason, these writers were not able to secure the same friendly reviews, heavy promotion, and posthumous reputation-construction that he was. To be great, it is not enough to focus on craft and hope that quality writing will eventually rise to the top. To illustrate what we mean, we'd ask you to imagine what Hawthorne's success must have looked like to the many other authors whose work appeared alongside his in gift book annuals. To their eyes, at least, his stories would appear no more finely crafted than theirs, so why should he enjoy fame and fortune while they remained stuck in obscurity? The more cynical among these writers would surely see his connection to Longfellow as an unfair advantage, and we imagine they would have scoffed at his preface to *A Scarlet Letter*—clearly a crass effort to cash in on scandal.

Second, the story of Hawthorne's ascent reveals the importance of collaboration within the context of publishing. In our last chapter, we discussed collaboration in relation to the writing process; it is equally—if not more—important within the literary marketplace. Part of Hawthorne's ability to become a successful writer depended on his collaboration with colleagues. Goodrich, Longfellow, and other editors essentially functioned as what Karen LeFevre would call reviewers and resonators, lauding Hawthorne's work in print and offering support, promotion, and publicity. Their work in these roles enabled the author to place his fiction in increasingly prestigious publication venues, and these venues then provided the frame within which readers would begin to recognize Hawthorne's work as important. However base it may seem, it was precisely this kind of social and career networking—the cultivating of important connections and endorsements that enabled Hawthorne to advance his writing in public markets.

Authors' need for these sorts of resonators extends into the present. Today, when we attend the annual writers' conference sponsored by AWP, the Association of Writers and Writing Programs, we hear attendees discuss the importance of emerging authors serving as good "literary citizens." This phrase comes up particularly in panels devoted to discussing first-book publication. Here, panelists tend to advise up-and-coming writers to actively support the careers of other writers, to work toward building community with peers and publishers, and to serve as readers or volunteers for nonprofit independent publishing projects. The idea is that if you act as a resonator for others by being supportive of their projects, you are more likely to have your own career supported in turn. Acting as a literary citizen in the capacities mentioned above offers you entrance into a collaborative network that may help facilitate your own authorial aspirations: you may get to know people who are currently, or soon will be, in a position to support the publication of your own manuscript.

Indeed, collaborative networking remains vital for emerging authors' careers. This is particularly true because the enterprise of creative writing sustains a structure of elitism and hierarchy. Let us explain what we mean through a comparison to academic publishing. Today, the latter tends to rely on the "blind review" of manuscripts: editors remove the author's name and identifying features from an article or scholarly monograph before they send it to a panel of anonymous reviewers, who are specialists in a given subject. In ideal circumstances, this procedure means the reviewers don't know the identity of the author, and the author doesn't know the identity of the reviewers. An effort to enact an ethical and democratic review process, the procedure works against what might be called academic nepotism, as it provides little if any advantages to individuals already enfranchised within powerful networks, or academic family trees, if you will. The integrity of the system works against the very idea of friends doing favors for friends, reviewers doing favors for authors and vice versa.

Personally, we often wish the procedure for reviewing creative writing manuscripts functioned in a similar fashion. At present, however, literary publishing is decidedly less democratic and tends to offer advantages to authors who have already made a name for themselves. For instance, most top editors and agents simply refuse to review unsolicited submissions. If they don't know you, they won't look at your work. Further, apart from the case of some literary contests and a few rare journals, all identifying features are kept on submitted manuscripts. As you might suspect, given these circumstances, known authors carry literary capital; unknown authors do not. This predicament makes it all the more difficult to publish a first book without the necessary contacts, hence the advice about finding your way as a literary citizen within established communities. Having a contemporary equivalent of Longfellow in your corner certainly doesn't hurt.

At the same time we want to cultivate the value of literary citizenry, we feel a responsibility to caution emerging writers about the potential dangers of networking in creative industries. As we drafted and revised this manuscript, the #metoo movement exposed how damaging abuses of power within artistic networks can be. Powerful people in many creative industries—including literary publishing—have been exposed for using their positions to prey on emerging talent. A number of celebrity authors (including Sherman Alexie, Junot Diaz, James Dashner, Jay Asher, and others) have recently been accused of sexual harassment or misconduct—with the merit of these accusations being sometimes freely admitted and sometimes fiercely denied. Our point here is less to invoke fear but rather to acknowledge the reality that in writing and publishing—as in most entertainment-affiliated industries—perpetrators exist who may attempt to exploit or manipulate efforts at what we are calling literary citizenship. That is, they may review or promote an emerging author's work, thus offering the benefits of name affiliation, only to later exert pressure for inappropriate forms of reciprocation. This behavior, of course, enrages us and we'd like to be clear that when we advocate literary citizenship we are in no way suggesting that anyone suffer unwanted sexual advances or feel manipulated into actions that run counter to their conscience. For us, advocating literary citizenship is not about feeling indebted for "favors" granted by enfranchised male authors; it is about seeking out and establishing supportive and trusted networks that may indeed promote healthy communities and perhaps in this capacity even serve as watchdogs for abuses of power. The more open and less isolated networking can be—through commitments to transparency, honest and open representation on social media, and help from advocacy organizations like VIDA: Women in Literary Arts—the harder it is for abuse to continue.

The Elephant in the Publisher's Closet

Before we get to our third issue (the importance of context) we should probably address a rather glaring omission. One thing we've left out of our discussion of Hawthorne's rise to national literary superstardom and his relevance to the present is, of course, his status as a white guy. His identity as cisgender Caucasian male enabled his enfranchisement within the literary culture of nineteenth-century New England, and he enjoyed the privileges of this culture, which remained largely inaccessible to those who did not share his identity—due to systemic race, gender, and class discrimination. While the diversity and demographics of the publishing industry have certainly changed since the time of Hawthorne's writing, they remain a very real concern for contemporary writers.

We may want to believe that, today, publishing is a meritocratic or egalitarian enterprise, but it isn't. In a recent forum on equity in publishing, Amy King suggested the following regarding the contemporary US publishing scene:

> Publishing carries on as if it is solely premised on merit and that everyone is simply out to publish the best work going. This presentation—this oft cited guise—parallels the notion that everyone in this country was born with the same rights, accesses, and means across the board. It's delusional to pretend . . . that we aren't living in a country that has yet to fully address and rectify a holocaust that ravaged and destroyed many people of color . . . [W]ho gets to speak . . . has always been determined by a violent hierarchical ranking. To pretend that somehow publishing is built on simply locating and advancing the 'best voices' is to pretend that the literary world is somehow removed from a country that ranks and others and decimates entire

populations—so too does the literary world, which is made up of the same country's citizens.

QTD. In Aiello

The problem King illuminates is backed by statistics. Recent surveys found that among US publishers roughly 90 percent of books were penned by white authors (see CCBC, Gay, Low). This astonishing number clearly points to a systemic problem. Indeed, many argue that the demographics of the publishing industry itself serve to perpetuate a lack of diversity among the books it publishes: white acquisitions editors look for books that reflect the tastes of white acquisition editors. Like King, Caroyln Reidy, CEO of Simon & Schuster, conceptualizes the lack of diversity as a problem of legacy: "The large American publishing companies . . . were established by relatively wealthy white men, and they sort of perpetuated their own kind" (qtd. in Neary). This statement largely rings true, but we need to complicate it a little bit. Over the last several decades, the internal makeup of publishing houses has shifted in at least one fairly dramatic way. The old boys club is no longer a boy's club—at least when it comes to employees. The majority of individuals working in acquisition, editorial, marketing, or managing positions now identify as female. Roughly 80 percent of the workforce is comprised of women. However, about 86 percent of the workforce still identifies as white (Milliot).

As Daniel José Older has suggested, this radical imbalance too often means that writers of color must get their work past a "white gatekeeper" in order to gain entry to a publishing house. Indeed, many individuals and organizations have been pointing to this problem and demanding reform. Over the last few years, We Need Diverse Books, a nonprofit literary organization, has been engaged in an influential Twitter campaign that calls for more diversity in children's book publishing. Akashic Books, an independent literary publisher in Brooklyn, has made "reverse gentrification of the literary world" their official motto (qtd. in Neary). According to Older's thinking, the problem comes down to representation inside the publishing industry: "We need diverse agents, we need [diverse] editors, we need diverse book buyers . . . and we need diverse executives and CEOs at the top, too" (qtd. in Neary).

The case of N K Jemisin and her struggle to get her first sci-fi/fantasy manuscript published sheds further light on the need Older identifies. Jemisin shopped her first novel around in 2006. *The Killing Moon* (TKM), set in a politically and culturally complex alternate Egypt, landed Jemisin an agent, but no publishers would bite. As we've suggested, rejection is a normal part of being an author, especially an author of a first novel, but Jemisin's rejections came loaded with extra freight: "There were these little dog whistles, these coded notes," she told the *New Statesman*. "I was being told that they weren't sure how to publish a book like this, they didn't know who would buy it"

(Barnett). By "dog whistles" Jemisin refers to phrases meant to signal racist ideas without overt racist expression. In this case, *we don't know who will buy your book* was whistling *sci-fi readers don't buy books by black women*.

"That was a hard year for me," Jemisin later wrote in a blog entry entitled "Contemplation, at the end of a season": "I almost quit writing, to be honest." As she considered prematurely ending her writing career, Jemisin remained confident in her skill: "I knew full well TKM wasn't a second-class book . . . and that the reasons for its rejection had nothing to do with the work's quality." Jemisin didn't feel like giving up because she questioned her own skill but because the industry's gatekeepers were all turning her away.

But Jesimin didn't give up. She now knew without a doubt that she wasn't fighting for acceptance on a level playing field. As she put it in the same post, "If a white guy's novel gets rejected, he probably doesn't wonder whether systemic racism or sexism played a role. If a white guy chooses to self-publish, it's probably not because he thinks there's no place for someone like him in this genre." So Jemisin kept on writing, hoping her next book might somehow get past the publishing world's gatekeepers.

Fortuitously for Jemisin, while she was hard at work, science fiction and fantasy fandom underwent some major changes. Early in 2009, sci-fi author Elizabeth Bear posted advice on her Livejournal about how to write characters who belong to cultures not your own. This post became the epicenter of a widespread and heated debate about representation and cultural appropriation in speculative genres, which came to be known as "racefail." While some commenters lauded and shared Bear's advice, many others critiqued her post on the basis that Bear's fiction performed exactly the same appropriation and poor representation she advised against (see, for example, Willow). Defenders rallied to Bear's side. Critics rallied in opposition, and soon fandom was awash in conversations about race and representation. As racefail went on, and its critique became more widespread, publishers took notice of two key points: a) that appropriative and insensitive works would no longer pass without criticism by fans and b) that there was a sizeable market for diverse speculative fiction. Jemisin later commented on racefail, noting that "massive discussions about race and gender had begun to take place, spurred by early social media . . . and these were a clear signal to the SFF establishment that there *was* an audience out there for the kind of stuff I write. There always has been."

By the time she was ready to shop around her new novel, publishers were much more open to Jemisin's queries. This time, nobody told her, "We aren't sure how to publish a book like this," and nobody said "We don't know who would buy it." Instead, they were already looking for work just like hers and were eager to read her manuscript. *The Fifth Season*, Jemisin's first published novel, debuted in 2015. The next year it won speculative fiction's most prestigious award, the World Science Fiction Society's Hugo Award for Best Novel, making Jemisin the first black woman ever to win that award. Her sequel, *The Obelisk Gate*, took home the Hugo again the next year. And the third title in her trilogy, *The Stone Sky*, made Jemisin the first person ever to win the Hugo for Best Novel three years in a row. In this case, a combination of factors—Jemisin's own resilient fight against racism, the power of the reading public, and the zeitgeist of the era—enabled publishing insiders and outsiders to eventually recognize her trilogy of novels as great books.

Claiming *Your* Context

The cases of Jemisin and Hawthorne shed light on our third issue: the importance of publishing work in the right venues. Today, when we the encounter the covers of Jemisin's novels, which promote her status as a Hugo Award winner, we recognize her as a master of speculative fiction. Similarly, when we see Hawthorne's work reproduced within the *Norton Anthology*, we recognize him not as an anonymous gift book scribbler but as an erudite canonical American author, whom we are (for some reason) supposed to study. If we borrow language from Tompkins, we might say "the conditions of dissemination . . . interpret the work for its readers" (23). In other words, the context for publication matters significantly, for it effectively instructs readers how to approach, understand, and categorize the work in front of them: i.e., the context tells them how to read it. This insight is especially crucial for emerging writers, who must place their work appropriately, targeting the right journals, websites, and presses, to ensure that it reaches their intended audience. If we want to make our claim on an audience of readers—say we want readers to treat our novel as a particular kind of fiction—that claim will succeed or fail based on whether readers can recognize our work appropriately. If our work does not arrive to readers in a context that signals "traditional mystery," "feminist literary narrative," "avant-garde fiction," "true crime novel," "young-adult paranormal romance," or whatever type of book we are shooting for, readers will not recognize our work the way we want them to, and our claim will likely fail. For any creative writer, then, decisions about how and where to publish a piece of writing are as important as decisions about how to craft the piece itself.

Of course making this claim on audiences is a complicated process that requires not only an author's assertions but also the activities of agents, editors, marketers, and a whole host of others. Complicating the process further—especially for writers of color—is the problem of gatekeeping we outlined above. Jemisin knew exactly who her audience was and where she wanted to publish her work but, faced with systemic racism, she initially struggled to get it past the gatekeepers of those venues. Thankfully, over the last few years we have seen an emergence of individuals and organizations who work directly with writers to address this very problem. For instance, Kima Jones, owner of Jack Jones Literary Arts, is a publicist and self-described "queer black girl from Harlem" who specializes in culturally-specific marketing. Describing her work, she states, "The agency partners exclusively with writers who have been historically underrepresented in publishing," particularly those from the African diaspora. She estimates that 95 percent of her clientele (several best-selling authors among them) are writers of color, whom she helps find broad and diverse audiences by navigating the complexities of the publishing world. While Jones recognizes the disproportionate issues of representation in contemporary publishing and the adversity faced by writers of color—perhaps more astutely than others—she also recognizes improvement: "[W]e're in a time in the history of publishing where we're starting to get more representation and pay for our work, getting the awards for our work, getting recognized" (qtd. in Ho).

In our current market, making a successful claim on an audience requires not only locating appropriate publication venues but also reaching out to the right people (maybe Kima Jones of Jack Jones Literary Arts? maybe Johnny Temple of Akashic Books?). It also requires remaining tenacious when faced with adversity. Finally, it demands significant research. If you're aiming for literariness, you probably don't want to submit your work to the contemporary equivalent of a gift book publisher. You might not want to rush to submit your work to the most prestigious of big presses either, for they will likely file your manuscript in the circular file if it is not an invited submission. Between these extremes may reside an appropriate venue for your writing, and we'd like to help you conduct the research to find it—along with the right people to help you get it there. Of course, we can't try to place your work without being familiar with the style, genre, and idiosyncrasies of your writing, and without understanding your specific motives for publication: how exactly do you want to identify yourself to the publishing world and what specifically do you want to achieve by having your work appear in print?

Given this predicament, we don't think it would be effective for us to catalogue publication venues, issue blanket advice, or assume familiarity we don't have. (Plenty of resources already offer lists of relevant resources). Rather, we think we can be most helpful by dedicating this section of our book to looking at the three major categorical contexts for publication that define the contemporary literary marketplace—(1) commercial publishing, (2) independent or small press publishing, and (3) self-publishing—and asking you to reflect on the nature of your writing to decide which might be most appropriate for you. We think it's incredibly useful to understand the way these three markets function before attempting to target specific journals, presses, editors, agents, and others.

Discussion Questions

1. We asked this question rhetorically above, but we'd like you to spend a little more time thinking about it here, for we consider it of crucial importance to anyone seeking to place their work: How exactly do you want to identify yourself to the publishing world and what specifically do you want to achieve by having your work appear in print?

2. Are you particularly interested in selling your creative work? To whom? What do you hope to achieve personally or professionally through book (or related) sales? And what kinds of readers do you hope to attract?

3. What kinds of things do you already do that might qualify you as a literary citizen? What kind of things would you like to start doing to this effect? What particular communities would you like to support and be supported by? Also, what steps might you take to protect yourself and other emerging writers from potential predators or abuses of power?

Your Turn: Questions, Concerns & Creative-Critical Comments

1. ______________________________

____

____

____

2. ______________________________

____

____

____

3. ______________________________

____

____

____

Writing Experiments

1. Write a rejection letter to your favorite author. You'll have to invent the particulars, but we'd like you to imagine you are an editor at a top publishing house reviewing a specific manuscript this author submitted, preferably during the earliest stages of their career: i.e., before gaining any kind of reputation or notoriety. In your letter, state specifically why you find the work unsuitable for publication. You might opt for a serious route and personify an editor with impeccable standards trying to represent the aesthetic integrity of their publishing house. Alternatively, you might take a comical approach and create a caricature. Perhaps you'll be so obsessed with grammatical correctness, you will fail to see the brilliance of the manuscript's content because of a comma splice on page 17. Obviously, there are a myriad of reasons to refuse publication; the more particularly you can identify your reason, the better. Regardless of the direction you take, we hope this activity will strengthen your own resiliency when faced with the inevitability of rejection. There is no better way to boost your confidence than to humble your heroes, to knock down an immortal (like Hawthorne) from the heights of canonicity. We're feeling better already, and we hope you are too.

2. Find creative ways to publish your work without a publisher. Choose a finished work—probably something relatively brief—that you feel is ready to be shared. Then, rely on methods considered unconventional by traditional literary standards to get it in front of readers. Like a street artist, you might use guerilla tactics and wheatpaste it in strategic locations all over town. (Think of Swoon's life-sized figures on Brooklyn's streets or Shepard Fairey's early Andre the Giant sticker campaign. Or, if you want to get really old school, think of Martin Luther nailing his *95 Theses* to the church of Wittenberg Castle in 1517.) If you prefer a more contemporary approach, use social media: Tweet it in a series of Twitter posts; DM it to friends; spam it to email inboxes; post a version on YouTube. Write up a comprehensive strategic plan and while doing so consider what methods would be best to reach your particular audience.

3. Create and then fill out an application for citizenship in a utopian nation of writers. You'll have to determine what exactly this application looks like—its categories, headings, and subheadings. Regardless, you should probably offer space to do the following:

- **a.** Identify the nation you wish to join and state why you want to join it. Are you looking to enter the United Republic of Literary Flash Fiction, or the Isle of Eco-Conscious Sci-Fi, or the Nuyorican Poets' Secessionist Collective? What exactly makes this nation appealing to you?

b. Identify some of this nation's prominent citizens, real or imagined. Who writes and publishes here? In what particular journals or venues? At what conferences do these members congregate? Who are the less-acknowledged people working behind the scenes to create a solid infrastructure?

c. Explain what will make you a good citizen of this nation. What might you pledge to do for your country? And what might you expect your country to do for you?

After you've designed your application, fill it out and share your results with your writing group.

Deep Reading

1. Peruse the articles in the second section of David Richter's *Falling Into Theory: Conflicting Views on Reading Literature*. Pick and read at least three of them. These essays and excerpts (including an excerpt of Jane Thompkins's book) discuss the literary canon, the process by which books are canonized, and the merits and potential for establishing a new canon or abolishing the canon altogether. These essays are not about publication exactly, but they are about how to decide which published works should be given the kind of attention and longevity Hawthorne's works enjoyed. This is an important issue that we were not able to discuss at length in this chapter. The essays will have special relevance for those of our readers who hope to publish the kind of work that becomes assigned reading in classrooms.

2. Since our anti-handbook doesn't exactly offer traditional "how-to" advice on writing and publishing, we thought we'd—begrudgingly—point you in the direction of some allegedly useful guides. Can you sense our resistance? The industry standards in the US and UK, respectively, are *The Writer's Market* and *The Writers' and Artists' Yearbook*. Both of these books, which offer new editions annually, combine a list of publication venues with practical advice. Readers seeking to learn more about how to represent themselves to publishers, editors, and agents, might also be interested in the *The Writer's Digest Guide to Query Letters* by Wendy Burt-Thomas and *Formatting and Submitting Your Manuscript* by Chuck Sambuchino. If you're not particularly interested in shelling out significant cash for these books, we'd suggest simply searching online for similar content. Let's just say the web is crowded with free advice—often from the very same people who are writing these guidebooks. We'll leave it to you to separate the proverbial wheat from the proverbial chaff.

7

Commercial Publishing: Cumulative Advantage and Marketing Magic

To consider commercial publishing is to think big. Really big. Extraordinarily big.

Let us explain the kind of big we're talking about. At the time of our writing, the five giants among commercial publishers (commonly referred to as the "big five") include Penguin Random House, Simon & Schuster, Harper Collins, MacMillan, and Hachette Book Group. This last organization is part of a French company (Hachette Livre) that acquired Time Warner Book Group from the Time Warner Company in 2006, Hyperion Books from the Walt Disney Company in 2013, and the Perseus Book Group in 2016. As their example suggests, most of these and other large publishing houses are currently owned by enormous global media conglomerates worth billions of dollars. CBS owns Simon & Schuster, News Corp owns Harper Collins, Pearson PLC and Bertelsmann own the newly merged Penguin Random House, and Holtzbrinck Publishing Group owns MacMillan. Each of these giants has dozens of imprints. For instance, MacMillan houses Farrar, Straus, and Giroux; Henry Holt & Co; Picador; Bedford/St. Martin's; Minotaur Books; and a whole slew of others, each of which specializes in titles of a particular type aimed at a particular reading public. In short, a small number of consolidated parent companies run a huge percentage of the commercial publishing industry, producing over two-thirds of books in the US alone (Kachka).

This is not to say that there aren't highly successful smaller commercial publishers, but it *is* to say that the market is dominated by a select few mega-companies. Successful authors who publish with these and other large or mid-range commercial publishers might expect not only to sell books in print and electronic venues but also to go on national or international reading tours;

make radio, television, and internet appearances; and in some cases prepare their work for movie adaptations and related spin-off merchandise. While writers' personal definitions of success may vary, authors who want to distribute their work through traditional commercial publishing must contend, to some extent, with the definition of success offered by this market. And this is, for the most part, a mainstream market concerned above all else with bottom lines and profit margins: in a word, *sales*.

Indeed, book sales are big business. *BookMap* estimated the value of the global book market at $143 billion dollars in 2017 (Williams), and the Association of American Publishers tracked over $26 billion in sales for US publishers in the same year (Association of American Publishers). The authors who do well in this market may make a comfortable living from their creative work. However, the chances of success are not high; nor are the means of achieving success straightforward or predictable. The commercial book market is *not* a meritocracy. Neither the hardest workers nor the "best" writers necessarily rise to the top. And yet, commercial publishing remains one of the primary means to financial success available to authors, so there is value in analyzing how this market works and what writers might do to establish an advantage for themselves within it. For this purpose, we investigate the rise of two superstars of commercial publishing, examining the factors that contributed to their ascent.

The Wizard that Almost Wasn't: Pushing and Pulling Young Harry

The case of J K Rowling sheds light on several issues related to commercial publishing. While we find it somewhat difficult to separate the popular myth from the historical fact of her authorial development—there are many competing and hyperbolic narratives of this billionaire's initial ascent into literary stardom—we'll do our best to try. We know for certain that Rowling began her foray into the literary marketplace as an unconnected author in search of an agent. She had very little social capital, even less actual money (she was on government welfare at the time), and no network of literati. Nevertheless, she managed to secure representation. Specifically, she copied names of literary agents and publishers from *The Writers' and Artists' Yearbook*, which she accessed for free in the Edinburgh Central Library. She then queried agents on this list. According to legend (at least the way Susan Gunelius tells it in *Harry Potter: The Story of a Global Business Phenomenon*), Rowling's writing sample wound up in the rejection pile at the Christopher Little Literary Agency. However, Bryony Evens, an administrative associate, caught a glimpse of the unusual cover and binding, which stood apart from the rest of the sea of plain white paper, and found herself suddenly drawn to the work. After requesting and subsequently reading Rowling's full manuscript, which she adored, she recommended the work to her boss. Christopher Little decided to take a chance on the work and made Rowling what amounted to the agency's rather typical offer to new clients: they would take 15 percent from her net proceeds of UK book sales and 25 percent of foreign and film rights (5). To be clear, we may never know what really happened behind the scenes at the Little Agency: would Harry Potter really have never made it to print if the glint of difference on Rowling's cover hadn't caught the eye of an administrative associate? Could bedazzling the cover of a manuscript actually be a *good* idea? Regardless, we *do* know that Rowling agreed to the terms of the contract, and Little began the work of trying to place her manuscript with an appropriate publisher.

During Little's search, Harry Potter was rejected a dozen times by large and mid-sized publishers, including Penguin, Harper Collins, and Transworld. Finally, after roughly a year of rejections, Little managed to sell the work to Barry Cunningham at Bloomsbury, which at the time was a newish and relatively small publishing house, nowhere near the scale of the five giants, nor even close to a mid-sized publisher like Hyperion. Initially, Bloomsbury made Rowling a rather tepid deal; she received an advance of $6,500, and the initial print run of Harry Potter was restricted to 500 copies (Gunelius 6). While the original deal didn't exactly exhibit extreme confidence or anything remotely approaching an extraordinary financial investment in Rowling, it offered her the advantage of the publisher's systematized promotion and marketing procedures. Part of Bloomsbury's strategy included exhibiting new and forthcoming titles at international book fairs. Through this mechanism, the company was able to get *Harry Potter* into the hands of Arthur Levine, the editorial director for Scholastic Books' US division, who encountered the book at the Bologna Children's Book Fair, where he was perusing international titles for potential investment. Specifically, he was looking to buy the rights to new children's books for US markets. To make a long, complicated story absurdly short, let's just say he was the right person with the right hands, and the book fortuitously landed in them. He bought the rights to *Harry Potter* for a significant sum of money and dedicated himself to aggressively promoting the book among US audiences while Rowling worked on the rest of the titles in the series. Due to these key transactions, sales figures transcended the number Bloomsbury had initially anticipated, and Rowling and Potter eventually made their way to superstardom.

Of course, this success didn't happen easily or by chance. After the book's initial launch, a number of market factors enabled Rowling and Potter to make their ascent. Before we get to those factors, however, we should acknowledge that prior to *Harry Potter* even being published, the market was primed for its release; there was a pre-existent demand for it or, at least, for a book like it. As Gunelius explains, in the late 1990s—a time that witnessed an unprecedented proliferation of new media and emerging internet technologies—parents who feared a culture of declining literacy found themselves actively searching for exciting, unusual books that would succeed in "luring children . . . away from television and videogames and back to reading" (xii). Perhaps because most entertainment and media companies were so invested in newer technologies, their focus on books waned. In other words, when the marketing teams at Bloomsbury and Scholastic were promoting the story of the awkward young wizard, the demand was already there, but the competition was not. Rowling's work happened to be uniquely attuned to the cultural zeitgeist of the era. Her timing was just early enough to precede the radical expansion of titles in children's and YA literature. This timing proved to be as important as the content of the story itself.

More important still were the promotion and marketing teams behind *Harry Potter* and their effective mixture of traditional and nontraditional advertising strategies. In addition to offering copies at book exhibits like the one in Bologna, Bloomsbury and Scholastic used what Gunelius calls the "tried and true" method of marketing books, which includes "sending galleys out in advance of publication to generate early reviews" and "sending complimentary review copies to newspapers and magazines . . . to create awareness of the new author's work and generate early sales" (26). In other words, as publishers had done for over a century, the Bloomsbury and Scholastic teams spent money and resources to create hype within the conventional venues of print culture. To further extend this hype, the teams also "sold" the mythology of the author's own story, or at least a fairytale-like version of it that capitalized on Rowling's transformation from a single mother on the dole to a successful and increasingly famous children's author. As Gunelius emphasizes, the marketing teams knew very well that "promoting the Cinderella story of J K Rowling would bring added publicity to and interest in the Harry Potter book" (14). She writes:

> People were intrigued and touched by the story of J.K. Rowling as a single, poverty-stricken mother, which in many ways mirrored the story of her character, Harry Potter. Like the Harry Potter character, J.K. Rowling was a good person struggling to overcome difficult circumstances who succeeds in the end. It's the kind of Cinderella or rags-to-riches story that people have always loved, and it was a public relations dream come true. Once the PR juggernaut took hold, there was no turning back.
>
> 25

To ensure that this story functioned to facilitate book sales, promotion and marketing teams booked Rowling in various mainstream media outlets that were popular at the turn of the twenty-first century, including the *Today Show* and the *Rosie O'Donnell Show*, where she could promote the Potter series by disseminating this sound bite version of her life to a mass audience. Much the way that Coleridge's story of mystical inspiration, Kerouac's story of spontaneous composition, and Hawthorne's story of political scandal were used as marketing vehicles, Rowling's story of her financial struggles and subsequent success was used to promote the budding Potter empire.

In addition to relying on these means of traditional "push" marketing, familiar methods for propelling a product or brand into the thoughts and minds of potential buyers, the Bloomsbury and Scholastic teams also took advantage of newer forms of "pull" marketing, strategies of capitalizing on existing consumer demand. They did so most effectively within what were, at the time, nascent experiments with online forums. As readers became fans of Harry Potter (in large part because of traditional marketing strategies), they began to share their experiences of the young wizard and his story on websites, in internet chat rooms, blogs, and developing venues for social media: i.e., the precursors to forums like Facebook, Tumblr, Twitter, Snapchat, and Instagram in the earlier days of the internet. While Rowling, Bloomsbury, and Scholastic at first made the mistake of aggressively guarding their intellectual property rights and seeking to squash unlicensed uses of Harry Potter, they quickly strayed from their policing tendencies as the series progressed, for they learned the value of allowing fandom to take hold. As Gunelius argues, by allowing fans to interact with the story of Harry Potter and create their own relationships with the characters from the novels, they encouraged their audience to "personalize the [Potter] brand" on a whole new level (29). In other words, because this sort of interaction tends to encourage "deep emotional attachment as consumers relate the product to their own lives," it also tends to create "brand loyalty" (29). In turn, this brand loyalty tends to encourage further word-of-mouth marketing and viral promotion of the product. In fact, rather than squash unlicensed uses of Harry Potter, marketing and publicity teams began listening in on internet conversations and actively seeking to find key influencers within online Harry Potter fan communities. Gunelius explains: "The team behind Harry Potter embraced those influencers and encouraged them to continue the conversation by sending them insider information, inviting them to movie sets and more" (33). In this manner, the marketers developed incredibly effective viral pull-marketing campaigns. The result? As Gunelius states, "fans were becoming walking advertisements as they communicated the Harry Potter brand's benefits to people across the world via the internet" (41).

Cumulative Advantage as the Invisible Hand

The push and pull strategies used by Bloomsbury, Scholastic, and partner media companies were particularly attuned to the means by which the world of commercial publishing tends to function: in a phrase, what sociologists call the principle of *cumulative advantage*. If there is anything consistently guiding the economy of commercial publishing, it is perhaps this principle. Sometimes known as "the Matthew Effect," the idea has it roots in the work of Robert Merton, who, in the late 1960s, was interested in the sociological applicability of the following verse from the Gospel of Matthew: "whoever has will be given more, and they will have an abundance. Whoever does not have, even what they have will be taken from them" (NIV Matt. 25.29). In essence, this well-known verse suggests that the rich get richer and the poor get poorer. Merton and more contemporary sociologists have expanded this idea to explore not only the ways in which money begets more money but also the ways in which social capital begets more social capital.

Before we apply it directly to Rowling and Potter, let's take a look at an example of how the principle has worked in the twenty-first century marketplace. In 2006, Matthew Salganik, Peter Dodds, and Duncan Watts crafted an empirical study of the principle of cumulative advantage. They gave a pool of 30,000 participants access to free music downloads from unknown artists. The control group explored this music library with no feedback other than their own interest, while the experimental group was presented with information about how many times each song had been downloaded by other users. The experimental group was also divided into eight "worlds" or sub-groups. Participants assigned to a world only had access to the download data from other participants in the same world. In this way, the researchers could study whether the same song would gain popularity across worlds and groups, or whether popularity would beget further popularity somewhat randomly.

The results clearly supported the principle of cumulative advantage. Watts explains:

> [W]hen people could see what other people liked, the inequality of success increased, meaning that popular songs became more popular and unpopular songs became more unpopular. Second, and more surprisingly, each song's popularity was incredibly unpredictable: One song, for example, came in first out of 48 we sampled in one 'world,' but it came in 40th in another.

When participants received a strong signal about the popularity of a song—when they were given a ranked list instead of extra data on an unranked grid—the results demonstrated greater inequality and less predictability. In other words, the more obvious it was to participants what others were downloading, the greater the difference there was between frequency in downloads for any given song from one world to the next. A small initial increase in downloads put some songs on top of their world's rankings early on, and this early advantage led to ever-increasing downloads in relation to other songs. Popularity begat popularity at random.

The strategizing and spending of the marketing teams behind Harry Potter reflect a sophisticated understanding of this principle. Contacting key cultural influencers with the objective of increasing Potter's popularity in the online sphere was no accident; this is merely one method by which marketing teams were essentially seeking to create a kind of cumulative advantage for their product. While they weren't dealing in number of downloads, they were hoping to increase the frequency of product mention and the likelihood of brand name recognition, factors proven to affect the popularity of the product and hence, according to the sociological principle under study here, increase sales successfully. These teams were also spending significant sums to assure the advantage in purely economic capital: i.e., cold hard cash.

As the book series developed and expanded into different media, near record spending—not inherent greatness—is what led to record sales. In addition to the strategies already mentioned (exhibitions, publicity, author appearances, and viral marketing), the teams at Scholastic, Bloomsbury, and their partner media companies paid for advertising, direct marketing, sales promotions and contests, sponsorships, product placements, and merchandising (Gunelius 40). Here is a list Gunelius includes of only the selected "global advertising spend estimates for Harry Potter":

> Book advertising: $3.5 million
> Movie advertising: $142.7 million
> DVD/video advertising: $68.5 million
> Merchandise/cross-promotion advertising: $54 million
>
> 46

Any doubt that the success of Potter was dependent on marketers' ability to exploit the principle of cumulative advantage can be assuaged by examining a related issue. In an article for *Bloomberg*, Watts explains that the results of the music download study we just mentioned apply directly to literary success and, even more specifically, to Rowling herself (or at least an alternate version of her identity). He points to the publication of her novel *The Cuckoo's Calling* as a real-world recreation of the download experiment. In 2013, seeking to escape the pressure of her authorial reputation and experiment freshly with crime fiction, Rowling sought anonymity, so she decided to publish a book entitled *The Cuckoo's Calling* under the pseudonym "Robert Galbraith." If the novel had sold well and made Robert Galbraith famous, it would have suggested that the inherent quality of the writing, and not the social influence of Rowling's fame, was the determining factor in its literary success. But this was not the case. Watts points out that "Until the news leaked about the author's real identity, this critically acclaimed book had sold somewhere between 500 and 1,500 copies. . . . Had the author actually been Robert Galbraith, the book would almost certainly have continued to languish in obscurity." Conversely, after Rowling was revealed as the book's true author, *Cuckoo* shot to the top of Amazon's bestseller list within hours. It went from number 4,709 to number 1, and sales rose by 150,000 percent (Hern).

The radical nature of this transformation suggests the astonishing power of literary celebrity within a marketplace that runs according to the principle of cumulative advantage. Initially, *Cuckoo* didn't sell remotely as well as Rowling's other books because it wasn't published with the Rowling label or brand—the author's name and all its accumulated social capital. Thus, Rowling as Galbraith found herself back in the position of an unconnected debut author trying to break into the closed circles of literary success. By the way, we understand that Rowling (as Galbraith) was initially rejected when she tried shopping the *Cuckoo* manuscript; rather than give up all of her advantage and struggle anew to get her pseudonymous work into print, she eventually decided to spare herself labor and heartache and simply go with her regular publisher, who was in on the gag ("JK").

What's in a Name? Cumulative Advantage and Collaboration of a Different Beast

Rowling is not an isolated case. The career of James Patterson similarly reveals the significance of cumulative advantage as well as the value of name recognition within the world of commercial publishing. Currently, Patterson is a best-selling author whose US sales, according to Nielsen BookScan data, surpass Stephen King, John Grisham, and Dan Brown *combined* (Mahler). This wasn't always the case. When Patterson first began writing and publishing thrillers, his sales were roughly on par with Robert Galbraith's, if a little bit higher. Between 1976 and 1992, Patterson released six books while working his day job as copy writer and director for the J Walter Thompson advertising firm, where he invented popular slogans like "I'm a Toys 'R' Us kid." During this 16 year-run, not one of his six books ever exceeded sales of 10,000 copies. While his numbers were often quite good, they didn't meet the ambition of an author who had aspirations to see his titles appear on best-seller lists. As an advertizer, Patterson knew that if he wanted to expand his readership and sell more books, he would have to spend more money up front. More specifically, he would have to invest more heavily in mechanisms of marketing and promotion.

When his 1992 novel *Along Came a Spider* was ready for publication, Patterson tried to persuade his publisher Little, Brown "that the best way to get the book onto best-seller lists was to advertize aggressively on television" (Mahler). When they balked, he wrote and produced a commercial with his own money. (With all his years in corporate advertising, he wasn't exactly strapped for cash.) After seeing the ad, Little, Brown executives agreed to share the costs of putting it on air. The decision reaped wild success, for, upon its publication, *Along Came a Spider* rose to ninth on the *New York Times* bestseller list. From there, further advantages accumulated. As Mahler explains, the book's status as a bestseller ensured it "favorable placement near the entrance of bookstores, probably the single biggest driver of book sales [at the time]. It rose to No. 2 in paperback" and eventually sold more than five million copies.

With the success of subsequent books in his Alex Cross series, the initial triumph of *Along Came a Spider* became what Mahler calls a "booming franchise." Patterson was relentless in pursuing an ever-larger market share for his books, so much so that he started collaborating with other writers in order to increase his productivity, which in turn would increase his chances of capitalizing on name recognition in the marketplace. His process has worked something like this: Patterson produces a long, detailed outline and then passes it off to a co-author to flesh out a draft and return it; then, Patterson sweeps through the book, making edits and changes as he sees fit. This process allows him to be amazingly prolific, a quality that further bolsters his status as a bestselling author, for more books mean not only more potential book sales but also, as Mahler suggests, "greater visibility, ensuring that Patterson's name would almost always be at the front of bookstores, with the rest of the new releases." To be clear about the kind of numbers we're talking about, we should mention that Patterson tends to release nine new hardcover fiction titles every year. Further, these nine hardcovers are "only the beginning" of the Patterson franchise. As Mahler states, "Nearly all of those books are published a second and third time . . . as traditional paperbacks [and] then as pocket-sized, mass-market paperbacks," so his name appears on the hardcover bestseller list, and then again on the paperback bestseller list, with multiple titles gaining premium shelf space in different parts of major bookstores and premium visibility on online stores like Amazon and iBooks. These sorts of advantages have led to some rather astonishing statistics. Since 2006, Patterson has written "one out of every 17 hardcover novels" purchased in the US. He has also penned 51 *New York Times* best-sellers; 35 of these have reached number one (Mahler).

As in the case of Rowling, the case of Patterson reveals how the principle of cumulative advantage structures the economy of commercial publishing:

money begets more money, popularity begets more popularity, and literary celebrity begets more literary celebrity until an author's very name begins to function as a commodity. As this structure suggests, commercial publishing has begun to look more and more like an oligarchical enterprise, offering concentrated success for a very select few. As we suggested in the previous chapter, this select few is overwhelmingly white. In "Where Things Stand," Roxanne Gay discusses the nature of this problem. She argues that the whiteness of commercial publishing appears to be self-replicating, leading to situations where vastly more books by Caucasian authors are reviewed (often by Caucasian reviewers) than by any other race. In a survey she conducted, she found that approximately "90% of the books reviewed by the *New York Times*" were "written by white writers." Of course, this kind of discrepancy is not limited to the *New York Times* nor is the underrepresentation of minority authors limited to the kinds of books reviewed by the *Times* (largely traditional fiction and nonfiction). Writers of color are radically underrepresented in many genres. As the Cooperative Children's Book Center reveals, in 2017 roughly 7 percent of children's books released by commercial presses in the US were written by Native, Latinx, and African-American authors *combined.* Bea and Leah Koch offer similar statistics for the genre of romance. In their survey of 3,762 commercial romance novels published in 2017, they found that just over 6 percent were written by people of color.

Surely, you noticed that both of our examples of authorial superstars in this chapter were of white authors, and that is not by choice. A quick glance at a list of all-time best-selling authors will turn up mostly white names, Patterson and Rowling chief among them. While we can't show specifically in the cases of Rowling and Patterson if or how their whiteness boosted their careers, we do wonder if readers would have been equally "intrigued and touched" by the story of a "single, poverty-stricken mother" if J K Rowling were a person of color. Likewise, would publishers have been as receptive to Alex Cross, Patterson's black protagonist, if Patterson himself were black? We wonder about these questions, in part, because Lee and Low's Diversity Baseline Survey found that 79 percent of publishers and 89 percent of book reviewers identify as white (see Baker). We can only speculate, but the state of the publishing industry would seem to suggest that whiteness is itself something of a cumulative advantage.

At the same time, we should point out that we have focused on ultra-super-mega success in this chapter, so we did not account for the many successful authors, who make decent and more-than-decent livings in this market: the many "mid-list" authors who publish with big-name imprints but don't make anybody's best-seller list. There are many ways to define "success," and the pool of writers looks a little more diverse as your definition includes mid-list and other sales figures. All of this is to say commercial publishing is undoubtedly in need of reform, but we hope we have not discouraged anyone—regardless of race, gender, nationality, social or economic position—from taking a shot at placing their work in this market. Our intention here is not to dissuade or dispirit but to inform. We trust that a better and more critical understanding of exactly how this market functions—flaws included—will help diverse writers find their way within it. Indeed, if you are interested in commercial publishing (with its low percentages, high risks, and potential for lucrative payoff)—and we can see why you might be—you'll probably want to gain as much critical awareness and practical knowledge as possible to improve your chances of success. To this end, we'd like to dedicate the next section to exploring more direct strategies for breaking into the market. This process usually begins with understanding how to get your work in front of an acquisitions editor at the one the big five publishers.

The Paradox of Representation and the Problem of Agency

Many authors who publish with commercial presses begin with well-financed promotion and marketing campaigns from their publication's earliest pre-release. So how does an emerging author gain this advantage? The catch-22 here is that, in the vast majority of cases, in order to be represented by a major commercial publisher, authors must already have secured representation. In other words, they must have an agent. As actors have Hollywood agents and professional athletes have sports agents, most writers who publish with commercial presses have literary agents, individuals who work behind the scenes within a network of contacts to get an author's manuscript into the hands of the right people at the right publishing houses. While they have a range of responsibilities, which include selling the rights to an author's work and negotiating terms of contracts, we'd say that their most important function boils down to initially matching an author's manuscript with the appropriate publisher. In this sense, they take on the work of brokering or arranging working relationships between authors and presses.

So, then, how do you initially land an agent? On a cynical day, we'd recommend that if you don't have friends in high places, you try to make some. We might loathe ourselves for sounding like the ghostwriters of Dale Carnegie's *How to Win Friends and Influence People*, but we're only partially kidding here. Until creative writing adopts a large-scale blind-review mechanism, we fear that who you know will remain an overpowering influence in determining literary success. In our less cynical moments, we'd suggest a slightly less smarmy approach to gaming the system: reach out to others within your network to see who may have relevant contacts or advice and simultaneously research literary agencies and agents to determine whose representation might be appropriate for you.

There are several ways to begin this process of research. But before we discuss two of them, we have to offer a bit more bad news for some of you. Literary agents rarely, if ever, represent poets unless they have already established a significant name for themselves (often through work in more saleable genres like fiction, nonfiction, or drama) and garnered a sizeable following of devoted readers: i.e., a poet seeking representation must already be a literary celebrity to a relative degree, or maybe even a celebrity in some other domain, like a rock star. While there are some exceptions, the market for contemporary poetry simply isn't profitable enough to interest most commercial publishers and remains restricted to small, independent and university presses. If you're a poet, please understand that we don't intend to ostracize you here, but you might not need to consider finding an agent an immediate priority. Please prove us wrong! Or, at least, please be patient with us until we get to our next chapter. In the meantime, do not pass Go, and do not collect $200. (We hope you're idealistic enough to be in this for the love of language, not the love of money? Gulp.)

For the rest of you, one of the most practical ways to begin a search for an agent is to take a look at the Acknowledgments pages of recently published books that you strongly admire or that you feel come closest to representing your style of writing. Here, authors often pay tribute to the agencies and agents who have helped them bring their work into print. You might consider culling a list from these pages and then going online to see what you can discover about the names you've written down. The second way to find an agent—the one Rowling followed—is to search through existing lists or databases designed for this purpose. Writer's Digest puts out an annual book entitled *Guide to Literary Agents*. *Literary Marketplace* is another annual resource; however, at over $300 a copy, the book is cost-prohibitive, to say the least. We don't particularly recommend buying it. Instead, maybe check and see if a friend or a local library has a copy you can borrow. Or, try an alternative: *Poets and Writers* offers a free online database on their website, as do Agent Query and Query Tracker. There are also a number of blogs dedicated to this service. Some of these lists are arranged alphabetically, some by genres represented. If you opt to consult any of these documents or databases, you should probably understand that you are likely to be surprised by the number of entries listed and the superficiality of these listings. You will probably need to narrow your search and investigate individual agents or agencies more thoroughly since this is really only the preliminary step in a larger process of research. That said, before you get too far into this process, you should be aware of a few issues.

First, as in any profession, there are good and bad agents. It is crucial to take your time in finding a good one. Consult the resources mentioned above, maybe check out Michael Larson's *How to Get a Literary Agent* from your library, talk to literary friends and mentors, and invest in the process of carefully vetting potential candidates for representation. If you decide the market of commercial publishing is right for you, it means you really want your work to circulate, and finding the right agent to enable this circulation should be a considerable priority.

Second, you should know something about the economics of working with agents to aid in this vetting process. Agents usually arrange their fee structures so that they take around 12–15 percent of an author's earnings. While we'll allow you to ultimately judge the merit of this commission system for yourself, we will say that it offers a certain advantage, for it encourages agents to invest in your work and motivates them to lobby on your behalf. The more books you sell, the more money your agent earns. If you encounter an agent who asks for significantly more than 15 percent for domestic book sales (rates for international contracts and alternate media venues tend to be higher), you should probably be suspicious. If you encounter an agent who attempts to charge you some sort of initial reading fee or asks you for any money up front, you should probably turn and run away. Do not pass Go. Do not allow them to collect $200 or any of your hard-eared cash. Instead, maybe get in touch with the Better Business Bureau. Asking you to front money may not necessarily be illegal, but it is a far cry from conventional practice within the enterprise of literary publishing, and it may represent a deliberate scam or an amateur operation. Be assured that no reputable literary agent will charge you any sort of start-up costs. In fact, many agents in the US are members of the Association of Authors' Representatives, which has its own Canon of Ethics that explicitly prohibits members from charging reading fees ("AAR").

The final issue you should probably understand as you begin your search for an agent is the competitive reality of securing representation. While the proliferation of MFA programs has created more writers, it hasn't necessarily created more commercial publication venues, so literary agents currently find themselves faced with more potential clients competing for roughly the same amount of publishing opportunities. In "A Right Fit: Navigating the World of Literary Agents," Michael Bourne explains the reality of this predicament by reflecting on the research he conducted at Folio Literary Management, a top agency based in Manhattan. In describing his observations of daily practices at Folio, he writes:

> [T]he agency receives roughly 100,000 unsolicited queries a year, or about 200 a week for each of the nine Folio agents who accept unsolicited queries. Hoffman [the agency's co-founder] has taken on four new writers

in the last year, only one of whom came in through the slush pile . . . When I sat down with another agent, Michelle Brower, as she read her slush pile, I watched her power through 19 query letters in 14 minutes, rejecting 18 of them and putting one aside for more consideration.

Yes, agents and editors refer to the collection of unsolicited queries and manuscripts they receive as a "slush pile." This term probably originates from the days of writers leaving unsolicited manuscripts on or near publishers' doorsteps, where they were sometimes subject to wintery weather conditions. It's not necessarily meant to be unflattering, but the image speaks for itself. It's hard to feel flattered when your work is lying beside the sole of someone's wet shoe. And, yes, agents receive loads of unsolicited queries. The odds listed above are terrible—probably worse than the odds faced by aspiring Hollywood actors, would-be arena rock stars, or prospective intergalactic cosmonauts. And, yes, even if you were skeptical at first, you can probably now understand precisely why we started our section on publishing with a conversation about rejection.

We offer the perspective above not to discourage you, but to prepare you. And to emphasize the importance of not contacting agents until you are absolutely ready to do so, for your work must stand out immediately from its competition. It should shine like a gemstone from Jupiter. It should carry the echoing heat of crystalized magma from Mars. It should offer readers the promise of heretofore unknown jewels from a galaxy further than far, far away. That is what Alan Dean Foster's work must have done to initially get the

attention of sci-fi agent Virginia Kidd, who, in turn, helped him secure the gigs of novelizing the film scripts to *Star Wars* and *Star Trek*.

A bit more practically, we might say that your manuscript should be so refined that you can't imagine making it any more ready for publication. (Sure, you'll have to revise again later when you work with your publisher's editor, but at this stage you should have gone through so much obsessive revision that you think it is perfect.) The query letter that you send before any other documents—the brief, one page piece of correspondence that introduces you and your work—should also be perfect, as carefully crafted as one of Shakespeare's sonnets or Wali Gujarati's ghazals. After you send an initial query to an agent, you don't get a do-over.

In the meantime, if you are finding yourself suddenly crestfallen, you should know that despite what may seem like terrible odds, many ordinary people regularly succeed in securing agents and going on to publish acclaimed and popular works of literature. We have many colleagues who have managed to get representation. One colleague secured his agent with the help of connections he made through his book-review blog. Another colleague managed to secure representation by—in her words—"stalking her prospective agent on Twitter" after submitting her initial query and writing sample. She went on to gain a lucrative contract for a very successful YA novel series with an international publisher. Before their successes, these colleagues faced terrible odds and many rejections, but with a little help from ardent research, twenty-first century social media, and unrelenting tenacity, they managed to persevere. On the other hand, if the commercial book market's definition of success—with its unrelenting capitalist drive—makes your soul ache (and we can see why it might) you may want to consider the alternatives we offer in our next chapters.

Discussion Questions

1. Given what we've discussed about commercial publishing, is this the venue in which you would like to publish your work? Why or why not?

2. In this chapter we've offered case studies of Rowling and Patterson. What sort of myths or legends have you heard about the means by which other famous authors achieved their commercial success? How accurate do you think these stories are?

3. Consider the ways in which Rowling and Patterson (or their marketing teams) created particular advantages that helped them achieve popularity. With the resources you have at your disposal, what might you do to create a kind of cumulative advantage for your work?

Your Turn: Questions, Concerns & Creative-Critical Comments

1. ____

____

____

____

2. ____

____

____

____

3. ____

____

____

____

Writing Experiments

1. For this exercise, we'd like you to take some time to further develop your response to discussion question #3 above. Dream big—perhaps bigger than you did a moment ago—and free-write a future for yourself in commercial publishing. Now that you've been exposed to the stories of Rowling and Patterson, it's time for you to chart your own path to commercial success. Write the story of your rise to fame. Poets: don't hold back! Reveal how you will become a rare twenty-first century bestselling bard. Put yourself on the cover of *Time* and the *New York Times* and the *New Yorker*—all in the same week. Regardless of the particulars, make sure that you outline or narrate how you will create advantages for yourself in the literary marketplace, focusing specifically on whatever key moments or big breaks will advance your career (something akin to Patterson's TV ad or Rowling's sale to Scholastic). You might play by the rules of cumulative advantage or you might reject these

rules outright and game the system in some other capacity. Whatever your choices, think about what exactly will launch your career the way you want it to be launched. Perhaps you will become a living, breathing corporate franchise like Patterson, or perhaps you will dismantle the system that keeps his name at the top.

2. If the previous exercise is a little too fantastical for you, try a more practical approach and draft a query letter to an agent. First, go online and browse one of the agent databases we mentioned earlier, perhaps Agent Query, Query Tracker, or Poets & Writers' list. Do your research and select an agent who is a good fit for the kind of work you produce. Also, do your best detective work—without contacting the agent directly—and try to discover what exactly this person wants to see in a query and writing sample. Next, take a look at examples of successful query letters. You can find many of these online. In particular, Writers' Digest offers several web pages and blogs that provide aspiring authors with model queries, many of which were actually used by writers who succeeded in gaining representation. When you're ready, address your letter to this agent and start writing. We'd like to offer a crystal clear disclaimer to this exercise. Earlier in the chapter, we suggested that you should not contact a literary agent before you are absolutely ready to do so. This advice still applies. We think generating a query letter—without sending it—is a useful exercise in its own right, as it provides practice in authorial self-representation, a necessary skill almost anywhere within the literary marketplace. Of course, if you are unequivocally determined to use this letter to contact an agent ASAP, we can't do anything to stop you. But, really, we highly recommend you slow down and get a literary mentor or someone enfranchised within the publishing industry—who knows the business well—to review your documents and make recommendations before you send them off. First impressions really are everything in this business. Some authors spend almost as much time on their query letters as their actual manuscripts.

Deep Reading

1. Trends in publishing change from year to year. To keep on top of the latest news and developments, we recommend that you get online and follow the blogs and Twitter feeds that cover the publishing topics specific to your interests. Look for agents who have landed contracts for authors you admire and/or who work in your genre. Follow publishers and editors you are interested in. We also suggest that you become a regular reader of websites that cover the publishing industry as a whole like Publisher's Weekly.

2. For a big-picture look at commercial publishing, we recommend John Thompson's *Merchants of Culture: The Publishing Business in the Twenty-First Century* and Albert Greco, Jim Milliot, and Robert Wharton's *The Book Publishing Industry*.

3. For a deeper look at the relationship between race and publishing, consider John Young's *Black Writers, White Publishers* and Cécile Cottenet's edited collection, *Race, Ethnicity, and Publishing in America*. For an examination of how marginalized groups have created their own pathways to publishing and literary acclaim, check out Elizabeth McHenry's *Forgotten Readers: Recovering the Lost History of African American Literary Societies*.

8

Small Literary Publishing: Understanding the Pitfalls of Prestige at Independent and University Presses

Welcome back poets! Your ship has come in! Your glory days have arrived! Your . . . Well, sort of. While we're tempted to say that literary publishing offers a kinder, gentler world—especially for poets—we should offer a few caveats. After all, we don't want to mislead you into thinking that when compared to commercial publishing, this world is entirely utopian. The principle of cumulative advantage still reigns, albeit to a lesser degree, and while the odds of publication are a bit better, they remain a far cry from encouraging. As we described the advent of creative writing as a beautiful impossibility in our first chapter, we might describe contemporary literary publishing as a gorgeous mess. Like an unkempt garden, it offers the *potential* for an Edenic existence amidst a reality of rotting flowers and overgrown weeds. Somehow, it can simultaneously cultivate awe and hot stank. We know these grounds well because we publish here: James as a writer of narrative and criticism, and Steve largely as the faculty advisor for a small literary journal and also as an essayist and poet—yes, all those seemingly sadistic digs at poets were really just instances of misdirected self-deprecation.

While far from perfect, this world is indeed smaller than that of its commercial counterpart. It is often more personalized than profit-driven, and it is definitely much less exclusively driven by capital. In fact, there is significantly less money involved overall. We're not talking about huge multimedia conglomerates here, but rather individuals, small writers' communities, educational institutions, and nonprofit organizations devoted to the integrity of the literature they produce. While all of these publishers face what can be intense pressure to meet bottom lines, they tend to prioritize their devotion to authors' work over quests to stretch profit margins. In other words, this is a far cry from the world of James Patterson's booming authorial franchise—both in structure and style. The work being published in this context tends to be more akin to the sort of poetry, literary fiction, and creative nonfiction you might see coming out of traditional MFA programs. In fact, MFA programs fuel much of the small publishing scene, which as we will soon reveal can be both a blessing and a curse. While university presses and small independent publishers have much in common, they also have enough substantial differences to warrant separate treatment; below, we've decided to discuss each of these publication contexts in turn before treating them collectively.

Small, Independent Presses: Ephemera in Red and Black

By their very nature, the publishers in this category tend to resist easy definition; as independent entities, their very identities hinge on their ability to set themselves apart from others. Perhaps the best way to think about them is as eclectic operations that remain unaffiliated with universities or larger commercial publishing houses. They tend to be founded by individuals or small collectives seeking to change the literary landscape by publishing work of a certain aesthetic and fostering the careers of the writers they truly believe in—regardless of how popular or unpopular, conventional or unconventional, these writers may appear to be. Incidentally, literary modernism may never have come into being without indie publishing: Gertrude Stein, Ezra Pound, T S Eliot, Mina Loy, Ernest Hemingway, and many others may not have made names for themselves if editors of independent literary magazines had not taken a chance on their work. For instance, *The Little Review*, an early twentieth-century indie lit journal edited by Margaret Anderson, introduced American readers to poems, stories, and essays by Hart Crane, HD, Emma Goldman, Sherwood Anderson, and William Carlos Williams, in addition to serializing James Joyce's *Ulysses*.

Somewhat ironically, most independent publishers in the US are now decidedly dependent upon a larger service organization, the Council of Literary Magazines and Presses, or CLMP, which helps them facilitate the merger of art and business that is necessary for their survival. CLMP has described the goals of this mode of publishing as follows:

> Independent literary presses are mission-driven not market-driven. The motive to publish is to enrich the literary culture by bringing works by

> important and often neglected writers to the widest possible audience. Manuscripts are selected and books are published as part of a press's fulfillment of its mission.

These missions, of course, vary from publisher to publisher. For instance, BlazeVOX seeks to "publish the innovative works of the greatest minds writing poetry today . . . regardless of commercial viability." In contrast, the literary journal *Apogee* articulates a more specialized goal. It seeks to publish "fresh work that interrogates the status quo" or as the editors suggest in more detail, "literature and art that engages with identity politics, including but not limited to race, gender, sexuality, class, ability, and intersectional identities." *Apogee* also strives to "provide a platform for underrepresented voices, prioritizing artists and writers of color" ("Mission"). *Fence*, which started as an avant-garde literary journal and has since moved into book publishing, looks for "challenging writing distinguished by idiosyncrasy and intelligence rather than by allegiance with camps, schools, or cliques" It seeks "to encourage writing that might otherwise have difficulty being recognized because it doesn't answer to either the mainstream or to recognizable modes of experimentation." ("Fence Books"). While these publishers offer different aims for different audiences, they are united by their ability to prioritize larger cultural functions over immediate commercial aims, despite their immediate dependency on selling books and magazines. By the way, these three representative publishers are only a handful of hundreds. According to CLMP's estimate, small or independent publishers currently produce around 600 active print journals, a statistic that does not include the 400–700 periodicals that are produced irregularly and the increasing number of online literary magazines. Further, this estimate leaves out book publishing altogether.

While certainly a smaller world than that of its commercial counterpart, independent publishing offers a diverse range of possibilities in size and scope. On the low-budget end of the spectrum, we find tiny independent presses started by ambitious writers or editors who work full- or part-time day jobs and devote their spare time to publishing and promoting the work of writers aligned with their missions. The products they offer might range from cheap, photocopied zines and staple-bound chapbooks to the kind of glossy, slick, perfect-bound books you'd find at your local independent bookstore. One of our favorite indie book publishers is BatCat. In a rather unique arrangement, they started out by producing limited editions of gorgeous hand-crafted books—works of art in and of themselves—that students in a publishing course at Lincoln Park Performing Arts Charter School helped edit and design. Regardless of format, the works that small presses issue tend to be filled with literature that appeals more to specialized readers than a mass audience.

The example of Mud Luscious Press, an indie lit standout from 2007 to 2013, reveals the sort of operation characteristic of low-budget indie publishing. When J A Tyler started the press, he found himself reading through piles of submissions on his living room floor and clearing off his kitchen counter to layout book designs, literally and figuratively making room for the press in his already crowded life as a devoted parent, teacher, husband, and writer. His operating expenses reveal a sharp contrast to the world of commercial publishing, especially the figures devoted to promotion and marketing. According to Tyler's estimate, Mud Luscious would typically spend the following amounts for each of its titles: "$100–150 in cover design, $100–150 in interior layout/design, . . . $150–$250 in advertising, $3–8 per book printed, . . . $3–5 per book shipped (stateside), $12–15 per book shipped (overseas), 8–10 percent royalties, paid in advance." In addition to these costs, Mud Luscious would pay for ISBNs and additional miscellaneous expenses (Robinson). Although these costs may be miniscule in comparison to what was spent by the publishers of J K Rowling and James Patterson, we can imagine how they nonetheless must have presented challenges for a press with few external financial resources. In the case of Mud Luscious, these challenges stretched a shoe-string budget (i.e., Tyler's wallet) to produce print runs of 100–500 copies. Given these conditions, presses like Mud Luscious tend to rely heavily on word-of-mouth marketing, social media, and favors from friends. They also tend to have relatively short, unstable existences, as exemplified by the now defunct status of Mud Luscious. For it, six years was a good stretch.

On the middle-to-higher end of the small press scene are literary journals and presses with long-established reputations and reliable sources of funding from grants and patrons. Publishers in this range tend to have budgets that afford them a small staff, allow them to hire a distributor (often SPD, or Small Press Distribution), and enable them to offer literary prizes to the tune of $1,000–$5,000. Red Hen Press, the largest independent literary publisher on the US's west coast, is a non-profit organization (501(c)(3)) that supports itself largely through annual fund-drives and donations. In 2017, it raised $457,894 exclusively from contributions and grants ("Red Hen"). One Story, a Brooklyn-based non-profit publisher devoted to the short story, works on an operating budget of approximately $320,000, a figure that combines sales, donors' contributions, and grants from the NEA, Amazon, and The New York State Council on the Arts ("One Story"). Unlike these two examples, other independent publishers—especially those that rely on wealthy benefactors—can afford to remain in the red. Francis Ford Coppola's *Zoetrope* comes to mind.

Perhaps the most extreme anomaly for independent publishing (at least related to budgetary issues) is *Poetry* magazine. While it has gone through numerous budget crises in its relatively long history—struggling, in fact to stay afloat on various occasions since its founding in 1912—it has since 2002 enjoyed a bequest of over one hundred million dollars from the late pharmaceutical heiress and philanthropist, Ruth Lilly. We find it quite apt that Lilly's relationship with *Poetry* began with rejection—she received handwritten notes from the journal's editor when she submitted her work in the early 1970s. While perhaps initially upset by this rejection, Lilly nonetheless appreciated the care and conscientiousness with which reviewers treated her work. Later in her life, she sought to ensure the journal's existence in perpetuity because she believed in its cultural purpose and value: to promote the work of newer voices alongside established poets whose work may not otherwise reach a substantial audience of readers. The Poetry Foundation, a nonprofit organization that functions as the journal's advisory board, was created to oversee her mission (Curdy).

Needless to say, this kind of stability is exceedingly rare in the world of independent publishing; most journals and presses do not enjoy this luxury as they struggle to cover their basic operating costs. In fact, the world of indie lit publishing tends to be so ephemeral—especially during our current moment in history as we transition from print to electronic publishing—that we're not sure the publishers we've mentioned here (apart from the Poetry Foundation) will continue to be in business when you happen to be reading this book. For many of them, the idea of "lingering in obscurity" might, indeed, be a long-term goal.

University Presses: Show Me the Prestige

While scholarly publishing traditionally specializes in critical research, many university presses have significant departments dedicated to contemporary literature. Their general operations and their mission-driven approaches to publishing tend not to be all that different from those of mid- and high-range independent presses, apart from the fact that they are affiliated with institutions of higher education, tend to be larger in size, and in many cases have enjoyed longer histories and, hence, more established traditions of readership. In this sense, they may offer what are perceived to be more prestigious venues for publication. For instance, Yale University Press offers the acclaimed Yale Younger Poets Prize, the University of Pittsburgh publishes the much-lauded Pitt Poetry Series, and Carnegie Mellon's Series in Short Fiction garners many accolades. These, of course, are just a few of many examples. Depending on the particular institution with which it is affiliated, a university press may range from essentially a several-person operation that is housed within a larger institution to a multimillion dollar entity with numerous departments and large teams of editors, proofreaders, interns, and marketing professionals.

Regardless, university presses often share independent publishers' tendency of claiming nonprofit status and providing literature to small, specialized audiences. Over the last five years, university presses have been responsible for about 1 percent of sales in the US book market (AAP).

While independent publishers tend to use CLMP as their parent organization, university presses tend to belong to AAUP, or the Association of American University Presses. According to AAUP's statistics, at the time of this writing, "ninety-two university presses . . . publish on the order of 11,000 books a year, and . . . 700 learned journals" (Givler). Thus, the tiny percentage of the overall US book market that falls to university presses is nonetheless composed of significant numbers; this kind of production relies on great variation in financial backing. While we hesitate to attempt to calculate a representative average budget—we trust neither the idea of "average" nor our rudimentary math skills—we can suggest with confidence that the budgets of most university presses fall far, far below that of the Poetry Foundation and far, far above that of Mud Luscious Press. (Many operational budgets tend to range between the high hundred-thousands and the low millions). Regardless of their size, university presses usually rely on book sales and a combination of institutional support, donors, and grants (especially those from the NEA and NEH) to meet their bottom line. Like independent publishers, their goal is not to make money hand over fist but to break even or gain a small surplus while advancing what they consider important works of creative and intellectual merit that contribute to culture.

While being affiliated with a university might seem to offer these publishing houses more stability, this is not necessarily the case. Since the US recession of 2008, this market has been characterized by increasing volatility and contradiction. While some presses have reported increasing sales, others have fallen so far into the red they have had to close their doors. In 2018, the University Press of Kentucky had its funding cut, and at the time of this writing, the University Press of New England is scheduled to close. Perhaps the unpredictability of this market is best exemplified by the differing fates of two presses: Southern Methodist University Press and the University of Missouri Press. In 2010, the former announced plans to suspend its operations. Then, after much community rallying, the press attempted to reopen in 2011 with a revised budget and business plan. Unfortunately, the changes were not enough; in 2015, it shut down permanently. In contrast, the University of Missouri Press survived its initial threat of closure. In 2012, the University's president, Timothy Wolfe, announced plans to discontinue the press. Amidst community outcry, he rescinded these plans, and the press adopted strategies more characteristic of commercial publishing. In addition to laying off workers and cutting expenses, it grew book sales by decreasing its emphasis on academic monographs and increasing its concentration on the salability of manuscripts more popular among regional and national audiences. As Emma Pettit reports, the press has been able to survive by increasing its bottom line (by about $100,000 annually) through the kinds of marketing approaches commercial presses use to gain cumulative advantage. She writes, "The [UMP] marketing staff has sharpened its collection of metadata, enabling it to predict the terms most likely to bring books to the top of online search results." According to Pettit, the press has also adopted an algorithm similar to Amazon's to analyze "information about customers" and target them more directly. As the vulnerabilities and adaptations of UMP's story suggests, the pressures of the changing marketplace have infiltrated the so-called ivory tower.

These market changes concern not only issues of technology but also revenue sources. It used to be that university libraries consistently purchased new titles from university presses; this is no longer the case. As Paola Corso explains, "In the past twenty years, university presses have experienced a shrinking library market . . . For some presses, library sales have plummeted from as much as 70 percent of sales to as little as 20 percent." She goes on to suggest that the reasons for this change involve "a demand for alternative media," such as subscriptions to electronic publications, audio and video materials, as well as a decrease in libraries' own budgets. In reaction to this radical change in sales demographics, some university presses have attempted to appeal not only to their traditional specialized audiences but also to a wider public. That is, they have "turned to trade publishing for a general audience." (24). To a certain extent, then, we are beginning to see a developing overlap between the worlds of nonprofit university presses and commercial publishing, especially when it comes to contemporary literature.

Given our culture's rapid changes in technologies and markets, we are at present in the midst of an unstable moment in publishing at large, and we're not sure how this overlap may develop or where its trajectory may lead. That said, we'd like to suggest that university presses, in their present incarnation, offer contemporary creative writers certain advantages. First, they tend to keep books in print longer than independent and commercial publishers. In other words, if you publish your book of creative writing with a university press it may have a longer proverbial "shelf life" than books published in other contexts (provided, of course, that shelves continue to exist—we have watched more and more of them disappear from our libraries over the last few years). Second, because of their connections to academic institutions, university presses tend to market their products, in part at least, to professors, and professors tend to adapt books in their area of specialty for classroom use. All of this is to say that publishing with a university press might allow you to tap into the classroom market, which comes with a built in, reliable audience of student-readers and, according to the most recent estimate, amounts to a 3.98 billion dollar industry (AAP). If your title appears regularly on course syllabi semester after semester, you may not only sell more books but also gain a kind of cumulative advantage in the academic sphere. Popularity might beget popularity within the interconnected worlds of colleges and universities, and you may find yourself subject to a kind of contemporary canonicity: in other words, the more frequently your work appears on class reading lists, the greater your chances of becoming the next Nathanial What's-His-Name, or David Foster What's-His-Face, or What's-Her-Krauss, or at least of gaining more widespread recognition among populations of academic readers. That's the dream, at least. Third, if the worlds of university and commercial publishing continue to intersect, you may have a decent chance of reaching a wider commercial audience without sacrificing the integrity, innovation, or quality of your work. Many writers who first published with university presses have gone on to larger commercial success. After publishing *Field Guide* through the Yale Younger Poets series in 1973, Robert Hass became one of the most popularly recognized American poets of the late twentieth century (not to mention the Poet Laureate of the United States from 1995 to 1997). Norman Maclean gained widespread acclaim after his breakthrough collection *A River Runs Through It and Other Stories* was published by University of Chicago Press. In fact, in the presence of these overlapping markets many authors have started to seek representation within this publication context. Agents are beginning to make their presence felt, and more "agented" submissions are landing on the desks of editors at university presses (and also independent publishers) than ever before.

Adding It all Up: The Unflinching Cruelty of Decimal Points

As we've suggested, while the realms of independent and university publishing might stand distinctly apart from the larger world of commercial publishing, they are not all that different from one other. Apart from the variations we've mentioned above, independent and university presses tend to offer writers similar experiences in a number of capacities. If you are considering publishing in either context, you might want to consider three overarching concerns: cash, competition, and contests.

First, as our analysis of their budgets might suggest, most university and independent publishers tend to offer more prestige than payment. This is not to say that money can't be earned, but it is to say that rewards tend to be modest. For instance, most literary journals, whether independent or university affiliated, offer contributors little more than a few complimentary copies of an issue and the pleasure of seeing their work in print. While there are, of course, exceptions—especially with higher-budget journals—a contributor's copy (instead of cold, hard cash) tends to be the common form of currency exchanged. Book publishing is a little bit different. Here, in addition to complimentary copies, publishers offer some sort of royalty arrangement. Mud Luscious's routine of offering these royalties up front is rather anomalous. Unlike commercial publishers, many independent and university presses offer no form of payment (or "advances") prior to actual book sales. In fact, to cover their own costs of production, some university presses require that their authors sell a certain number of books before royalty payments even kick in. If sales never reach this number, then authors do not earn money from their books. This arrangement may seem undesirable from a writer's perspective, but it represents a necessary effort for many nonprofit publishers to share the burden of financial risk in unstable times. It also has the effect of motivating writers to actively market their own work.

In fact, while university and many independent presses tend to have established audiences, they tend not to spend nearly as much money on marketing and promotion as commercial presses. They generate reviews by sending out complimentary books to appropriate periodicals, critics, editors, and related organizations, but most don't have the capital to invest in large-scale public advertising. In fact, they leave authors largely in charge of generating their own buzz. Frankly, if you are considering publishing a book of fiction or poetry in this context, it helps to be a bit of a hustler, as you may or may not have the advantage of veteran marketers or advertising teams working behind the scenes trying to establish your cumulative advantage. It also helps to have your own website and established social media presence—many publishers insist on these as a condition of acceptance—and to give up any hesitancies about being perceived as a shameless self-promoter. Being proactive about your writing on platforms like Facebook, Tumblr, and Twitter provides a prime means of self-marketing without the financial backing of a large commercial press.

In addition to encouraging authors to gain followers or fans through the regular use of social media, most independent and university presses also encourage their authors to do real-life reading tours. Usually, apart from several key events, the burden for arranging, publicizing, and financing these tours falls on the authors themselves. In a phrase, the typical arrangement is pay your own way. Of course, resourceful and trusting authors can always use social media to their advantage in this regard, perhaps reducing their travel expenses by arranging to crash on the couches of Facebook friends or other contacts established through online networking.

Our second concern is, in a word, competition. While the potential payoff in this market is nowhere near that of commercial trade publishing, the competition is almost as brutal. Certainly the odds of having your poem or story published by a reputable literary journal or your book published by an independent or university press are better than the odds of securing representation at a commercial agency like Folio (as we discussed earlier). However, the difference is not as great as you might imagine. In this context, acceptance rates hover at the extreme low end of the spectrum: i.e., only slightly above zero. Using a renowned fiction journal as an example, Joe Bunting puts the problem this way: "*Glimmer Train* literary magazine is harder to get into than Harvard." Unlike Harvard, which tends to boast a 6.2 percent acceptance rate, "literary magazines like *Glimmer Train* often have acceptance rates of under one percent." To be a bit more precise, *Glimmer Train*'s 2018 acceptance rate was less than 0.3 percent, according to Duotrope ("Glimmer"). No, we have not made an error: there is, in fact, a decimal point in front of the 3 in the sentence above. In real numbers, this means the editors of the journal accept approximately 3 out of every 1,000 submissions for publication.

Granted, *Glimmer Train* is one of the few indie lit journals to pay its contributors in significant cash money ($700 per story published), and it continually ranks near the top of fiction journals. At the end of 2018 (ironically, the year it announced it would cease publication), it came in at number five on Bookfox (Fox). In short, it represents a highly desirable publication venue for fiction writers. These odds, however, are not reserved for the top echelon of literary journals. Even journals that offer no cash payment and are not considered among the highest ranking have similar—sometimes lower—acceptance rates for standard submissions. Take the poetry journal, *Rattle*, for instance. While a solid journal, it carries neither the cachet nor cash reward of *Glimmer Train*. It ranks number 21 on Clifford Garstang's "2019 Literary Magazine Ranking—Poetry," and it doesn't appear at all on the list of top 50 literary magazines published by Every Writer's Resource. That said, *Rattle*'s editors read approximately 120,000 poems in 2018 and selected 250 of those poems for publication, making its acceptance rate 0.2 percent ("About Us"). In other words, roughly 1 in 500 submissions gets published. Again, we really wish these numbers were wildly inaccurate—a result of our terrible math skills. Unfortunately, they are correct.

The typical odds for publishing in respected literary journals—at or under 1 percent—are significantly worse than those for publishing in the crème de la crème of academic journals. In fact, most top-tiered academic publications accept 6–15 percent of submissions. Take, for example, *PMLA* (*Publications of the Modern Language Association of America*), arguably the most prestigious journal in the field of English studies. As Wai Chee Dimock states in his 2017 editor's report, "The overall acceptance rate for submissions is 7.2%" (2). The top two journals in the field of linguistics, *Language Learning* and *Applied Linguistics* have acceptance rates of 15–18 percent and 15–20 percent respectively (Renandya). A midrange literary journal can thus be around 15 times more difficult to get into than the venues publishing the most influential, cutting-edge scholarship today.

Book publishing at small and university presses is plagued by odds similar to those of journal publishing. Take, for example, Tom C. Hunley's Steel Toe Books, a tiny press (now affiliated with Western Kentucky University) that has been publishing books of poetry since 2005. It tends to receive 100–156 manuscripts during its open reading period and selects 1 for publication, thus bringing its acceptance rate to somewhere between 0.64 percent and 1 percent ("News"). While we might admire the quality of books produced by Steel Toe, we must admit that it is not yet prominently established as a top venue for contemporary poets. If anything, its numbers reflect more of a standard than an exception.

As all of these numbers suggest, low acceptance rates are the norm in literary publishing. Given the mission of many small presses—to promote work likely to be overlooked by mainstream trade publishers—this norm carries with it a bit of irony and paradox. CLMP describes the ideal or ambition of many literary publishers this way:

> Small presses are often pioneers, discovering talented new writers and bringing their work to the attention of reviewers and readers. They have also been the source for much experimental writing, works deemed too risky by other publishers. Minorities and marginalized voices, ignored by mainstream publishing, have long been mainstays of noncommercial presses.

We admire the intention of publishing new, experimental, and minority writers, and we wish it were regularly fulfilled. However, it is difficult to give voice to many marginalized voices when rates of publication are so low and rates of rejection so prevalent. In practice, the reality is that voices ignored by mainstream commercial publishers too often continue to be ignored by small press publishers, as the odds against getting published linger at over 99 percent. The truth is that a perhaps typical 1 in 200 chance of publishing with a small press is significantly better than the chance of securing a top commercial literary agent. Still, writers would probably face better odds betting on horses—even aiming for elusive trifectas—than trying to publish their work at a mid-or top-range small press. Again, we don't mean to be discouraging here but realistic. It is difficult for us to balance our factual account of the current publishing scene with our desire to motivate emerging authors. That said, we assume that if you've stuck with us this far, you have more of an interest in writing than gambling on horses, and you're probably willing to push through a storm of negative statistics to carry on bravely with your writing projects. After all, how many creative writers are concerned with statistics? And since when has reality prevented motivated individuals from succeeding?

Poet and fiction writer, Martin Ott, who has slogged through piles of rejection slips to achieve significant success within the context of small press publishing, embodies one of many examples of perseverance. He offers the following advice to emerging authors based on his own experience:

> By my best estimate, I have had a submissions acceptance rate of approximately 2% over the past two decades. This means that I have also had more than 10,000 rejections . . . Success comes with rejection, and writers who take submissions personally are missing the point: readers and tastes evolve constantly at each and every magazine. I have placed work at magazines that have rejected me ten times or more.

Succeeding in this arena clearly requires a level of resiliency. We'll leave it to you to decide whether to consider Ott a model of motivational excellence (i.e., the Tony Robbins of indie publishing) or a model of contemporary insanity (i.e., the Tony Robbins of indie publishing). Either way, we think it's safe to say that the 2 percent success rate he has achieved in this context has not earned him enough money to buy his own island. And, frankly, we like him better because of this.

If we suffer ambivalence about small press publishing—particularly the challenge of balancing statistical reality with optimism—we suffer it most acutely when it comes to literary contests, our third and final issue to address. On the one hand, contests have largely enabled the genre of poetry to survive. As popular readership of this genre has waned over the last several decades, contests have provided a means for financing the publication of poetry collections that would otherwise not be economically feasible to produce. The system works as follows: publishers charge entry fees (anywhere from $10–$35), offer some combination of publication and a cash prize (usually $1,000–$5,000) or some articulation of a royalty arrangement; then, they use the surplus of entry fees to cover the costs of printing the winning collection and other operating expenses. This tends to be how many poetry presses stay afloat in a larger cultural climate that seems to have forgotten the value of poetry. It is precisely through this mechanism that poets can afford to write for a niche readership of other poets—and not be required to sell great numbers of books—rather than taking on what may seem like a rather impossible task: finding a more mainstream audience that, shall we say, is elusive at best during our current moment in history.

We recognize this particular value of literary contests. Despite our irreverent humor, which places poets at the butt of too many jokes, we too want to keep poetry alive. On the other hand, we also recognize the financial and ethical nightmares that too often accompany the contest circuit. The vast majority of contemporary poets' first books are published through contests. In fact, it is quite difficult for younger poets to find ways around the contest circuit for first book publication, which has become the standard rather than the exception. As John Sutherland states rather succinctly, "To make a career in American poetry nowadays you must enter contests and work your way up the prestige ladder." The normative contest circuit carries with it not only the odds of small press publishing as described above (significantly fewer than 1 percent of entrants win contests), but also a hefty price tag. It is not uncommon for poets to spend thousands of dollars on entry fees, repeatedly entering contests in an effort to have their first book accepted for publication. One of our colleagues spent well over $5000 before her collection finally won the APR/Honickman Prize. Another colleague spent approximately $6000 before giving up on the contest circuit altogether. This sort of pay-to-play system inevitably recalls and complicates a history of vanity publishing. Here, in a topsy-turvy, through-the-rabbit-hole kind of universe, aspiring poets spend significantly more than it would cost them to self-publish their collections with not only no guarantee of acceptance but almost a guarantee of no acceptance. Yes, you read that correctly—absurd, isn't it? Essentially, aspiring poets pay top dollar for a less than 1 percent chance of being awarded the prestige of a contest win/publication. Systematically, then, the contest circuit is a rather classist affair, for it effectively reserves the genre of poetry for those with disposable income. Who else would have the means or will to spend this sort of money to see their work (not) appear in print? In this sense, the system of literary contests offers significant disadvantages in terms of financial strain and economic diversity.

That said, there might be significant advantages to contests—theoretically at least. Perhaps the most significant advantage would seem to be the proverbial leveling of the playing field: contests would appear to offer a mechanism for working against the principle of cumulative advantage, which otherwise structures the worlds of independent and university publishing almost as much as it does commercial publishing. As J K Rowling has an infinitely easier time getting published as J K Rowling than she does as Robert Goldbraith, so too do the celebrity authors of indie lit culture have an easier time getting published than unknown or emerging authors in this arena. Journals are far more apt to accept or solicit regular submissions from established names who have an established following of readers—e.g., Dean Young, Molly Peacock, Dave Eggers, Nick Flynn—than they are from unknown authors. In fact, if you peruse a selection of literary journals, you will find names like these functioning as marketing devices. They are often listed, celebrity marquee style, on front or back covers in an effort to attract readers: i.e., to sell journals. In this sense, the established names of indie lit function a bit like James Patterson's name functions in commercial publishing. They serve to market and brand, associating a particular journal with the prestige of a particular kind of author or group of authors who begets popularity and sales. Of course, the same is true for book publishing. Presses are far more apt to publish work by an author who already has an established following of readers than an unknown voice, regardless of the subjective assessment of that work's quality. All of this is to say that while the stakes, reputations, and price tags are much, much smaller in this arena, the reality of cumulative advantage still encourages editors to offer established writers preferential treatment in this manner when selecting content for publication.

In a sense, then, to enter a contest is to pay to avoid or disrupt the problem of cumulative advantage. Theoretically, an emerging writer who enters a contest should have as much opportunity for success as a celebrity author since the problem of selling has largely been averted through the surplus of entry fees used to pay for book production. If attracting an audience doesn't particularly matter, then the prestige of an author's name shouldn't matter. However, as we suggested earlier, many creative writing contests are not blind-reviewed. Authors' names remain on their manuscripts, and this significant detail, in conjunction with other issues, tends to prevent this theory from translating into practice while creating a whole host of related ethical problems. In fact, in the first decade of the twenty-first century, an organization called Foetry (fraud+poetry) investigated and reported on these problems, serving as an unofficial watchdog of sorts for the contest circuit. Their findings were alarming, to say the least.

At the time, Alan Cordle, the main figure behind Foetry, discovered that very few ethical guidelines governed contest procedures. Even the minority of contests claiming to offer blind reviews were not exactly blind: although names and identifying features may have been removed from manuscripts, judges often recognized the work of their students, friends, and colleagues, with which they were familiar, and awarded prizes accordingly. Because contests tended to rely on a single judge (usually a celebrity author) rather than a juried panel—even though the latter might bring more integrity to a shared review process—the potential for favoritism and corruption was paramount. If what occurred did not exactly represent the dark side of cumulative advantage, it represented a smarmier shade of nepotism, in which established authors used their position of power to select their own in what journalist John Sutherland describes aptly as "cronyism."

In the two most dramatic cases to be uncovered by Foetry, contests run through the University of Iowa Press and University of Georgia Press exhibited egregious ethical problems. Steven Ford Brown discusses these cases in an interview entitled "Foetry.com and What Academia Doesn't Want You to Know About the Creative Writing Industry." As he reveals, in 2004–2005, the

University of Iowa Press charged entry fees to between 1,500–2,000 writers who entered their annual fiction and poetry contests. All of the screeners and judges for these contests were affiliated with the University of Iowa; all four of the four winners selected "had intimate connections to the university," as they were "graduates, former teachers, or current employees of the [Iowa] Writers' Workshop or University of Iowa." Knowingly, the judges selected their own students or colleagues as winners, contest ethics be damned. Brown goes on to state with candor,

> It frankly seemed to me that the situation was specifically tailored to benefit Iowa Writing Workshop grads, that it was an affirmative action program for Iowa Writing Program graduates subsidized by the contest entry fees of unsuspecting writers and taxpayer dollars (the fiction competition is underwritten by an NEA grant and the University of Iowa receives federal and state tax dollars).

Why is it that when we finally hit upon some decent odds—4 out of 4, or 100 percent—these odds describe a level of corruption rather than legitimate acceptance percentages? So much for the proverbial leveled playing field.

Even more disturbing was the case of the University of Georgia Press. For years, the press's poetry series kept the identities of its contests' judges secret and refused repeated appeals for transparency. After being legally forced to reveal this information through an Open Records request, it was confirmed that "the contest at Georgia featured multiple judges secretly selecting friends and former students as winners in the literary competition . . . In many of those years, open literary submissions to the contest had no chance of winning" (Brown). In one instance, when Cordle investigated the press's 1999 poetry competition, he discovered that the judge, Jorie Graham, recommended the award be given to Peter Sacks, Graham's former student—a man whom she was dating at the time and whom she married in 2000, several months after the award was issued. Yes, you read that statement correctly: Graham selected her former student and future husband for the prize. The poetry series editor, Bin Ramkin, then subsequently awarded the official prize to Sacks. But that is just the beginning. It turns out that Sacks had not even entered the contest. In other words, after accepting entry fees from hundreds of aspiring poets, the University of Georgia Press awarded its prize to a writer who, initially, had neither entered the contest nor paid the requisite entry fee. Brown explains:

> Correspondence from the director of the poetry series to the editor of the University of Georgia Press . . . indicated that he [Ramkin] selected a winner of the competition for that year before he had read all the submitted manuscripts. The eventual winner (who never entered the contest but was

> solicited outside of the contest) was connected to the judge for that year [Graham]. This kind of activity at Georgia was secret for twenty years until Foetry.com obtained the records. That means that for twenty years unsuspecting writers annually sent in fees to subsidize this activity.

Brown approximates that during much of this time, the University of Georgia Press accepted somewhere between $15,000 and $25,000 in entry fees, essentially cheating entrants out of their money while offering them no chance of winning the press's contest. Again, we're not statisticians, but we think that 0 percent (while not terribly far from 1 percent) is significantly worse than the odds we've been describing. In all seriousness, when the news broke, we were ashamed of the press and its unethical treatment—in a word, abuse—of writers. And we can't believe this kind of abuse went largely unnoticed and unpunished (at a university, nonetheless) until the intervention of one watchdog group.

We think the case of the University of Georgia is the exception rather than the norm; in fact, since the work of Foetry, there has been a significant effort to reform contest ethics. As a result of the Georgia scandal, Jorie Graham stopped judging poetry contests, Bin Ramke resigned from his position as editor of the press's poetry series, and the press reconfigured its contests in an effort to avoid such egregious conflicts of interest. Many other presses subsequently adopted what was at the time informally deemed "the Jorie Graham rule," which prohibited writers who had a relationship with a contest's judge—be it most immediately defined as former student, current lover, future husband, or, more simply, friend or colleague—from entering that contest.

These developments eventually led the Council of Literary Magazines and Presses to establish official guidelines largely aligned with the ideals of transparency underlying Alan Cordle's initial vision at Foetry. Their specific code of ethics now reads as follows:

> CLMP's community of independent literary publishers believes that ethical contests serve our shared goal: to connect writers and readers by publishing exceptional writing. We believe that intent to act ethically, clarity of guidelines, and transparency of process form the foundation of an ethical contest. To that end, we agree to 1) conduct our contests as ethically as possible and to address any unethical behavior on the part of our readers, judges, or editors; 2) to provide clear and specific contest guidelines—defining conflict of interest for all parties involved; and 3) to make the mechanics of our selection process available to the public. This Code recognizes that different contest models produce different results, but that each model can be run ethically. We have adopted this Code to reinforce our integrity and dedication as a publishing community and to ensure that our contests contribute to a vibrant literary heritage.

Currently, many independent and university presses offer this exact statement or variations thereof in their contest submission guidelines. Undoubtedly, their very offering of this statement represents a step in the right direction. That said, we don't think the Code goes quite far enough, especially when it comes to the issue of assuring ethical compliance in the absence of watchdogs. Let us explain.

Foetry ceased its operations in 2007. It was really only a side project of Cordle, who was a librarian by trade, and whose poet-wife had been frustrated by the contest circuit. Since 2007, there has been no prominent watchdog group; rather, as the Code suggests, presses themselves (and not CLMP) are responsible for monitoring their own ethical compliance. This follows the kind of logic that Republican lawmakers used in the early twenty-first century when they were able to arrange for industrial polluters (and not the Environmental Protection Agency) to be responsible for monitoring and policing their own levels of pollution. In other words, we have suspicions, to say the least, about the efficacy of this system. Whatever the criticisms leveled against Foetry—many writers enfranchised within indie and university publishing criticized the vitriolic tone of Cordle's reports—we think there needs to be a watchdog either in the form of CLMP itself or an outside party to better evaluate levels of transparency and ethical compliance.

Also, while we understand the Code's need for rather generalized language (so that it can be adapted by numerous presses and applied to variant publication contexts), we'd like to see several more specific recommendations. At the very least, the Code should explicitly prohibit judges from awarding prizes to close affiliates while mandating a blind-review process so that emerging authors have more of an equal chance of success. As we suggested, many presses have adopted such a mandate as the unofficial "Jorie Graham rule"; we'd like the Code to make it official—and also to rename it.

We'd also like the Code to require that contests be judged not by an individual author but by juried panels consisting of three or more people. We think this arrangement offers two advantages. First, the presence of others actively discourages an individual judge from engaging in the kind of favoritism or cronyism or blatant nepotism exemplified by Graham. In other words, it makes cheating more difficult to get away with. Second, it potentially leads to more transparency and productive dialogue about the problems associated with assessing the quality of literature. In the past, presses have protested that because evaluating creative writing is a highly subjective activity, it is much easier for an individual celebrity judge to simply award a prize according to his or her taste than try to get a small group to agree upon a winner. We don't think the conversation should begin and end here—with a mere shrug of the shoulders. Rather, we think jury members should be encouraged to undergo rigorous processes of debate as they winnow down lists of finalists to collectively agree upon a winner based not on whim or arbitrary characteristics but on articulated criteria of assessment. By no means are we suggesting any formulaic or quasi-mathematical procedure here, but we are insisting that there is plenty of productive and collaborative space between the poles of the purely subjective and the purely objective. In fact, the model of the juried panel that we are advocating has been practiced in the discipline of fine arts for decades, where it has worked quite effectively. It is often used to curate museum shows, judge painting and sculpture contests, decide upon admissions to MFA programs and artists' residencies, and award various grants and prizes. In some ways, we wonder if the old Romantic myth of single authorship has been a factor in preventing presses from moving toward the juried fine arts model in this regard. It seems to us as if maybe inheritors of this mythology expect that a celebrity judge (like the Romantic author of old) should work in isolation—as if they can't be brought out of their private loft to engage in debate or address worldly ethical concerns.

Finally, we'd also like to see a mandate that requires juries or judges to, indeed, select a winner. As judge of the Yale Younger Poets' Contest in 1998, W S Merwin refused to do so, claiming that none of the hundreds of manuscripts entered in that year's contest were worthy of the award. Merwin's decision, which understandably caused an uproar at the time, represented not only an instance of absurd arrogance but also one of fiscal irresponsibility and deception. Yale University Press accepted thousands of dollars in entry fees and failed to fulfill its promise of actually issuing a prize. In the interest of protecting contest entrants, we think it is perfectly reasonable to ask that CLMP require sponsors of writing contests to actually award the prizes they claim to offer. This seems like the most basic of contractual obligations.

Again, we want to stress that we think (and hope) the ethical breaches we've discussed here represent the exception rather than the rule. In good faith, we believe that the vast majority of contests are probably designed to support rather than exploit emerging authors, and indeed offer a legitimate means of contesting the effect of cumulative advantage while raising the funds necessary to support the continuing cultural production and circulation of poetry and literary fiction. That said, we value transparency highly, and we want to make sure you are aware of both the boons and burdens that define this context for publication. Thus, we'll conclude our reflection on small press publishing and all of its accompanying issues with neither empty hosannas nor dogmatic jeremiads. We won't suggest in *Chicken Soup for the Soul*-like fashion that you ignore the realities of odds and ethics, act like an ostrich with your head in the sand or gaze myopically at your computer screen, and simply "do what you love." We also won't offer any prophecies of doom that suggest this market will inevitably leave you fated to a penniless writing career of merciless fire and brimstone, in which cronies' chosen few are rewarded and innocents punished like Job. Instead, we'll leave it to you to make your own informed decisions about the worth of small press publishing in relation to your own ambitions as a writer. We are firmly rooted in this context and, frankly, we have a love/hate relationship with its conditions of existence. In all honesty, we'd like to make it a better place, as we've invested a good chunk of our personal and professional lives here, and we'd like you to help us do so. That said, it is not our position to recruit you. Instead—and at the risk of sounding like the authors of a terrible pop-psychology personality survey—we'll end with a few questions that might help facilitate your own decision about publishing contexts. Depending on how you answer these questions, you might want to consider self-publishing, our next subject of discussion.

Discussion Questions

1. Do you enjoy intense competition? How do you handle rejection? Do you think you are resilient enough to work in an environment in which "success" means being rejected about 99 percent of the time and rewarded about 1 percent of the time? How might you have to change (or what might you have to sacrifice) to accept these odds?

2. How much does the prestige of a publishing venue matter to you? And how important is it to you to get paid for your writing? Are you more concerned with your literary reputation or your ability to earn cold hard cash? Are you in a position to risk *losing* money? Or are your priorities somewhere else entirely?

3. Based on our discussions of commercial and small press publishing, what context do you think would be more appropriate for you? One or the other? Both? Neither? What more information would you like to know before making this decision?

Your Turn: Questions, Concerns & Creative-Critical Comments

1. ____

____

____

____

2. ____

____

____

____

3. ____

____

____

____

Writing Experiments

1. In our commentary on literary contests, we only grazed the surface of what is really a much broader and more complicated issue, one that we feel deserves further exploration. Have you had any experiences with literary contests? If so, what were they like? If not, why not? Either way, what do you find intriguing and/or off-putting about the contest circuit? More importantly, what qualities do you think make a literary contest fair? With this last question in mind, we'd like you to reread the Council of Literary Magazines and Press's "Contest Code of Ethics," which we reproduced above. After becoming familiar with this document, we'd like you to draft your own code of conduct for a literary contest. To do so, please select one of the two following options: (1) play it straight and offer an ideal model that, indeed, aims for an irreproachably ethical system of behavior; (2) treat this assignment satirically and propose the worst code of conduct you can imagine, one that is morally reprehensible. If you select option #2, feel free to draw examples from the actual history of corrupt contests we've touched on in this chapter, or invent as many repugnant qualities or indefensible behaviors as you see fit.

2. Imagine that you and a several of your peers are founding a new small press and/or literary magazine and are writing its mission statement. What will the focus of your small press be? Whom will it serve? What kinds of work will it publish and why? What is your press/magazine going to do that will set it apart from the other hundreds of journals and presses in the contemporary marketplace? Write up a draft of your mission statement. Please keep in mind that precision and brevity are important here.

Deep Reading

1. Now that you've learned a bit about commercial publishing and small press publishing, we'd like to direct your attention to *MFA vs NYC*, a collection of essays edited by Chad Harbach. Harbach's title essay suggests that, while there is much overlap between the two, MFA publishing (represented by universities, contests, and small presses) and NYC publishing (represented by big publishing houses) represent two distinct cultures and offer writers two very different ways of being in the world. The rest of his collection attempts to flesh out the differences and the overlap between these cultures. For example, Eric Bennett's essay "The Pyramid Scheme" presents an interesting take on the history of MFA programs: he finds that the discipline received early funding from the CIA. In "How to Be Popular," literary agent Melissa Flashman presents one of the most insightful essays we've read about what it takes to make a literary work successful. Carla Blumenkranz gives us "Seduce the Whole World," an essay that sheds light on what it was like to take a fiction workshop from Raymond Carver's editor/collaborator Gordon Lish (spoiler: it was awful).

2. If you're looking to publish with a small, independent press, we recommend that you become familiar with *Poets & Writers* and *The Writer's Chronicle*. Each issue of these magazines contains a section of literary contests and calls for submission. We also recommend looking at directories like *Writer's Market* and *The International Directory of Little Magazines and Small Presses*. These will provide more than enough publishing venues to occupy an entire career. We also suggest that you go to your library and read through the two or three most recent issues of the literary journals that are in stock. When you find a journal you like, or which is publishing work similar to your own, take note of their submission guidelines and send them some of your work.

9

Self-Publishing in the Internet Age, or the eBook that (Nearly) Ate the World

On April of 2013, James Patterson placed a full-page, wraparound advertizement on the cover of *Publisher's Weekly*, calling for government intervention to save the American publishing industry. "The Federal Government has stepped in to save the banks, and the automobile industry," said the ad, "but . . . who will save our books?" (Patterson). Patterson's ad references the US government's response to an economic recession in 2008, during which several major banks and car-makers were on the verge of bankruptcy. Five years later, according to Patterson, the book publishing industry was now in exactly that kind of crisis. But why was he so nervous about the state of publishing? And who or what was responsible for putting literature at risk? Patterson's ad does not name a culprit, and the economic downturn he cites was more or less stabilized by the time of his ad. So what happened between 2008 and 2013 that made Patterson so scared for books?

In a word: Amazon.

Founded in 1994, Amazon.com quickly became *the* go-to online bookseller, and its share of the book market steadily grew, eating into the profits of brick-and-mortar bookstores, including nationwide megastore chains like Barnes and Noble and Borders. While Barnes and Noble found a way to adapt to the rise of internet booksellers, Borders closed the last of its stores in 2011. For many folks in the industry, Borders's closing looked like terrible news. Amazon was wiping out physical bookstores in large numbers, and—worse still—it was threatening to eliminate physical books as well.

In 2007, Amazon launched the Kindle, a portable device for reading books in electronic format. Prior to the Kindle, ebooks existed mostly as CDroms or on public-domain sites like Project Gutenberg. According to Publishing historian John Thompson, ebook sales at that time, "represented around 0.1 percent of . . . overall [book] sales." But once the Kindle launched, "the same trade house that had seen ebook sales grow by 50 percent in 2007 now saw its ebook sales leap by 400 percent in 2008" (319). In 2009, Barnes and Noble released the Nook, and in 2010, Apple unveiled the iPad, selling 15 million units worldwide. By 2011, the market was saturated with portable e-reader and touchscreen devices, with many millions of users seeking content. While ebooks represented 8 percent of total revenues of book publishers in 2010, they grew to upwards of 22 percent in 2011 (Thompson 321). By the end of 2011, the US market for ebooks totaled $2.1 billion, and in the first quarter of 2012, net sales revenue from ebooks surpassed that of hardcover books by more than $50 million (Boog "eBook"). By 2013, James Patterson felt it was time to hit the panic button. He and many other authors and publishers worried that, if this trend continued, the ebook would soon eliminate all physical book sales. Major publishers would go belly up, and the book market would be completely dominated by self-published authors.

Yes, fairly recently, some commentators viewed self-published authors as a real and rising threat to the Big Five book publishers (and to the institution of Literature itself). As Amazon laid waste to physical bookstores and its Kindle chewed into the market for hardcopy books, its CreateSpace service provided a platform where anyone could upload and sell ebooks about whatever they wanted—no agents, editors, or publishers required. As a result, the book market witnessed a surge in self-publishing. Between 2006 and 2012, the number of self-published titles produced every year grew 287 percent, with a record 235,000 self-published print and ebooks hitting the market in 2012 alone (Bowker). Critics like Laura Miller saw the ebook-fueled self-publishing boom as a dangerous trend. For Miller, the radically democratic nature of platforms like CreateSpace effectively meant that the public would be subjected to an unfiltered flood of books, a flood in which most readers would simply drown: "If . . . reading is something you turn to, seeking fun or transcendence, during your precious hours of free time, how long will you persist when book after book has exactly the opposite effect, crushing your spirit instead of refreshing it? How long before you decide to just give up?" Without traditional publishers holding firm at the floodgates and only letting truly worthy titles pass through, all the literary gems would be lost in a sea of stinkers.

While this sort of alarmism about digital technologies may seem silly to us now, the concerns of folks like Patterson and Miller were prevalent in their time. It really did look to many like publishing was going to change dramatically, and probably not for the best. Of course, we could poke many holes in these old arguments: they rely on the idea that publishers are somehow objective arbiters of good taste rather than for-profit enterprises that give market advantage to titles they think they can sell; they ignore the way internet communities select and promote books according to their own visions of quality; and, of course, they completely misunderstand the nature and effects of electronic media. But we won't bother picking an old fight here. In the years since Patterson's front-cover cry for help, publishers and hard-copy books have proven their resiliency in the internet age, the Big Five have learned to adapt to the existence of electronic media, and ebooks have settled into a sizable but not world-ending corner of the book market. As of this writing, self-published ebooks account for about 27 percent of all ebook sales, a number that has held since 2015 (Author Earnings). Oh and by the way, who do you think topped Author Earnings's list for dollars earned by ebook sales in 2017? Here's a hint: He had a title count larger than the next three authors on the list combined. Yep. James Patterson.

Though the alarmism has quieted since Patterson bought the cover of Publisher's weekly, the "frightening" trends of the early 2010s may still be marching forward at a slower pace. (See, for example, Mike Shatzkin's "A Changing Book Business: It All Seems to be Flowing Downhill to Amazon" for lingering concerns). Further, cultural markets can be volatile places. There is no telling how the book publishing businesses might change between our writing of this chapter and your reading of it. All we can say is that in the moment we are writing this book, the ebook market looks pretty good for self-published authors. Let us back up a bit and explain why.

To Self-Publish Is Not (Necessarily) to Perish: A Perspective of Advocacy

In 2010, Author Joe Konrath published a novel with Grand Central Publishing, an imprint of Hachette Book group, which sold 50,000 copies in all formats. According to the *Wall Street Journal*, Konrath "earned about $30,000 in total. But if he sold [his work] as an ebook on his own, he could make that much in 18 months by selling 800 ebooks a month" (Fowler). In other words, by self-publishing, he could earn at least double the money, selling the same number of books. And so, Konrath gave up publishing with commercial presses to earn his living almost exclusively through ebook publication. He estimated his annual income from sales of self-published ebooks for 2011 at $200,000 (Konrath "You"). Further, he has stated that "he's already earning more from Kindle books that New York publishers rejected than from his print books" (Fowler).

On his blog, *A Newbie's Guide to Publishing*, Konrath argues against the kind of alarmism voiced by Patterson and Miller. In Konrath's view, Amazon and ebooks are not a bane but a boon to readers and book publishing. Rather than discouraging readers from buying books, "ereaders are actually increasing the number of books bought, and causing people to read more" (Konrath "Tsunami"). Rather than issuing in an unfiltered flood of material, outlets like Amazon, with their user reviews, do a decent job of sorting out good titles from bad. All that's happening here is that one system of distribution is being replaced by another: "Bookstores, libraries, passionate editors, and publishers don't write books. They help books find readers. Like Amazon does, by connecting readers and writers. Except Amazon has no barriers to entry, and gives writers a better royalty rate." (Konrath "Konrath on Patterson"). Konrath's point about royalties is no joke. In the summer of 2010, Amazon's royalty rate for ebooks priced between $2.99 and $9.99 doubled, moving from 35 percent to 70 percent, where it has since remained. This is a whopping figure compared the typical rate of 10–12 percent for authors working in traditional publishing contexts. In purely economic terms, this means that self-publishing authors can sell fewer books at a lower cost than authors under contract with traditional publishing houses and still make more money—potentially, at least. Because they represent themselves, they are also able to hold on to more of their earnings; they are not required to forward any percentage of their royalties to an agent.

According to Konrath, financial gain is far from the only benefit of self-publishing. He tells the story of John Kennedy Toole, whose *A Confederacy of Dunces* won a posthumous Pulitzer, to argue that what he calls the "legacy publishing" system is not always a good thing for literature. According to Konrath, Toole "was rejected by publishers, was supposedly very upset about it, and eventually killed himself." Konrath is not claiming that editorial rejection was the direct cause of a suffering author's decision to end his own life. But he is saying that the ebook market removes frustrating and sometimes destructive barriers between writers and the public. As Konrath argues, "rather than go through what Toole—and no doubt countless others—had to go through with the legacy system, they [authors] now have the opportunity to publish works themselves." What authors need, he states, is "less mentoring, fewer roadblocks, and more opportunities to get . . . published. Which self-publishing allows" (Konrath "Konrath on Patterson").

Thanks to the advent of the ebook, writers have direct access to the book market and no longer need to appeal to publishers or agents to participate in the making of culture. In other words, largely because of ebooks, publishing has become more decentralized, with power flowing out of the hands of the big five publishers and into the hands of authors/readers. This phenomenon mirrors similar processes in other media. In the music industry, an increasing number of bands have been refusing to court industry executives or rely on record labels in traditional fashion; instead, they are functioning independently, producing their own music, selling their songs directly on iTunes, Bandcamp, or similar venues, and, in many cases, retaining more creative control than would otherwise be possible. Filmmakers are relying less and less on major Hollywood studios and, instead, producing their own films and pedaling them independently on the film festival circuit. Similarly, many visual artists are relying less on gallery representation and selling their work directly on Etsy, Deviant Art, and other websites. Instead of hoping that their work gets noticed by an elite group of industry ambassadors, the culture-makers—the authors, musicians, filmmakers, and artists of the world—are testing their own fate by presenting their work directly to the public. For us, this paradigm shift does not by any means signal the death of literature or music or, more broadly, the arts. Nor does it offer an ultimate panacea for all the ills of the publishing and entertainment industries. Rather, it signifies an exciting time for experimentation and reinvention—or, more precisely, an excitingly uneasy time.

Let us explain what we mean by *uneasy*. As the path to successful authorship through self-publishing is full of new possibilities, it is also fraught with its own set of complications, especially for unknown and emerging authors. You've probably noted that Konrath, the author we've been focusing on thus far, started out with one of the big five publishing houses before he decided to transition into self-publishing. His success as a self-publisher may be largely contingent on this crucial detail: when Konrath switched to self-publishing he had the advantage of having already been branded and marketed by a team of professionals who spent considerable time and money on this process. Through this mechanism, his work had found an established audience, which made all the difference in the world. Just as it was much easier for Radiohead to self-release the album *In Rainbows* as a donation-based download in 2007 after they had already achieved popularity through a traditional path in the music business (which began with a major label during the early 1990s), it was much easier for Konrath to dare to self-publish after establishing a reputation through the traditional "legacy" model of publishing. As Edan Lepucki notes, "Konrath already had an audience from his traditionally-published books by the time he decided to take matters into his own hands. It's much harder to create a readership out of nothing." While the case of Konrath might be useful for us in understanding the changing market of ebooks, it sheds less insight on what is perhaps the biggest challenge for emerging authors planning to self-publish: the uneasy question of finding an audience. Luckily for us, three other cases offer insight into this particular issue.

Excitingly Uneasy: Amanda Hocking, Zane, E L James, and the Question of Audience

One of the go-to stories for self-published success is that of Amanda Hocking, a 28-year old who made millions publishing fantasy ebooks on Amazon. Her success story is important precisely because it reveals the challenges facing an unknown author in both traditional publishing and electronic self-publishing contexts. Hocking's struggle to be published by traditional means began at the age of seventeen, when she received her first rejection letter for her first novel. Hocking continued writing and gathering rejection letters over the years until she reached a somewhat desperate moment. Ed Pilkington, who profiled Hocking for *The Guardian*, explains: "She was frantic to get her first book published by the time she was 26, the age Stephen King was first in print, and time was running out . . . So while holding down a day job caring for severely disabled people, for which she earned $18,000 a year, she went into a Red Bull-fueled frenzy of writing at night, starting at 8pm and continuing until dawn." We should be careful to note that while Pilkington's clipped journalistic style may tend to reinscribe Romantic ideas of frenzied artistic production, Hocking's process was hardly akin to the fabulist account of Kerouac's scroll. This was not another myth of spontaneous genius pouring out unfettered in a convulsive burst of creativity, but an obsessive workaholic's continual labor of love. Hocking wrote regularly and repeatedly night after night—for a period of nine years—until she had produced seventeen novels. Granted, this is a tremendous output, but Hocking herself admits that, in retrospect, her manuscripts may not have been adequately edited or revised (Hocking "Some").

All of her seventeen novels were rejected by publishers and remained unpublished until April of 2010, when Hocking heard that a museum exhibit about Jim Henson and his Muppets would soon be coming to Chicago. A huge fan of Henson's work, Hocking wanted to attend the exhibition, but had no money for the trip. Having read up on self-publishing online—indeed, she studied Konrath's blog—Hocking decided to post one of her novels to Amazon, hoping that over the course of the year, it would sell enough copies, mostly to family and friends, to earn the $300 she needed for her trip. What she hoped would garner a few hundred bucks turned into an incredibly lucrative career.

Hocking could not possibly have picked a better moment in history to experiment with self-publishing ebooks. As we suggested earlier, the period of 2010 through 2011 marked a rise in ebook sales that took the segment from 8 percent to around 22 percent of total book sales revenue. This was a time when major publishers were noticing but not yet fully responding to the uptick in sales. Amazon's Kindle had been available for several years, and the iPad made its debut in the same year Hocking did. Her book entered a market where demand was rising rapidly and supply had not yet caught up. "Within a few days," states Pilkington, "she was selling nine copies a day . . . By May she had posted two further books in the series . . . and sold 624 copies. June saw sales rise to more than 4,000 and in July she posted *Switched* . . . It brought in more than $6,000 in pure profit that month alone, and in August she quit her day job." By October of that year, Hocking had made $20,000. By 2012, she had sold "1.5m books and made $2.5m." without "a book agent or publishing house or sales force or marketing manager or bookshop anywhere in sight" (Pilkington).

So how did she do it? Granted, her timing was impeccable, and in this sense she was aided by a combination of factors beyond her control: history, technology, and chance. Getting her work into the e-marketplace was easy—simply a matter of formatting her work and using Smashwords to make it available to Sony, Nook, Kindle, and iBook users. But what things did she do specifically to find and establish her audience? We'd like to suggest that three strategies enabled her breakthrough. First, to put the matter rather crassly, she appealed to the cheapskate in all of us. She made her work so inexpensive that almost anyone could afford it. Rather than compete with the prices of ebooks from traditional publishers (often upwards of $9.99), she priced her work at $.99 and $2.99. In fact, she adopted these price points quite strategically, offering the first book in a series for just less than a dollar to lure readers, and then upping the price for subsequent books to $2.99. The high royalty rates we discussed earlier are precisely what enabled Hocking to price her work so low and maintain profitability. (They are also what would lead many other self-publishers to offer their work at a similarly low cost.) Second, she borrowed a traditional marketing strategy from print publishing and adapted it to the online sphere. Instead of sending out advanced print copies of her work to noted critics and established reviewers (the practice of traditional publishers), she emailed influential book bloggers and asked them to review or recommend her work. Hocking credits this factor, perhaps above all others, for her ability to quickly find readers and gain popularity. When offering a month-by-month account of her breakthrough year, she writes:

> In June, something truly magical happened. I discovered book bloggers . . . These people take time out of their busy lives to talk about books and have contests and connect with followers and writers and other readers . . . I asked several if they would be interested in reviewing my books, and most of them said yes, even if they didn't generally review self-published work.
>
> HOCKING "An Epic"

Thanks to the free publicity generated by book bloggers, Hocking gained an advantage over other similar titles, and this advantage became cumulative as more readers began to discover and discuss Hocking's work. It was quickly and widely circulated within contexts for review until Hocking's name achieved a certain status; once recognized, her name acquired the power to regenerate its popularity in a market that had yet to become terribly competitive. Of course, it didn't hurt that Hocking worked in a genre with widespread appeal: what we may have called fantasy at the time of its release and what we would now (in our increasingly specialized market) most likely call paranormal YA romance.

Hocking's third and equally effective strategy was to market herself aggressively through other forms of social media. She continually posted entries on her blog, cultivated followers on Twitter and Facebook, redirected these followers to websites reviewing or selling her titles, maintained an active online presence through constant updating of webpages, and responded tirelessly to emails from her developing fan base. In the absence of an agent or a publisher's marketing division, these means of self-promotion proved economical and essential to her success. They also proved laborious and draining. In one blog entry, she wrote, "I don't think people realize how much work I do . . . The amount of time and energy I put into marketing is exhausting. I am continuously overwhelmed by the amount of work I have to do that isn't writing a book" (Hocking "Some"). Because Hocking already had an archive of seventeen novels (and didn't need to spend time producing new work), she was able to devote almost all of her energy to marketing and networking, and this is exactly what she did. The time she spent advertising her books through social media amounted to more than a full-time job. This commitment led her to feel, perhaps, less like she was a writer and more like she was managing her own PR firm. Taking on the combined work of writer, editor, publisher, and publicist eventually prompted her to conclude: "It's harder to be a best-seller self-publishing than it is with a [publishing] house" (Hocking "Some").

And, indeed, in a rather ironic turn in 2012, Hocking—one of the world's most successful self-publishers—decided to revert to traditional publishing. Burned out by her business responsibilities as a self-publishing author, she signed a deal for $2.1 million with St. Martin's (in the US) and Pan Macmillan (in the UK), which enabled her to relax a bit and leave most of the business of publishing to her publisher. Of course, she would never have been able to secure such a deal if she had not gotten her name into print on her own accord and dived headfirst into her self-fashioned ebook publicity blitz. Her success in self-publishing is precisely what enabled her to gain the attention of the commercial publishers that had previously rejected her work. Their editorial tastes suddenly changed when they learned of her sales figures.

The lesson for emerging authors seems to be two-fold: (1) it is possible—although not at all easy—to build an audience from scratch; (2) under the right circumstances, self-publishing might provide a gateway into commercial publishing. In broader terms, the case of Hocking suggests that self-publishing ebooks does not signal the death of literature or traditional publishing at all, but may, in fact, wind up reinforcing the so-called "legacy" system. Here, self-publishing and traditional publishing enjoy more of a symbiotic than confrontational relationship.

This symbiotic relationship also applies in the cases of best-selling erotica authors Zane (*Addicted* and *The Sex Chronicles*) and E L James (*Fifty Shades of Grey*). Regardless of your feelings about the work of these authors (or the genre of erotica in general) you can probably appreciate how they launched their multimillion dollar writing careers by self-publishing and building their audiences online. When Zane (the pen name of Kristina Roberts) started writing erotic fiction, Amazon did not exist. Nor did Twitter, Facebook, or YouTube. Social media as we know it today was only a latent possibility of the early internet. And so, in 1997, when Roberts wrote her first piece of erotic fiction, she posted it to an AOL chatroom for a few of her friends, "and the next thing you know," Roberts told the *Washingtonian*, "I started getting e-mails from complete strangers—just like, 'Oh, my gosh, your story was the hottest thing I've ever read'" (Moser). Roberts, an African American woman, wrote her stories about African American women and shared them with other African American women, for whom representations in romance novels and erotica were in short supply. With a marketing degree from Howard University, Roberts understood the business potential in this response. She took on her pen name, set up a website and an email newsletter, and she offered to mail out 50 photocopied pages of fiction for $13. According to the *Washingtonian*, "The response was tremendous: Zane estimates she sold more than a thousand copies of the collection. She'd spend all day at Staples, she says, copying and collating pages." Bolstered by this success, Roberts self-published her first book, *The Sex Chronicles: Shattering the Myth*, followed quickly by *Addicted*, each of which sold 50,000 copies in their first year (Patrick). This success attracted the attention of major publishers, but Roberts turned them down. Roberts told *Time* magazine that these publishers would say, "You're one of the best writers we've ever read, and we'll offer you a deal today, but we need to tone you down" (Sachs). Roberts held out, continuing to increase her sales numbers as a self-published author until she got an offer from Simon & Schuster that didn't insist on modulating her tone. The deal with Simon & Schuster gave her access to the marketing and distribution power of the firm, which led to increased sales, a TV series with Cinemax, and Robert's own imprint, which has published well over 30 of her novels along with work by 150 other authors. In her chapter in *The Cambridge History of African American Literature*, Candice Love Jackson describes Zane as a trailblazer, who "led black erotica from the shadows into the clearing of the mainstream" (675).

Roberts (as Zane) may also have blazed a trail for mega-popular erotica in general. In fact, it's not really a stretch to say that Robert's insistence on not "toning down" her work—and the subsequent success of her novels—alerted publishers to the notion that the general public was ready for something like E L James' *Fifty Shades of Grey*, which sold more than 70 million copies worldwide and was followed by two bestselling sequels. Like Zane's fiction, James's novels were originally self-published online. In this case, though, the *Grey* novels were not posted as original content to an AOL chat forum, but as *Twilight* fan fiction to Fanfiction.net, a public archive for stories that appropriate characters and settings from popular media. *Twilight* and its sequels were a super-successful YA paranormal romance series in the early 2000s, and James's fiction (then called "Master of the Universe") recast Bella, the female lead, and her vampire love interest, Edward, into the roles of college newspaper reporter and wealthy entrepreneur with somewhat vampiric sexual kinks, roles that James later renamed in order to avoid copyright claims from

Stephanie Meyer & Co. *Twilight* fan fiction, with its large base of avidly reading and writing followers, provided a perfect location for James's trilogy-in-the-making.

In fact, James was able to build her audience precisely by appealing to the culture of fandom. Within this online community, fans read and review each other's stories, and authors of fan fiction grow in reputation in part due to the quality of peer-review relationships that they establish with other fans. In this context, it is worth mentioning two things. First, in order to establish what would eventually become the core of her own fan base, James may have had to practice literary citizenship of the kind we discussed in Chapter 6, supporting other fan-fiction writers, offering feedback on their work, and graciously accepting their comments on her own drafts. This tends to be how the culture of fan fiction works in general, though we don't personally have access to James's early drafts or any exchanges she may have had with other fans. In any case, fandom enabled James to develop a particular kind of invested audience: readers who may have functioned in some capacity as contributors to her work and who, in any case, shared a passionate interest in its source material (i.e., *Twilight*). According to Jason Boog, who broke the story of Fifty Shades' origins for NPR and Galleycat, "Master of the Universe" garnered over 37,000 reader reviews over the course of its stay on the site; it was later removed from the database for its explicit content (Boog "The Lost"). These reviews served the function of promoting James's work, increasing its popularity in fandom, and enabling it to gain a kind of cumulative advantage, which, to a certain degree, transferred to a different context and enabled the work to reach a larger audience.

When "Master" was complete, James retooled it with new titles and character names and sent it off to publishers. The manuscript was eventually accepted by The Writer's Coffee Shop, a small publishing house with a limited marketing budget that publishes only ebooks and print-on-demand paperbacks (an odd business model, since these are the very things authors can now easily do for themselves). According to the *Huffington Post*, the trilogy sold 250,000 copies at the publisher, which gained the attention of Hollywood studios, attention James was able to convert into a deal with an agent, who then landed her a seven-figure deal with Vintage Books, an imprint of Random House (Sales). It is most likely that James's early sales at The Writer's Coffee Shop were to fans she had gained in fandom, the invested audience she built through collaboration and networking. The cultivation of this audience provided the demonstrated interest—the base of readership—that garnered the interest of larger commercial publishers and made her ascent to mega-best-selling-author possible.

We don't relate the stories of Hocking, Zane, and James here because we want to encourage the notion that posting creative work online will guarantee success. You're not any more likely to get rich quickly on ebooks or self-published fan fiction than you are to strike gold in traditional publishing (well, maybe the tiniest bit more likely, but not much). Regardless, we want to be clear that Hocking, Zane, and James are exceptions rather than the rule. Most of the many thousands of self-published ebook and fan fiction authors make little or no money from their work. And, we should add, many have no desire to: they're in it for the pleasure of developing and sharing stories, and they treat their writing more as a labor of love than a career pursuit. This being said, while the cases of the authors we've profiled here are by no means typical, they demonstrate a path to successful publication that was neither viable nor hardly imaginable 20 years ago. It is now possible to self-publish online and develop a writing career. If writing and selling books is your goal, self-publishing in the ebook market is a feasible option for you now. Although copyright law limits what authors may do with derivative works, writing fan fiction is an option too. In fact, E L James's experience suggests that if you want to publish and sell erotic fiction—or genre fiction of any type—fan fic is a legitimate starting place. Together, Hocking, Zane and James's very different stories make clear that authors needn't appeal to major publishers in order to develop a following of readers and sell their work. If you understand the politics and procedures of self-publishing, you can write and then publish (whether to the ebook market or to a peer-to-peer fiction sharing environment like fandom) in order to build an audience. And, if your work finds enough readers this way, there is a chance that traditional publishers—even those who've rejected your work—may just seek you out.

But What About Literary Fiction? The Talk of a Self-Published Tome

You may have noticed that all three of the examples we discussed above were of authors of what might be called "popular genre fiction": that is, they write things like paranormal romance and erotica. We did not single these authors out for this commonality. Rather, the fact that our examples of highly successful self-published authors all wrote in popular genres is a reflection of the market for ebooks, which is dominated by popular fiction, and so self-published authors in these genres stand a better chance of becoming successful. Fiction, broadly understood, is by far the most popular category in the ebook market, with various fiction subcategories dominating the top four slots on Author Earnings' list of US ebook sales. Topping the list is "Literature and Fiction," with over 70 million ebook sales and a market share of over $330 million. "Mystery, Thriller & Suspense," "Romance," and "Science Fiction &

Fantasy" take up spots 2–4 on Author Earnings's list with a collective total just under 114 million sales and a $450 million share of the market. In other words, "genre fiction" (comprised of mystery, romance, sci-fi, and fantasy combined) sells twice as well as literary fiction and makes about 1.5 times the profit. So it shouldn't come as a surprise that early success stories resulting from the rise of the ebook were all authors in popular genres.

That said, literary fiction has made its way into ebooks as well (although the market is smaller). John Thompson found that "while the shifts are strongest in commercial fiction and especially genre fiction, there has been a strong shift in literary fiction too." Citing a particular example, he writes, "Jonathan Franzen's *Freedom* . . . sold around 750,000 copies in hardcover and 250,00 ebooks in the US during its first year, so ebooks comprised around 25 percent of its frontlist sale" (323). The ebook market has also become a home for literary titles that don't fit well anywhere else. George Saunders, for example, released his story "Fox 8" as a Kindle Single at the suggestion of his publisher at Random House. The story, meant at first as a children's book, was deemed not fit for that market, and then, when preparing the manuscript of *Tenth of December*, Saunders had trouble making the story fit his collection. "Every time I got to this one," Saunders said of "Fox 8," "it was asking one stretch too many from the reader. So I took it out, and then my editor said to me, 'Would you like to revisit that story as a stand alone release?' I didn't even know you could do that" (qtd. in Ulin). The story now sells for 99 cents on the Kindle store.

Ebook sales of titles by authors like Franzen and Saunders demonstrate a market for electronic literary fiction, a market that has also recently demonstrated an openness to self-published titles. Of course, literary self-publishing has a rich history that extends much further back than our current electronic age. Whitman self-published *Leaves of Grass*, Proust self-published *Swan's Way*, and a whole host of authors got their work into readers' hands with the help of so-called "vanity" presses. Sergio De La Pava has added his name to this history as the first breakthrough literary fiction author to find acclaim self-publishing online. De La Pava's novel *A Naked Singularity*, a 700-page postmodern dismantling of the US justice system—De La Pava is a full-time public defender—was rejected multiple times over the course of three years. No publisher or agent would take on the work as it was. In fact, 88 agents rejected it (Keller). According to Garth Hallberg of *The Millions*, De La Pava found some interest when he first sent out excerpts of his work, but then nearly every interested agent expressed concern about the marketability of his full manuscript: "the response to the sheer bulk of the complete manuscript was, 'You've got to be kidding.' De La Pava, having poured seven years of his life into the book, wasn't ready to see it chopped into something smaller and less risky." In fact, De La Pava describes his response as follows:

"My attitude was, I'll take my ball and go home" (qtd. in Hallberg). "Going home" looked like putting his manuscript up on Xlibris as a print-on-demand paperback.

Like Konrath, Hocking, Zane, and James, De La Pava took proactive steps to get his self-published book in to the hands of the right readers, largely by tapping into appropriate contexts for review. In this case, his partner, Susanna De La Pava (also a public defender), more or less functioned as his agent and publicist in her spare time, sending emails to reviewers, bloggers, critics, and other online literary figures, informing them of the work and suggesting they read/review it. Her particular strategy was to target people "who had written about *Infinite Jest*, offering to send them something they might like" without revealing her identity as the author's partner (Hallberg). Capitalizing on the late David Foster Wallace's popularity and seeking to entice some of his more high profile fans with a promise of similar work, she sought to generate a buzz, or what Julia Keller has called a kind of "literary scuttlebutt." Unlike Hocking, she opted not to canvass a large populace of potential readers but to discriminately target a small group of key literary influencers. Her approach worked.

A simplified version of the book's success story goes something like this: After reading an essay by Scott Bryan Wilson and learning of this critic's "love for long, complicated books," Susanna De La Pava sent Wilson a review copy of *Naked Singularity*. Wilson then wrote an overwhelmingly positive review of the book for *The Quarterly Conversation*, a widely-read literary webzine. Sparing few words, he called the labyrinthine text "one of the best and most original novels of the decade." Similar positive reviews followed in *Open Letters Monthly*, a popular review of arts and literature, and other online journals. This nascent buzz led to more interest, more reviews, and eventually book sales (around 100 a month by De La Pava's estimation). Perhaps more important than the conversion of hype into sales figures were the conversations about the book that took place between figureheads in literary publishing. According to Julia Keller's version of the story, after reviewing *Naked Singularity*, Wilson began talking the book up to his friend and colleague, Levi Stahl, who worked as the publicity manager/promotions director of the University of Chicago Press. Stahl subsequently read and loved the book; he pitched its publication to his colleagues at the press—an unusual proposal for a press that rarely publishes new fiction. As it made its way through stages of review at Chicago, the book was greeted with overwhelming approval. Its advocates were excited about the prospect of "discovering" the literary talent of De La Pava and rescuing his book from what they saw as potential self-published obscurity. The board of directors voted in favor of publication, and the press offered De La Pava a traditional book deal.

Since its publication with Chicago, *Naked Singularity* has not found the same kind of financial success as the work of Hockney and James, but then literary fiction doesn't necessarily aim for the same sales numbers as genre fiction. It tends to measure its worth in critical praise, literary reputation, and adoption in academic courses. De La Pava has garnered many such accolades. His prose has been compared to the work of Dostoevesky, Henry James, and Thomas Pynchon. And his novel was awarded the PEN/Robert W Bingham prize for a debut work of fiction in 2013. His second self-published novel, *Personae*, was also picked up by University of Chicago, and his third, *Lost Empress*, was published by Pantheon. Given his atypical path to literary success, De La Pava is critical of literary folks who would turn up their noses at self-published work: "If I tell you this book is self-published, your first response is: 'It's not going to be a good book,'" he told the *Wall Street Journal*, "But if I tell you this filmmaker made this movie using his credit cards, you'd have an opposite reaction" (qtd in. Catton). His story not only reveals that crossing over from vanity to university press is indeed possible, but it also addresses the merit of self-publishing in a saturated literary marketplace, encouraging us to reexamine our preconceptions about who self-published authors are. Twenty years from now, when scholars are studying the historical trend from traditionally published to self-published literary fiction, De La Pava's books might just be required reading.

To Be or Not to Be Self-Published? That is Your Question

All of the self-published authors we have surveyed in this chapter were successful because they spent time researching and then targeting their audiences appropriately. While this is no guarantee of success, it is the common thread linking the stories of these radically different writers. It is also, more or less, a prerequisite for those aspiring to earn any kind of living by self-publishing. If you decide to you want to write, publish, and sell your own books, you will need to spend time and energy cultivating an audience. We can say this with certainty. On the other hand, we can't say with any kind of certainty whether the self-publishing path to authorship is appropriate for you. Only you can make this decision. So, instead of trying to nudge you in one direction or another, we'll close this section by recapping some of the advantages and disadvantages of self-publishing in the electronic age.

Let's start with the positives. First, self-publishing obviously allows you to escape the heartbreak of rejection. If you don't have the resiliency to accept editors regularly saying no to your work in a market that defines a successful author as someone who places around 1–2 percent of their submissions, you may want to consider taking matters into your own hands. In the case of Hocking, self-publishing not only offered a practical solution but also facilitated a kind of redemption; it ultimately allowed her to place her work with a commercial publishing house that, previously, wouldn't even consider her writing. We imagine it must have felt pretty great to be courted by a publisher who had to eat some proverbial crow and admit their earlier mistake.

Second, self-publishing allows for a much timelier public release of your work. Instead of engaging in the process of finding and securing an agent who will, in turn, engage in the process of trying to sell your manuscript to a publisher, who will, in turn, engage in the process of finding an editor to assist in further developing your work (processes which, collectively, tend to take years), you can post your writing almost immediately to Amazon, Barnes and Noble, or another ebook seller's website. Third, self-publishing may prove to be a more lucrative endeavor than traditional publishing. As we suggested earlier, royalty rates for self-published authors tend to be significantly higher. Further, as a self-published author, you won't need to share any percentage of your earnings with an agent. Depending on the kind of writing you do, it may also be worth taking into consideration the cost of the contest circuit in traditional literary publishing as a point of comparison. As we've suggested, emerging authors often spend hundreds or thousands of dollars in entry fees trying repeatedly to place their manuscripts in increasingly competitive literary contests. Self-publishing allows you to avoid this expense entirely. Fourth, self-publishing enables you to have more control not only of pricing your work but of a range of other issues including cover art and editorial decision-making. Initially, De La Pava decided to self-publish because he didn't want to carve up his postmodern tome of a novel into a more saleable market-friendly product. For him, self-publishing represented a choice for personal integrity over prospective agents' advice.

Lastly, self-publishing lowers the bar of entry into the book market, which means that authors and subjects previously spurned by editors and agents now have an opportunity to find their audiences. The importance of this advantage is perhaps best articulated by self-published African American children's book author Zetta Elliott, who expresses her reasonable frustration with the big five's focus on white, middle-class readers and their interests:

> How many children's books do we have about police brutality—mass incarceration—lynching—HIV/AIDS? Homelessness and suicide among queer youth of color? How many books show Black children using magic and/or technology to shape an alternative universe? These are the kinds of stories that I write and am forced to self-publish, because they are rejected over and over by (mostly white) editors.
>
> ELLIOTT

In other words, there are books that need to be written and read, and the traditional publishing industry is not currently well disposed to produce them.

On the flipside, there are, indeed, a number of disadvantages to publishing without the assistance of a traditional press. First, unless you start out in the world of commercial or literary publishing (ala Konrath), you will not be able to depend on a publishing house's established audience; nor will you have the advantage of being marketed by a team of professionals working to create or brand your authorial identity with a particular population of readers. Second, because of this absence, all promotion, publicity, and marketing will fall to you. If you have the personality, gumption, and fortitude to take on this kind of work—not to mention the serious investment of time it requires—you might find yourself reasonably engaged. If you don't, you might find yourself courting disaster. Third, although you may get your work into readers' hands more quickly by forgoing the steps of securing an agent and editor, you may also find yourself missing the editorial support a traditional press offers. This factor played a significant part in Hocking's decision to move toward commercial publishing. She valued the developmental commentary that an experienced editor could provide. She has stated repeatedly that she feels her work became much stronger with this kind of support (Hocking "Some"). Fourth, while options for and attitudes toward self-publishing are changing, there is still often a stigma associated with the practice. Some less open-minded readers consider it the province of hacks, wannabes, or inferior writers. Sometimes this prejudice can emerge in rather unexpected places. After acquiring the rights to *Naked Singularity*, the University of Chicago Press declared they would not look to adopt any more self-published titles. They consider the quality of De La Pava's work an anomaly rather than a potential new norm (Keller). Of course, we are not suggesting that there is merit to this attitude. From their particular vantage points in history, people tend to harbor inaccurate prejudices on a fairly regular basis. Rather, we are merely suggesting that a bias against "vanity" publishing continues to exist. Fifth, and finally, the market for self-published ebooks, at present, remains limited in a few capacities. As we've suggested, there is not, as of yet, tremendous demand for literary fiction (although this appears to be changing), and there is almost no market for poetry. By no means does the current climate suggest that there shouldn't be or can't be room for work in these genres; however, if you want to pursue self-publishing this kind of work, you'll have to be a bit of a trailblazer in building and strengthening its market, especially when it comes to poetry. (Stay with us, poets. We'll talk a bit more about options for innovative forms of electronic poetry in the next chapter.)

Perhaps we are naïve idealists; regardless, we're looking forward to a day when writers may not necessarily need to make a choice between self- or traditional publishing, but can navigate or switch between contexts like the authors surveyed above. That is, they can opt *to be and not to be* self-published. Perhaps because of the work of Konrath, Hocking, Zane, James, and De La Pava, this more inclusive option—what now seems like a rather strange way of doing things—may soon become perfectly ordinary. In the meantime, we leave it to you to decide where to make your work available and how to invent your future.

Discussion Questions

1. What has your attitude been toward self-publishing and where have your ideas about the practice come from? Now that you've read this chapter, have your ideas changed at all? If so, in what ways? If not, why not?

2. What exactly are your goals as an author? How do you think these goals might or might not be met through self-publishing?

3. What do you think it would take for audiences to stop discriminating against self-published works? And what would it take to build or expand an audience for self-published ebooks of poetry and literary fiction?

Your Turn: Questions, Concerns & Creative-Critical Comments

1. ____

____

____

____

2. ____

____

____

____

3. ____

____

____

____

Writing Experiments

1. Take a look at Project Gutenberg and browse through their catalog. All of the works posted on the site are in the public domain (at least if you live in the US, otherwise check your local copyright laws). Public domain works are available to you for free, and you may use them however you like. You can change them; you can rewrite them. You can cut them up and paste them back together into surreal formations. And you can sell them, either in their original form, or in the remixed version you come up with. This is why Seth Grahame-Smith was able to add zombies to *Pride and Prejudice* and sell the result. If you browse online ebook sellers, you'll find many of the free titles on Gutenberg are also on sale at these sites. Find something on Gutenberg that inspires you, intervene in it, mash it up, add your own language, and post the product online (for sale or for free).

2. It's time to write some fan fiction. Pick a book or film or TV series that you like and look around online to see if you can find any fans writing stories about it. If you do find a fandom, make an effort to discover which stories and authors are most widely respected by its members. Read several stories, and comment on them. Be both supportive and honest in your response. Once you have a sense of the kind of writing that's happening in the fandom, try your hand at it. Post the results online where fans are likely to see it, and see what sort of response you get. This sort of self-publishing won't produce work that you can sell (unless you do what E L James did and change the names and circumstances of the characters), but it might gain you some friends who enjoy and support your writing.

Deep Reading

1. To get a sense of the kind of fiction that has found some success online, we suggest you read some. Head over to Amazon's ebook store or Apple's iBooks and look at the top ranked titles in various genres. Maybe download a few. You might also look up the authors of these books and see if they have a website that offers any insight into their marketing strategies. If literary fiction is your thing, hunt around on the site and see if you can find anyone following in De La Pava's footsteps.

2. Read Laura Miller's article for *Salon* ("When Anyone Can Become an Author") and also find Joe Konrath's responses to Patterson ("Konrath on Patterson") and his article "Tsunami of Crap." Who is right about the effect of internet publishing? Is it cheapening our standards? Does the loss of editorial gatekeeping lead to a loss in quality? In what ways are ebooks good or bad for the future of literature?

SECTION FOUR

What the Future of Creative Writing Might Look Like

10

Misbehaving On and Off the Page: Toward the Literature of Tomorrow

According to Ray Kurzweil's Law of Accelerating Returns, "the rate of change itself is accelerating" (Kurzweil). This deceptively brief statement contains loaded implications for understanding human progress. The more humans evolve culturally and technologically, suggests Kurzweil, the quicker the pace of their progress; instead of following a constant linear model of growth, this pace increases exponentially. When Kurzweil examines historical trends of progress and applies them to our current outlook toward the future, he suggests that "we won't experience 100 years of progress in the 21st century—it will be more like 20,000 years of progress (at today's rate)." A controversial futurist, Kurzweil is considered by some to be one of our greatest living thinkers. To others, he is a little bonkers—a contemporary caricature of Nostradamus. Of course, we should probably place him somewhere in between these two extremes. He is, after all, one of Google's top engineers.

Whether or not we trust entirely in Kurzweil's Law of Accelerating Returns, we can probably agree that even the near future will look significantly different from our cultural present. Given the rapid changes in technology and publishing that have occurred over the last decade alone, we're uncertain what the future of creative writing will look like; hence, we can't offer any sort of prescription for success. The best forward-looking advice we can offer to emerging authors is perhaps quite simple: you should do what you want. After all, you are the future of creative writing. Your own and successive generations will reinvent the art, and you will probably do so at a rate heretofore unimaginable. The most rational thing for us to do now is probably get out of your way and let the reinvention begin. But before we step aside to watch you improvize a course for where you are going, let's reflect briefly on where we have been and, in the process, qualify what exactly we mean when we say you should do what you want.

Throughout this book, we've tried to provide a broad, informed perspective on creative writing without pigeonholing you into a particular identity as a kind of writer who is supposed to *not* do this or *not* do that. At times, we may have failed to provide what you particularly wanted to hear—yes, there were heaps of depressing statistics in that last section on publishing—but we have done so with the understanding that creative people tend to defy depressing statistics on a daily basis. The more informed they are, the more effectively creative they are able to be. That's how innovation works. If you recall, when we started this book (what now seems like exponential ages ago), we were concerned with the way handbooks offered prohibitive *either/or* ways of thinking that confined writers to rigidly prescribed roles. Since then, we have tried to suggest that one of the problems with creative writing is its tendency to confine writers: to the trappings of aestheticism; to Romantic idealizations of spontaneous genius; to antiquated understandings of single authorship; to inherited systems of publication that privilege the already-enfranchised; to the boundaries of print culture; and to related mythologies that are not particularly honest or useful. We'd like to suggest that when you come upon these sorts of confining prescriptions about who writers are and what they should do, you assert your agency to defy them.

With this clarification in mind, let us return to the critique of handbooks we started so long ago in our Introduction and offer two final examples to suggest with a little more specificity how you might reimagine creative writing as we know it in a way that is less entrenched in a prohibitive past and more attuned to the productive uncertainty of the future.

Tapping, Trapping, or Trashing into the Future? A Recycling of Handbook Prohibitions

Even progressive creative writing handbooks that intend to avoid the pitfalls of the past still seem to wind up offering weird behavioral prohibitions. Take, for instance, Carol Bly's *Beyond the Writers' Workshop*, a text designed to reconceptualize the study of creative nonfiction. While attempting to provide an alternative to Iowa's workshop model, Bly nonetheless advocates aesthetic isolationism perhaps as fervently as the New Critics did in the 1930s. When issuing advice to emerging authors, she states the following in all seriousness: "Occasions come up in writing that are so unfair that we would do best simply to agree to ourselves aloud or in our journals, 'That is wildly unfair,' and not think about them anymore. Unless you mean to give up your writing to become the leader of a major psychosocial rebellion, thousands of horrible social situations can't be cured [sic]" (186). In this defeatist tone, Bly treats literary art and worldly struggle as incompatible; the function of creative nonfiction here is precisely *not* to resist injustice, *not* to intervene in social or political affairs, and *not* to attempt to change the world, much less inspire others to do so. Rather, writers of this genre should passively accept worldly "unfairness"—surely a euphemism for serious social and economic problems—or choose to abandon their art. One might become an activist or protestor *instead of* a writer but not adopt both identities simultaneously.

The second handbook we'd like to mention here, *What Our Speech Disrupts: Feminism and Creative Writing Studies*, is quite progressive—one of the most innovative we have encountered. In it, Katharine Haake pushes the perceived boundaries of creative writing, positioning herself to the left on the field's unacknowledged political spectrum. The book's orientation is more overtly theoretical than Bly's and appears to be more concerned with encouraging experimentation, largely in the form of enabling students to produce hybrid or unconventional texts that do not fit readily into traditional genres. Despite her differences with Bly in this regard, she too reverts to a defeatist tone in an effort to maintain creative writing's autonomy. In one aside, in which she discusses the problem of "writing dangerously" (i.e., subverting conventions for purposes of social activism), she reveals a desire to regulate students' text-making behaviors so that they are not aimed toward cultural intervention: "[W]riting dangerously is not so much a truly dangerous act as it is just not behaving yourself on the page . . . however much we might wish that we could change the world through our writing, it isn't very likely" (263). While Haake does not prohibit students from writing politically motivated texts quite as forcefully as Bly, she discourages them from doing so by stating their likelihood to be ineffectual. Here, attempts to engage in social struggle do not necessarily have to be entirely separated from the activity of writing, but the combination represents a rather futile exercise. Haake makes recurrent efforts to encourage this separation, expressing a desire to discuss creative writing "without conflating aesthetic and political purpose" (263).

Now that we've surveyed these last two examples, let us take a moment to issue a small bit of advice as clearly as possible: *When you come across prohibitions like these, we recommend that you misbehave all over the page.* Conflate aesthetics and politics, science fiction and sociology, math and music, physics and journalism, weather patterns and joy. Combine the art of your writing with anything and everything you see fit, even and especially if it seems impossible. Really, we recommend that you start "a major psychosocial rebellion" *with* your creative writing. The most successful authors do it all the time. Or, if they don't start rebellions singlehandedly, they at least contribute to their force. June Jordan did it when she collaborated with her students at U C Berkeley to create *Poetry for the People: A Revolutionary Blueprint*. As we've suggested, this guidebook and performance series brought poetry out of the classroom and into the community, successfully blending personal expression with grass-roots social activism. Jonathan Saffron Foer contributed to a rebellion against factory farming in the US *by writing*. His creative nonfiction book, *Eating Animals*, changed the world by making Americans more aware of the environmental, economic, material, and medical consequences of their eating habits in a way that is more imaginative and insightful than dogmatic or dull. We recommend you check out the work of these "psycho-social rebels" and innumerable other contemporary authors who continually redefine what creative writers can or should do through just the sort of conflations creative writing handbooks try to prohibit.

In addition to misbehaving all over the page, we also suggest that you consider straying from the page or abandoning the page altogether: i.e., misbehaving *off* of the page. If using other media will help you pursue what you want to do and reach the audiences you wish to reach, then by all means, make use of the technologies that align with your goals, regardless of how dangerous or innocuous handbook authors might suggest them to be. Given the history of handbooks' prohibitory advice that we've uncovered here, we are uneasy suggesting that you should or should not do much of anything at all, really. To this end, instead of issuing advice about appropriate or inappropriate behavior, we'll dedicate the rest of this final chapter to exploring expansive possibilities. These possibilities envision a future for creative writing specifically by way of platforms that facilitate misbehaving through innovations in computer technology, performance, and collaboration. We hope you will treat the work we survey in these last several pages as models that you may learn from, appropriate, transform, ignore, or reject as you see fit: i.e., in accordance with what you want to do.

Beyond Flash Poetics: Innovation as Intervention

Over the last decade or so we've encountered the work of many creative writers who use internet and ebook technologies for innovative purposes. Immediately, we think of early pioneers like Oni Buchanan and Thomas Swiss, who collaborated with computer whizzes to create animated and interactive HTML experiments that reinvented poetry for the screen. Swiss and Shaw's "The Language of New Media" manipulates icons to reveal issues of authority inherent to electronic reading and web browsing activities. Buchanan and Mazzoleni's "The Mandrake Vehicles" disrupts the reading patterns of print culture by transforming what at first appears to be an ordinary prose poem into multiple possibilities for verse through dazzling sequences of 3-D animation. A quick browsing of the internet reveals that these and many other writers have reinvented creative writing in ways that would suggest what visual poets Stéphane Mallarmé or Guillaume Apollinaire might create if they were alive today, talented coders, and experts in Adobe Animate. While we might survey any number of works here (and we know many that are as attractive to us as tinfoil is to magpies), we'd like to focus on one digital text that specifically combines technological innovation with cultural intervention and, in this sense, speaks even more directly to the benefits of defying the conventional wisdom of creative writing handbooks.

Voices of Haiti is a collaborative multimedia project that combines activism, journalism, documentary photography, filmmaking, recorded live performance, creative nonfiction, and poetry. It was made possible because Lisa Armstrong, Kwame Dawes, and a team of collaborators did exactly what Carol Bly suggests creative writers should *not* do in *Beyond the Writers' Workshop*. After a terrible earthquake devastated Haiti in January of 2010, leaving millions of people homeless—instead of agreeing to themselves "that is wildly unfair" and deciding not to think about the issue anymore—they opted to do something about it *with their creative writing*. Specifically, they approached the Pulitzer Center on Crisis Reporting and requested funding for an experimental reporting project that would capture the human aspect of the tragedy and bring further global attention to the particular needs of the people suffering from the quake's devastation. Namely, it would address issues of "development, poverty, displacement, HIV/AIDS, educational reform, and the role of international aid" ("In Haiti").

After their proposal was approved, they made numerous trips to Haiti. There, as Dawes suggests, they not only witnessed the devastation of the quake—nearly 300,000 people had been killed and 80 percent of structures had been destroyed—but became friends with displaced survivors who were living in impromptu tent cities in and around Port-au-Prince. The crew listened to their stories, sought to understand their individual experiences, and then attempted to capture their struggles, their feelings of loss, as well as their sense of resiliency in a variety of genres. Dawes, who was responsible for writing poems based on his interactions, describes his own process of creating a poetry of witness: "I wrote poems in response to what I heard and saw . . . as a way to process and a way to work through the experience." He claims to have chosen to report in this genre because it "gives us an intimacy in relationship with people" even if it is seen as a rather unconventional choice for reporting. As Dawes states, "I'm not your standard journalist" ("In Haiti").

In its final articulations, the project does not read as standard journalism or conventional literature, being more dynamic, more humanitarian, and perhaps more comprehensive than a single genre or medium might allow. We should note here that the final project actually takes two forms: *Voices of Haiti* is an enhanced ebook available for free through iBooks, and *Voices from Haiti* is a project housed on the Pulitzer Center's website. The former combines writings by Kwame Dawes and Lisa Armstrong with photographs by Andre Lambertson, music composed by Kevin Simmonds, and videos of live singing performances by Valetta Brinson. The latter eliminates the nonfiction and recorded live performances to focus a little more exclusively on the relationship between Dawes's poems and Lambertsons's photographs through what the authors call "video poems." Below, we'll offer an example of material that appears in both venues to give you a sense of how the project functions.

In the screen devoted to the poem "Storm," lines written in conventional text offer a catalogue of images. Dawes describes, "the narrow lanes, the gutters, / the stolen power lines, / the makeshift clubs" (6–8) and other sights that capture the mix of desperation, survival, cynicism and hope that define life just after the devastating natural disaster. Then, he leaps into imaginings of the future, revealing economic tensions that define questions of development and possibility for the outskirts of the city:

> [. . .] the admonitions
> to keep the place clean, as if
> someone hopes to restore
> this stripped down hillside
> to its glory as a golf course
> for expatriates, the moneyed,
> the diplomats, too far
> to see the constant cloud
> from wood fires and coal
> factories tucked into
> this city of improvisation

10–20

Accompanying these lines is a video poem that combines an audio recording of Dawes reading the work with a soundtrack of sparse notes offered by Simmonds and a representative slideshow of Lambertsons's documentary photographs. As Dawes's voice resonates over the music, the audience is presented with a series of pictures, including the following: a tent city, groups of Haitians lining a roadside, cement rubble, a person walking atop a vast garbage heap, a mother and child receiving communion, policemen gathered around a white sheet (presumably covering a corpse), a panoramic nature scene of hills outside the city, and three children standing at the edge of the ocean (Dawes et al.). In its approach to journalism as a form of creative writing, the work inevitably echoes projects like James Agee and Walker Evans's *Let Us Now Praise Famous Men*. While Agee and Evans used the technologies of the 1930s to combine lyrical writing with documentary photographs as they reported on the plight of destitute Alabama sharecroppers, Dawes and his colleagues use the technologies of our time to offer an innovative, multi-layered fusion of subjective experience and informed, empathic reporting. We suggest you check out their work (either through iBooks or the Pulitzer Center) and consider what sort of writing project you might conceptualize using the same sort of ebook or internet technologies.

The Politics of Place: From Enhanced Ebook to Augmented Reality

We'd also like you to imagine what *Voices of Haiti* might be like if it made use of slightly different technologies. Instead of accessing images of Haiti anywhere in the world through an enhanced ebook or website, what if you went to Port-au-Prince and your actual experiences of the city and its surroundings were enhanced by what has come to be called augmented reality, a hybrid space "consisting of the real world augmented with a textual layer" (Løvlie "Annotative" 246). Picture yourself walking near the arts district of Pétion-Ville. With each step, you not only listen to the sounds of the bustling streets but you also hear Dawes's voice in your ears and you see the physical lines of his poems hanging like sculptures from the rooftops above you. Lambertsons' photographs of rubble and debris are superimposed on the façade of a newly opened gallery. How would this experience affect your understanding of the relationships between creative writing, place, and the future of literature?

A number of writers have been breaking handbook prohibitions by experimenting with augmented reality and locative media to enable the sort of experience we describe above. Using some combination of Global Positioning Systems (GPS), Google Maps, MediaWiki, and/or custom software, they design projects that reinvent creative writing for users of mobile devices in ways that intentionally blur the lines between literary and material worlds. One of the foundational projects within this developing body of work is Jeff Knowlton, Naomi Spellman, and Jeremy Hight's *34 North, 118 West*. Participants experiencing this narrative walk through the Freight Depot area of Los Angeles, wearing headphones and holding a tablet equipped with GPS. The GPS tracks their movements and triggers audiovisual clips concerned with the location's past when they enter "hot spots" created by the authors (Barber 96). In this way, the project enables a hidden history comprised of visual images and recorded sounds to emerge within the present day of users' lived experience, enhancing their understanding of place with what Knowlton and colleagues call "sonic ghosts of another era" (Knowlton).

Since the development of *34 North, 118 West*, technologies have improved and similar projects have begun appearing in England, Norway, Australia, and elsewhere. In "Poetic Augmented Reality: Place-Bound Literature in Locative Media," Anders Løvlie describes the creation of *textopia*, a project that allows users to "listen to literary texts that talk about the places" they encounter in downtown Oslo through a smartphone app (21). Like *34 North, 118 West*, *textopia* relies on "a database of place-bound literary texts" that are triggered according to users' precise geographical locations (21). Interestingly, this database was started through a creative writing contest. An open call for submissions invited writers to submit stories and poems "identified with a specific place in downtown Oslo" (21). Finalists were then selected—not by a single celebrity-author (American-style)—but by a three-person jury who walked the city while listening to submissions; finalists received a cash prize and their texts were added to the database. Among these texts are genres that Løvlie classifies as "stray voices," or "stories that move from place to place, requiring the user to traverse the landscape" of the city "in order to traverse the text of the story." Løvlie categorizes other texts as "counterfactual placetexts," which "describe future or alternative realities" (22). As an example of this work, Løvlie cites the contribution of a writer who created "a series of texts consisting of absurd, Monty Pythonesque fictional historical accounts of mundane downtown buildings" (24).

Marsha Berry's project, *Poetry4U: Pinning Poetry to Place*, relies on similar strategies to create experiences of locative literature in Melbourne, Pilbara, and Geelong. When first creating the project, she and her team "found a way of pinning creative artefacts in the form of Twitter length poems to a city landscape" with help from an annotated Google map (117). While the contents of these poems vary, they tend to reflect "landscape features, sensory responses, and spiritual and emotional concerns" connected to life in a particular region. (123). She describes the ambition of the Melbourne project this way: "We had a vision of poetry text floating over buildings in the city that would be visible using a smartphone camera. The poems would be lined up with particular buildings, and we could use GPS coordinates to set up bounds for each poem" (117). Throughout the development of the project, Berry has maintained a concern with providing users the capacity to serve not only as consumers but also as producers of these poems. Specifically, she states, "We envisaged a second phase of app development where a user could contribute poems . . . to designated locations" (117).

This comment reflects a larger, shared goal of many individuals working with combinations of augmented reality and place-based creative writing, who value users' ability not simply to access a database of stories but to continually add to it as authors. In this sense, they view the possibilities of their innovation as much more a democratic ideal than a slick technological gimmick. Løvlie suggests that "locative literature" (like the *textopia* project) provides users "a new kind of power to shape the cultural landscape of their own environment" (26): i.e., to affect communities' thinking about their material surroundings from a diversity of perspectives and thus enable them to literally change their realities through augmentation. In this sense, it might be considered a form of cultural intervention capable of challenging inherited, monolithic, or unquestioned narratives of place. He believes in the power of literary production to reconceptualize a public space as "malleable by its inhabitants" (26), and he sees the future of locative literature doing just this.

Indeed, the vision underlying *textopia* and related projects involves a perpetual and seamless linking of digital narratives to material places. Løvlie writes, "If users have the opportunity to contribute their own texts, it is possible to cover every inhabited space with texts and allow users serendipitous exploration of a textual universe overlaid onto their everyday worlds" (252). We admire this ideal. We like the collaboration inherent to the production of locative literature. We appreciate the possibilities that might arise when poets and techies and citizens from all walks of life work together to invent the futures of their cities through creative writing. That said, we find ourselves fighting back some uneasiness about covering "every inhabited space with texts." Although we don't consider ourselves Luddites, we sometimes fear the potential transformation from *textopia* to dystopia. And we are not certain about how exactly this technology might be used or abused as it develops further. Will locative literature reach its lofty democratic ideals or offer little more than strange and glorified walking tours? Are some of its incarnations "little different from a Fodor's guidebook," as Mark Sample has suggested (72)? Can this technology empower citizen-authors to transform decrepit shopping arcades into lasting versions of Arcadia? Or will it be easily reduced to the newest cultural craze, a faddish literary reiteration of Pokémon Go? While it is certainly in vogue at the time of this writing, we're not sure whether it will stick around or go the way of Google glasses. Although unable to predict its future, we will say that if you find yourself skeptical, you are not alone. And if you find yourself suddenly yearning for an old school offline experience, one that values competition without subjecting you to a reality augmented by an omnipresent, ubiquitous, and perpetual overlay of competing narratives on every available surface, you might consider the following un-augmented phenomenon from Latin America.

The Performance of Misbehavior: Toward Real-Time Fiction

One of our favorite lower-tech approaches to taking creative writing off of the page comes from Peru. It's called Lucha Libro. The term is a play on the Spanish phrase Lucha Libre, which literally translates as "free fight" and is more commonly used to describe the art and sport of Mexican wrestling. You've probably seen Mexican wrestling matches before: Luchadors who go by pseudonyms hide their identities under intricately decorated masks and battle for supremacy in choreographed matches that are as much performance art as athletic competitions. In fact, Lucha Libre draws from a number of different histories of performance, conflating elements of medieval morality plays, vintage Hollywood camp, and various traditions of gymnastics, dance, and martial arts. The drama unfolds as clear heroes and villains hurl themselves at each other, grappling, kicking, punching and posturing until somehow a loser is eventually pinned for a three-count. Of course, the real drama occurs outside the parameters of the supposed rules of the match: wrestlers suffer the worst kind of defeat when their opponents commit the ultimate taboo of unmasking them. All of this is to say that in Lucha Libre, the art of misbehaving takes center stage.

With the change of one vowel, Lucha Libro conflates the tradition of Mexican wrestling with the fine art of flash fiction. The term translates literally as "book fight," or more loosely, "battle of the books." And, indeed, Lucha Libro contestants engage in literary wrestling matches, of sorts: live five-minute fiction writing competitions. In front of a crowd, masked contestants go head to head and laptop to laptop by typing furiously on their keyboards while their impromptu stories-in-progress are projected in real-time onto large screens behind them, their false starts, triumphant developments, and instant edits all visible to the audience. Here, the mess of the writing process transforms into a kind of practical pageantry; it is something to be admired (rather than disguised).

The structure of the match is straightforward. Just before the clock begins, competitors are given three random images or objects, which they must include in their work. Then, a referee counts to three, and the masked authors start inventing their stories frenetically. After their five minutes have elapsed, they read their narratives aloud. Subsequently, a panel of judges assesses their work and determines the winner, who advances to the next round of the competition. The tournament begins with 32 competitors and culminates, after an eight-week cycle, in a final battle. Here, a champion is selected and awarded the grand prize of a coveted book-publication contract.

Originally developed in 2011 by Christopher Vasquez and Angie Silva, Lucha Libro has brought serious excitement to Peru's literary scene. As Vasquez

describes the performance series, he states, "It's . . . about changing the idea that literature is boring. This turns it into an event." (qtd in Murphy, "Peru"). We never thought literature *was* boring, but apparently Vasquez and Silva turn the amps up to 11. We hear that they often begin Lucha Libro events by playing dance music and showing video clips of Mexican wrestling matches. Journalist Christopher Heaney has described the thrill of the live literary feuds, claiming Lucha Libro's entertainment value "lies in the way it turns literature itself into a spectacle, into a reality TV show whose format mines deep social anxieties" as "[b]eatings, murders, and acts of revenge . . . are drafted and redrafted in the ring" (10). He also recounts the spontaneous thrill of the performance, using the present tense to capture the drama of one occasion in which a competitor's speedy writing session almost ended in disaster. Heaney writes, "there is real joy to be found in hearing a Lucha Libro crowd member, after a contestant accidentally deletes his entire story with only thirty seconds remaining on the clock, urgently shouting: *'Control-Z! Control-Z!'*" (8).

Of course, the significance of Lucha Libro is not limited to its entertainment value. We might say the very invention of the art-sport is a political act: a way of using writing to change the world, or at least to disrupt the power dynamics of Peru's predominant literary culture. Vasquez and Silva created Lucha Libro, in part, to alter the economics of publishing and to further democratize the country's ideas about authorship. As Vasquez explains, Lima's literary scene "is still dominated by last names and social circles" (qtd in Murphy, "Lucha"). In other words, a privileged literati more or less controls the publishing industry, which makes it exceedingly difficult for outsiders to get their work into print—particularly those from lower economic backgrounds and even more particularly those from lower economic backgrounds who happen to be women. Heaney points to the problem of patriarchy: "Novels and short fiction overwhelmingly remain a boy's club in Peru . . . and book release parties are attended by a familiar cast of horn-rimmed hombres" (8).

Complicating the problems of sexism and classism is the exorbitant expense of producing books in Peru (where a paperback might retail for upwards of $25). Writers are often expected to absorb production costs. As Heaney states, "Most aspiring authors must pay to print their books, often with little editorial guidance. In America, this is considered 'vanity publishing.' In Peru, it's just 'publishing'" (5). Given these circumstances, you can probably imagine how and why conventional fiction writing remains a rather classist pursuit. Aspiring writers who are not already enfranchised within Peru's small literary circle are all too often advised to move out of the country if they want to pursue a writing career. However, as Heaney suggests, "Lucha Libro is fighting this state of affairs." He writes, "This isn't America's Literary Death Match, in which book lovers pay to watch famous or emerging writers competitively read their already polished work. Lucha Libro is for amateur writers without the access or capital to get even as far as self-publishing" (5). In fact, Lucha Libro is specifically aimed to provide opportunity to disenfranchised aspiring writers who have not had an opportunity to publish their work, a population Heaney describes as "the disadvantaged, the urban poor, the non-elite" (4). Competitors do not pay an entry fee; nor do they pay for their masks, which co-organizers Vasquez and Silva provide free of charge. Audiences also pay nothing. All of the event's costs are absorbed by media sponsors. Compared to the boys' club book release parties of Lima, the crowd at Lucha Libro events is diverse; further, roughly half of the competitors are female (Heaney 6, 8).

The masks themselves not only contribute to the drama of the event, combining kitsch and mystery so that audience members might enjoy the pseudonymous characters before them while wondering about their actual identities; in preserving anonymity, these masks also serve a democratizing function. As Vasquez states, "This [event] is democratic, because here you come together in front of a public made up of readers, and no one knows who's behind the mask" (qtd in Murphy, "Lucha"). Essentially, this arrangement allows Lucha Libro to achieve the ideal of functioning as a live blind-reviewed literary contest with no entry fees. Instead of authors' names being removed from print manuscripts, their faces are covered, their pseudonyms applied, and their work reviewed live by a panel of judges unaware of their true identities. And, did we mention—it all happens FOR FREE?! In this sense, it offers an ideal that US contests might learn from or aspire to—in theory at least.

There has been one significant hiccup in Lucha Libro's development. The event's contestant screening process is supposed to ensure that only unpublished writers are eligible to enter the tournament. In 2012, this screening process broke down. As Heaney reveals, a competitor going by the pseudonym Ruido Blanco, or White Noise, was allowed into the competition even though he had previously published a book of poems with the press, Mesa Redonda—the very same press that would be awarding a publication contract to the tournament's grand champion. In the year's final match, Ruido Blanco defeated the crowd favorite, Bucephalus, to receive this book contract. As Heaney states, given this result, it is "hard not to feel that Lucha Libro created an exciting new path to publication, but in 2012 forgot to screen out the advantages that rig the game *outside* of the ring, leaving the fight inside lopsided" (11). We're not sure whether this breach represents an honest mistake—a genuine oversight that allowed a contestant with a significant advantage to compete against those with significantly less advantage—or whether this competition was rigged from the start. The contest organizers suggested the former and committed themselves to assuring that tournaments have a more rigorous and enforced screening process (Heaney 10–11). We hope that the problem really was an organizational snafu, a symptom of Lucha Libro's infancy—it was only the second year of the competition—rather than a more nefarious kind of corruption. As far as we know, subsequent tournaments have remained scandal-free.

As Lucha Libro expands across Latin America, we hope it doesn't suffer the kind of corruption that has defined too many literary contests in the US, as we discussed in Chapter 8. We also hope it isn't absorbed by the mechanisms of twenty-first century entertainment industries to become an American Idol for aspiring writers. For now, Lucha Libro seems to have succeeded precisely because it has refused to play by the rules of Peru's old guard and antiquated notions of publishing. And as it continues to enjoy success, we hope it does, indeed, stick to the integrity of its idealism: i.e., its *potential* to offer aspiring writers a more genuinely democratic chance at publication. Lucha Libro doesn't have the strongest online presence we've ever encountered; still, we'd suggest you take a look at their website: www.luchalibro.pe.

Embracing the Hive-Mind: A Mandate for Open Collaboration Online

Have you ever heard of hitRECord? It's a collaborative production company with a huge web presence that was originally founded by the actor Joseph Gordon-Levitt. We might say that hitRECord misbehaves all the time, in the sense that it continually fails to function the way most people think a production company is supposed to function. Instead of making deals, supplying talent, and developing content behind closed doors, it invites writers, filmmakers, illustrators, musicians and others to collaborate openly on its website, which serves as a hive for creative activity. As Gordon-Levitt explains, "Anyone can participate . . . We use the internet to collaborate with artists from all over the world, and we form a community around the art that we make together." This art takes the form of stories, poems, scripts, films, illustrations, sound recordings, live performance, and a TV variety show. When inviting writers to participate in collaborative art-making, Gordon-Levitt describes the way this process works: "Writers, write us a short story or a script or a poem. Maybe another artist on the site will act that out, and that becomes a short film." This is just one example of the sort of cross-genre and cross-media collaboration that takes place on the website. As Gordon-Levitt suggests, "the hitRECord community collaboratively edits, builds upon, develops, and remixes each other's work" all the time. Often illustrators will render stories into a visual format or provide drawings to accompany text; in turn, animators will then animate these illustrations; and, in similar fashion, musicians will provide soundtracks until what started as written narratives transform into full multimedia productions.

Perhaps the results of this process are best exemplified through the story of how the book series, *A Tiny Book of Tiny Stories*, came to be. As the website developed, a hitRECorder who goes by the user name "wirrow" started a Tiny Stories collaboration forum. Here, writers and artists worked together to create all sorts of innovative multimedia micro-fiction. Gordon-Levitt and wirrow then enlisted the help of other contributors to serve as curators or selective editors. Working collectively, they sorted through about 2,000 Tiny Stories posted by the hitRECord community and chose works by 45 writers and artists to anthologize in an illustrated book, which they self-published. The success of this first book—enabled by a readymade community of readers and bolstered by Gordon-Levitt's celebrity—led HarperCollins to offer hitRECord a three-volume book deal. In the ebook versions of this series, traditional linear page-turning is disrupted by the insertion of video and audio, so that (much like in *Voices of Haiti*) readers navigate printed words, animated pictures, voice-overs, recorded live performances, and short films.

In brief, these ebooks are cool. We suggest you give them a look (and a read and a listen) not only to discover the way combined technologies may offer enhanced multimedia and multi-sensory reading experiences, but also to better understand the advantages of open collaboration. The hitRECord project reinvents co-authorship in ways that Raymond Carver and Gordon Lish could probably not have practiced in their time, as they toiled away in private correspondence, hiding their process of collaboration from the reading public.

Here, the anxieties and limitations that accompany illusions of single-authorship give way to the surprise and unpredictability of co-creation. In fact, when individuals join the hitRECord community, they must agree to the following condition: "You grant every user on hitRECord.org the right to modify, adapt, and remix your RECords" ("HitRECord"). This is a far cry from the portrait of the author working in an isolated garret. It is also a far cry from Lucha Libro or any literary competition that limits its prize to a single author.

What interests us about hitRECord is not limited to the possibilities it suggests for collaboration. Through its alternative business model, the production company also reveals new possibilities for emerging authors to become enfranchised within an arts community and publication network. It does so without relying on the format of the literary contest and while allowing writers to get paid for their work. Yes, you read that correctly, poets. Contributors get paid!

Here is how the system works. When a hitRECorders' work is selected for a monetized project like the *Tiny Book of Tiny Stories*, contributors share in fifty percent of the profits for that project. The other fifty percent gets redistributed by the company to cover expenses for new and ongoing projects. When compared with traditional publishers, hitRECord offers a generous package. Plus, their figures are relatively transparent—the bookkeeping is often displayed on the website for all to see. That said, their arrangement requires profitability. If a project's sales do not exceed the production company's initial expenses, then contributors don't get paid—but, then again, neither does the production company. As we've suggested previously, contractual arrangements with traditional publishers often have similar caveats about whether sales figures have to reach a certain amount before royalties kick in.

Regardless of these particulars, we find the arrangement promising, not only for the possibility of earning a small bit of cash, but perhaps more importantly for the access and exposure it offers emerging authors. If you post writing on hitRECord, your work instantly appears on a heavily trafficked website—regardless of whether it is ever selected for a monetized publication project. In other words, the venue provides a large and unique built-in audience, mostly of repeat users. These users are in no way an anonymous or passive reading public, but rather a network of artists and co-creators who are actively seeking to transform or reinvent the writing they encounter. When they read your work, they read it with investment. And their particular kind of investment, in a sense, conflates their identity so that they are simultaneously readers and potential (co)authors. Here, unlike in Barthes' world, there are not clear lines between a writer and a reader: i.e., one does not have to die so the other can live. Rather, both identities coexist in something akin to a state of superposition. Also blurred are the roles we discussed earlier: collaborator proper, reviewer, and resonator. If a hitRECorder chooses to transform your work, they will likely want to also promote that work, perhaps share its original and remixed articulations with others. Given the nature of collaborative investment, to promote your work is to promote their work and vice versa, so that the distinctions between self-interest and altruism also blur. What develops then—ideally, at least—is a powerful network of invested participants seeking to share and support each other's cooperative art and thereby foster each other's (and their own) success.

When we began writing this section, we were tempted to draw comparisons to the early stages of Nathaniel Hawthorne's career and treat Gordon-Levitt as a contemporary Longfellow of sorts, a figure who lends his celebrity to support the careers of emerging authors and artists. We suppose this comparison is somewhat apt. However, we realized that it wasn't Gordon-Levitt's name or authority, per se, that is helping emerging authors find larger audiences. Granted, his celebrity helps. But it is really the community itself, the hive Gordon-Levitt helps to maintain, full of collaborator-reviewer-resonators that has perhaps the most potential to facilitate career growth and establish new trajectories for how creative writers find audiences and form relationships with them.

Whispering from a Soap Box: How We Hope the Future Expands

Wherever you happen to find yourself now—online in Gordon-Levitt's hive, typing on stage with your face hidden beneath a wrestling mask, or enjoying some augmented fresh air somewhere else on this spinning planet that amazes us perpetually—we hope you will explore the freedoms (and constraints) that newer technologies for creative writing provide. Now that we have poems pinned to landmarks and ebooks with embedded movies, it seems impossible to sustain the illusion that genre is static or impermeable. Since we've moved past the conventions of print culture, it seems absurd to pretend that we should somehow remain impervious to change or somehow try to shelter ourselves from the big ideas that define technological and cultural progress. We find it too simple to recycle conventional workshop lore and advise each other to *show and not tell* in conventional print stories, consciously or unconsciously imposing Raymond Carver's style—which, as we've suggested, was never really Raymond Carver's style—onto our work, as if this particular aesthetic is universally appropriate. Similarly, we find it unproductive to recycle the ideology of Archibald MacLeish's "Ars Poetica" and suggest that our poems should somehow purge themselves of meaning. We think it's more than a little misguided to proclaim that the craft of fiction should or should *not* be this, or that the art of poetry should or should *not* do that. As we look toward the future of creative writing, we hope that the field will move beyond a mythological and rarified idea of literature that never really was. And we hope that as you engage in your own writing practice, you will use whatever genre, media, or technology you find most appropriate for your particular goals—regardless of what others tell you (including and especially us).

Discussion Questions

1. Have you ever thought that you *would* like to change the world with your writing? If so, how? If not, why not? What kind of project might you put together if you were to effect some sort of change, however large or small?

2. Think about your goals as a creative writer, a particular project you're working on, or the specific audience you would like to reach. What sort of technological platforms or kind of media might best serve your purposes?

3. Have you read any enhanced ebooks (with embedded video, music, or animation)? What did you think? Did you enjoy the enhanced features or did you find yourself wishing to return to a more traditional mode of reading? Can you extrapolate to determine what exactly might make a use of technology beneficial or detrimental?

Your Turn: Questions, Concerns & Creative-Critical Comments

3. ____

____

____

____

Writing Experiments

1. We suggest you try your hand at Flarf, a kind of poetry written with the help of an internet search engine. To write Flarf, pick a few terms (they can be as random as you like) and use them in an internet search. Your poem must be composed from the language you find online in response to your search. Flarf does not have to be good; in fact, the purpose of Flarf is to make use of language that is not usually considered poetic, or to use the poetic form to help us reconsider the language commonly used online. You might start by searching for "Flarf poems" to read some examples.

2. One important digital genre is interactive narrative—stories in which the reader has some say over the sequence and selection of events. In order to experiment with writing in this genre, we recommend becoming familiar with one or more composing platforms for this kind of work. Twine (twinery.org) is a self-described "open-source tool for telling interactive, nonlinear stories." This program is free to download, has a fairly intuitive interface and an active community of creators. It exports to HTML, so you can post your creations online. Another option is Storyspace, a program for composing interactive narrative designed at Brown University that was used to compose classic hyptertext works like "Afternoon" by Michael Joyce and "Patchwork Girl" by Shelley Jackson (http://www.eastgate.com/storyspace/index.html). If you want to allow your readers even more control over the narrative, making your fiction into a more fully realized "game," you might look at using Inform 7 (inform7.com), which is a platform for writing and reading Text Adventures (are you old enough to remember the Zork series?). Text Adventures allow users to read text and then type in commands like "move north" and "open the box" to which the game responds with more text, thus unlocking more of the narrative. Check out each of these platforms and then spend some time with one of them to see what you can create.

3. For this activity, we'd like you to imitate, in some way, the work of Kwame Dawes and colleagues. We want you to identify something "wildly unfair" and to "write dangerously" about it. Where is there injustice or inequality? Can you identify an event or some aspect of civic life in your community

that has placed a particular group at a disadvantage? Once you've settled on your topic, go out and document the experiences of community members who were affected by it. Interview and/or befriend them. Ask them if they'd like you to tell their story. If they agree, work together to take pictures and video, write poems and narratives. Piece together a multimedia work that represents the experiences of those you've interviewed. The final product of this activity might be a public reading, or a webpage, or an ebook, or all three. Make sure to include the community members you've befriended in the process. They may want to speak in their own voice, and so your project can offer them a platform from which their stories can be heard.

Deep Reading

1. In *Uncreative Writing*, Kenneth Goldsmith argues that the internet has brought about an age of writing defined by startlingly, and ironically, (un) original acts of appropriation, such as Simon Morris's blog "Getting Inside Jack Kerouac's Head," in which he retypes one page of *On the Road* each day. Goldsmith's own (un)creative writing includes work like *Traffic*, which is a transcription of traffic reports Goldsmith heard on the radio. We think it is worthwhile to consider Goldsmith's perspective on contemporary creativity, but we also strongly recommend that you look into Goldsmith's reading of "The Body of Michael Brown" and the ensuing controversy. Even "uncreative" acts take place in social contexts and have the potential to cause real harm. What do you think about Goldsmith's approach to (un)creative writing? And what are your thoughts on the consequences of recontextualizing prose?

2. Many scholars are writing about the cultural implications of electronic media. For a sampling of work in this area, we can suggest a few essay collections. Mark Bernstein and Diane Greco's *Reading Hypertext* assembles scholarly work specifically about linked text, including some examinations of hypertext fiction. N Katherine Hayles and Jessica Pressman's *Comparative Textual Media: Transforming the Humanities in the Postprint Era* collects the essays of scholars who attempt to reimagine academia, specifically the humanties, in response to digital media. Anouk Lang's *From Codex to Hypertext: Reading at the Turn of the Twenty-first Century* focuses on scholarly examinations of the contemporary reading experience as shaped by digital and social media. Lang's book has an impressive international scope, with essays on reading in China, South Africa, Canada, and the US, in addition to transnational spaces created for readers by services like LibraryThing. The

essays in Michael Dean Clark, Trent Hergenrader, and Joe Rein's *Creative Writing in the Digital Age* take a look at the implications digital media has for creative writing as a practice and an academic discipline. Glance at the tables of contents of these books, and see what strikes your interest. We imagine something will engage your intellect and stir your creativity.

Works Cited

"AAR Canon of Ethics." *Association of Authors' Representatives*, www.aaronline.org/canon

"About Us." *Rattle*, 2018, www.rattle.com/info/about-us/

Achebe, Chinua. "Africa and Her Writers." *Morning Yet on Creation Day: Essays*, Heinemann, 1975, pp. 29–46.

Ackroyd, Peter. *T. S. Eliot: A Life*. Simon & Schuster, 1984.

Adsit, Janelle. *Toward an Inclusive Creative Writing: Threshold Concepts to Guide the Literary Writing Curriculum*, Bloomsbury, 2019.

Aiello, Antonio. "Equity in Publishing: What Should Editors Be Doing?" *Pen America*, October 24, 2015. www.pen.org/equity-in-publishing-what-should-editors-be-doing

Armitage, Simon. "Rough Crossings: The Cutting of Raymond Carver." *The New Yorker*, December 27, 2007. www.newyorker.com/reporting/2007/12/24/071224fa_fact?currentPage=all

Association of American Publishers (AAP). "Book Publisher Revenue Estimated at More than $26 Billion in 2017." *Association of American Publishers*, July 20, 2018, newsroom.publishers.org/book-publisher-revenue-estimated-at-more-than-26-billion-in-2017/

Author Earnings. "January 2018 Report: US online book sales, Q2–Q4 2017." *Author Earnings*. January 2018, authorearnings.com/report/january-2018-report-us-online-book-sales-q2-q4-2017/

Baker, Jennifer. "First Diversity Baseline Survey Illustrates How Much Publishing Lacks Diversity." *Forbes*, January 26, 2016, www.forbes.com/sites/jenniferbaker/2016/01/26/first-publishing-diversity-baseline-survey/

Barber, John F. "Walking-Talking: Soundscapes, *Flâneurs*, and the Creation of Mobile Media Narratives." *The Mobile Story: Narrative Practices with Locative Technologies*, edited by Jason Farmon, Routledge, 2014, pp. 95–109.

Barnett, David. "Nora Jemisin: 'I would love to just write and not have everything turned into a political battle.'" *NewStatesmanAmerica*, September 1, 2016, https://www.newstatesman.com/culture/books/2016/09/nora-jemisin-i-would-love-just-write-and-not-have-everything-turned-political

Barthes, Roland. "The Death of the Author." *Image. Music. Text*, translated by Stephen Heath, Noonday Press, 1988, pp. 142–148.

Bennett, Eric. "How Iowa Flattened Literature." *The Chronicle of Higher Education*, February 10, 2014, www.chronicle.com/article/How-Iowa-Flattened-Literature/144531

Bennett, Eric. *Workshops of Empire: Stegner, Engle, and American Creative Writing during the Cold War*. University of Iowa Press, 2015.

Berlin, James. "Rhetoric and Ideology in the Writing Class." *The Norton Book of Composition Studies*, edited by Susan Miller, W.W. Norton & Company,

2009, pp. 667–684. Reprinted from *College English* vol. 50, no. 5, 1988, pp. 477–494.
Berlin, James. *Rhetoric and Reality: Writing Instruction in American Colleges, 1900–1985*. Southern Illinois University Press, 1987.
Berlin, James. *Rhetorics, Poetics, and Cultures*. NCTE, 1996.
Berry, Marsha. *Creating With Mobile Media*, Palgrave Macmillan, 2017.
"Best-Sellers Initially Rejected." *LitRejections*, 2015, www.litrejections.com/best-sellers-initially-rejected
Bible. New International Version. Bible Gateway.
Bishop, Wendy. *Released into Language: Options for Teaching Creative Writing*. NCTE, 1991.
BlazeVOX, www.blazevox.org
Bly, Carol. *Beyond the Writers' Workshop: New Ways to Write Creative Nonfiction*. Anchor Books, 2001.
Boog, Jason. "eBook Revenues Top Hardcover." *GalleyCat*, June 15, 2012, www.adweek.com/galleycat/ebooks-top-hardcover-revenues-in-q1/54094
Boog, Jason. "The Lost History of Fifty Shades of Grey." *GalleyCat*. Media Bistro, November 21, 2012, www.adweek.com/galleycat/fifty-shades-of-grey-wayback-machine/50128
Bourne, Michael. "Beyond the Page, Literary Magazines Find New Ways to Develop Literary Community." *Poets & Writers*, vol. 39, no. 6, 2011, pp. 78–82.
Bowker. "Self-Publishing Sees Triple-Digit Growth in Just Five Years, Says Bowker." *Bowker.com*, October 24, 2012, http://www.bowker.com/news/2012/Self-Publishing-Sees-Triple-Digit-Growth-in-Just-Five-Years-Says-Bowker.html
Bowker. "'The Right Fit': Navigating the World of Literary Agents." *The Millions*, August 15, 2012, www.themillions.com/2012/08/a-right-fit-navigating-the-world-of-literary-agents.html
Brooks, Cleanth. *Modern Poetry and the Tradition*. University of North Carolina Press, 1939.
Brooks, Cleanth, and Robert Penn Warren. *Understanding Poetry*. 4th edition, Holt, Rinehart, and Winston, 1976.
Brown, Steven Ford. "Foetry.com and What Academic Doesn't Want You to Know About the Creative Writing Industry: An Interview with Steven Ford Brown by Louis E. Bourgeois." *Left Curve*, 2005, www.leftcurve.org/lc30webpages/Foetry.html
Buchanan, Oni, and Betsy Stone Mazzoleni. "The Mandrake Vehicles." *Conduit*, 2006, www.conduit.org/online/buchanan/buchanan.html
Bunting, Joe. "How to Get Published in Literary Magazines: Interview with Glimmer Train Stories." *The Write Practice*, www.thewritepractice.com/glimmer-train
Catton, Pia. "Author Finds His Own Way, To Success." *The Wall Street Journal*, Dow Jones & Company, June 17, 2012, www.wsj.com/articles/SB10001424052702303836404577472763955160728
Cave Canem. *Cave Canem: A Home for Black Poetry*. www.cavecanempoets.org
Coleridge, Samuel Taylor. *Bibliographia Literaria: The Collected Works of Samuel Taylor Coleridge*, Volume 7. Edited by James Engell and W. Jackson Bate, Princeton University Press, 1985.
Coleridge, Samuel Taylor. *Collected Letters of Samuel Taylor Coleridge, Volume 3*. Edited by Earl Leslie Griggs, Clarendon Press, 1959.

Coleridge, Samuel Taylor. "Of the Fragment of Kubla Khan." *Christabel; Kubla Khan, a Vision; The Pains of Sleep*. 3rd edition, William Bulmer and Co., 1816, pp. 51–54.

Cooperative Children's Book Center (CCBC). "Publishing Statistics on Children's Books About People of Color and First/Native Nations and by People of Color and First/Native Nations Authors and Illustrators." *CCBC*, February 22, 2018, ccbc.education.wisc.edu/books/pcstats.asp

Corso, Paola. "Is a University Press Right for You? An Author Compares its Approach to That of the Big Commercial Houses and Finds Some Advantages Worth Considering." *The Writer*, vol. 122, no. 11, 2009, p 24. *Literature Resource Center*

Cottenet, Cécile. *Race, Ethnicity, and Publishing in America*. Palgrave MacMillan, 2014.

Council of Literary Magazines and Presses (CLMP). www.clmp.org

Clark, Michael Dean, Trent Hergenrader, and Joseph Rein, eds. *Creative Writing in the Digital Age: Theory, Practice, and Pedagogy*. Bloomsbury Academic, 2015.

Clark, Michael, Trent Hergenrader, and Joseph Rein, eds. *Creative Writing Innovations: Breaking Boundaries in the Classroom*. Bloomsbury Academic, 2017.

"Creative Writing Minor." Cal State Monterey Bay Humanities and Communication, www.hcom.csumb.edu/creative-writing-minor

Criona, Nicole. *Los Angeles Writers' Group*, 2014.

Cunnell, Howard. "Fast This Time: Jack Kerouac and the Writing of On the Road." *On the Road: The Original Scroll*, by Jack Kerouac, Viking, 2007, pp.1–52.

Curdy, Averill. "Poetry: A History of the Magazine." Poetry, www.poetryfoundation.org/poetrymagazine/history

Dawes, Kwame. "In Haiti, Writer Kwame Dawes Tells of Quake Aftermath Through Poetry." *PBS NewsHour*, January 4, 2011, www.pbs.org/newshour/arts/poetry/in-haiti-writer-kwame-dawes-tells-of-quake-aftermath-through-poetry

Dawes, Kwame. "Storm." *Voices from Haiti*. The Pulitzer Center, www.pulitzercenter.org/features/voices-haiti

Dawes, Kwame, et al. "Storm." *Voices from Haiti*. The Pulitzer Center, www.pulitzercenter.org/features/voices-haiti

DeMaria, Robert. *The College Handbook of Creative Writing*. 4th edition, Wadsworth, 2014.

Diaz, Junot. "MFA vs POC." *The New Yorker*, April 30, 2014, www.newyorker.com/books/page-turner/mfa-vs-poc

Dimock, Wai Chee. "Report from the Editor of PMLA for 2016–2017." *Modern Language Association*, January 6, 2018, www.mla.org/content/download/76300/2159890/Report-PMLA-2018.pdf

Donnelly, Dianne. *Establishing Creative Writing Studies as an Academic Discipline*, Multilingual Matters, 2012.

Dorantes, Dolores, and Flores Sánchez. "From *Intervene*." Mandorla: Nueva Escritura De Las Américas, no. 13, 2010, pp. 28–39.

Dorantes, Dolores, and Flores Sánchez. Interview by Guillermo Parra. *Best American Poetry Blog*, January 22, 2014, www.blog.bestamericanpoetry.com/the_best_american_poetry/2014/01/intervene-dolores-dorantes-and-rodrigo-flores-sánchez-by-guillermo-parra.html

Doyle, Nora. "Gertrude Stein and the Domestication of Genius in *The Autobiography of Alice B. Toklas*." *Feminist Studies*, vol. 44, no. 1, 2018, pp. 43–69.

Duhamel, Denise and Maureen Seaton. "Poetry and Collaboration" *Poets.org/ Academy of American Poets*, December 21, 2006, www.poets.org/poetsorg/ text/poetry-and-collaboration-denise-duhamel-maureen-seaton

Ede, Lisa, and Andrea Lunsford. "Audience Addressed/Audience Invoked: The Role of Audience in Composition Theory and Pedagogy." *Cross-Talk in Comp Theory*, pp. 77–96. Reprinted from College *Composition and Communication*, vol. 35, no. 2, 1984, pp. 155–171.

Eliot, T. S. "The Function of Criticism." *Selected Prose*, edited by Frank Kermode, Harvest Books, 1975, pp. 68–76.

Eliot, T. S. *The Waste Land*. Liveright Publishing. 2013.

Eliot, T. S. *The Waste Land: A Facsimile and Transcript of the Original Drafts Including the Annotations of Ezra Pound*, edited by Valerie Eliot, Harcourt, 1974.

Elliot, Zetta. "Black Authors and Self-Publishing." *School Library Journal*, March 16, 2015, www.slj.com/?detailStory=black-authors-and-self-publishing

Faigley, Lester. "Competing Theories of Process: A Critique and a Proposal." *The Norton Book of Composition Studies*, pp. 652–666. Reprinted from *College English* vol. 48, no. 6, 1986, pp. 527–542.

Farman, Jason. *The Mobile Story: Narrative Practices with Locative Technologies*. Routledge, 2014.

Feist Publications, *INC. v. Rural Telephone Service CO.*, 499 US 340. Supreme Court of the United States. 1991.

"Fence Books." *Poets & Writers*, February 17, 2017, www.pw.org/small_presses/ fence_books

Fenza, D. W. "Creative Writing and Its Discontents" *The Writer's Chronicle*, March/April 2000.

Fish, Stanley. *Is There a Text in This Class? The Authority of Interpretive Communities*. Harvard University Press, 1980.

Flood, Allison. "Junot Diaz Condemns Creative Writing Courses for 'Unbearable Too-Whiteness." *The Guardian*, May 19, 2014, www.theguardian.com/ books/2014/may/19/junot-diaz-attack-creative-writing-unbearable-too-whiteness

Flower, Linda, and John R. Hayes. "The Cognition of Discovery: Defining a Rhetorical Problem." *The Norton Book of Composition Studies*, pp. 467–478. Reprinted from *College Composition and Communication* vol. 31, no. 1, 1980, pp. 21–32.

Flower, Linda and John R. Hayes. "A Cognitive Process Theory of Writing." *Cross-Talk in Comp Theory*, edited by Victor Villanueva, NCTE, 1997, pp. 251–275. Reprinted from *College Composition and Communication* vol. 32, no. 4, 1981, pp. 365–387.

Foerster, Norman. "The Study of Letters." *Literary Scholarship: Its Aims and Methods*, University of North Carolina Press, 1941, pp.1–32.

Fowler, Geoffrey, and Jeffrey A. Trachtenberg. "'Vanity' Press Goes Digital." *Wall Street Journal*, June 3, 2010, https://www.wsj.com/articles/SB1000142405274 8704912004575253132121412028

Fox, John Matthew. "Ranking of The Best 100 Literary Magazines." Bookfox, www.thejohnfox.com/ranking-of-literary-journals

Fruman, Norman. *Coleridge, the Damaged Archangel*. George Braziller. 1971.
Frye, Northrop. *Anatomy of Criticism: Four Essays*. Atheneum, 1957.
Garstang, Clifford. "2019 Literary Magazine Ranking—Poetry." November 12, 2018, www.cliffordgarstang.com/2019-literary-magazine-ranking-poetry/
Gay, Roxane. "Where Things Stand." *The Rumpus*, June 6, 2012, https://therumpus.net/2012/06/where-things-stand/
Ginsberg, Allen. "The Dharma Bums." *The Village Voice*, November 12, 1958. The Village Voice, Voice Media Group, June 2, 2008, www.blogs.villagevoice.com/runninscared/2008/06/clip_job_allen_1.php
Givler, Peter. "University Press Publishing in the United States." *Association of University Presses*, www.aaupnet.org/about-aaup/about-university-presses/history-of-university-presses
Glass, Loren, ed. *After the Program Era: The Past, Present, and Future of Creative Writing in the University*. University of Iowa Press, 2017.
"Glimmer Train." *Duotrope*, www.duotrope.com/listing/29
Goldberg, Natalie. *Writing Down the Bones: Freeing the Writer Within*. Shambhala, 1986.
Gordon-Levitt, Joseph. "Joe's Intro Video." *HitRECord*, www.hitrecord.org
Graff, Gerald. *Professing Literature: An Institutional History*. University of Chicago Press, 1987.
Greco, Albert N., Jim Milliot, and Robert Wharton. *The Book Publishing Industry* 3rd edition, Routledge, 2014.
"Guide to Writing Programs." *Association of Writers and Writing Programs*, www.awpwriter.org/guide/guide_writing_programs
Gunelius, Susan. *Harry Potter: The Story of a Global Business Phenomenon*. Palgrave/Macmillan, 2008.
Haake, Katherine. *What Our Speech Disrupts: Feminism and Creative Writing Studies*. NCTE, 2000.
Hairston, Maxine Cousins. "The Winds of Change: Thomas Kuhn and the Revolution in the Teaching of Writing." *The Norton Book of Composition Studies*, pp. 439–450. Reprinted from *College Composition and Communication* vol 33, no.1, 1982, pp. 76–88.
"Haiti After the Quake." Pulitzer Center, www.pulitzercenter.org/haiti-after-quake
Hallberg, Garth Risk. "Outside the Ring: A Profile of Sergio De La Pava." *The Millions*, June 20, 2012, www.themillions.com/2012/06/outside-the-ring-a-profile-of-sergio-de-la-pava.html
Harvey, Matthea, and Amy Jean Porter. Interview by Erik Bryan. *The Morning News*, 1 June 2011, www.themorningnews.org/post/matthea-harvey-amy-jean-porter
Harvey, Matthea, and Amy Jean Porter. *Of Lamb*. McSweeney's Books, 2011.
Hazar, Kamran Mir, et al. "A Collaborative Poem for the Hazara." *Poems for the Hazara: An Anthology and Collaborative Poem*, edited by Kamran Mir Hazar, Full Page Publishing, 2014, pp. 522–539.
Heaney, Christopher. "Lucha Libro." *The Believer*, vol. 11, no. 4, 2013, pp. 3–11.
Hegamin, Tonya. "Inclusion and Diversity: A Manifesto and Interview." *Journal of Creative Writing Studies*, vol. 1, no. 1, 2016, http://scholarworks.rit.edu/jcws/vol1/iss1/3/
Hergenrader, Trent. *Collaborative Worldbuilding for Writers and Gamers*. Bloomsbury, 2018.

Hern, Alex. "Sales of 'The Cuckoo's Calling' Surge by 150,000% after J K Rowling Revealed as Author." *The New Statesman*, July 14, 2013, www.newstatesman.com/culture/2013/07/sales-cuckoos-calling-surge-150000-after-jk-rowling-revealed-author

"HitRECord Accord." HitRECord Terms of Service. *HitRECord*, www.hitrecord.org/terms

Ho, Jean. "Diversity In Book Publishing Isn't Just About Writers — Marketing Matters, Too." *Code Switch: Race and Identity, Remixed*. NPR, August 9, 2016, www.npr.org/sections/codeswitch/2016/08/09/483875698/diversity-in-book-publishing-isnt-just-about-writers-marketing-matters-too

Hocking, Amanda. "An Epic Tale of How it All Happened." *Hocking Books*, August 27, 2010, http://www.hockingbooks.com/an-epic-tale-of-how-it-all-happened/

Hocking, Amanda. "Some Things that Need to be Said." *Hocking Books*, March 4, 2011. www.hockingbooks.com/some-things-that-need-to-be-said/comment-page-23/

"Innovative Writing." *University at Buffalo, Department of English*, http://www.buffalo.edu/cas/english/graduate/certificate-in-innovative-writing.html

Jackson, Candice Love. "From Writer to Reader: Black Popular Fiction." *The Cambridge History of African American Literature*, eds. Maryemma Graham and Jerry W. Ward, Jr., Cambridge University Press, 2011, 655–679.

JAXA. "Space Poem Chain." *Japan Aerospace Exploration Agency*, iss.jaxa.jp/utiliz/renshi/index_e.html

Jemisin, N. K. "Contemplation, at the end of a season." nkjemisin.com, November 12, 2013, http://nkjemisin.com/2013/11/contemplation-at-the-end-of-a-season

"J K Rowling Revealed as Author of the Cuckoo's Calling." *BBC News*, July 14, 2013, www.bbc.co.uk/news/entertainment-arts-23304181

Jordan, June, et al. *Poetry for the People: A Revolutionary Blueprint*. ed. Lauren Muller, Routledge, 1995.

Kachka, Boris. "Book Publishing's Big Gamble." *The New York Times*, July 9, 2013, www.nytimes.com/2013/07/10/opinion/book-publishings-big-gamble.html?_r=0

Keller, Julia. "The 'Naked' Truth: An Author's Improbable Leap from Self-Published Obscurity to—Maybe—Literary Stardom." *Chicago Tribune*, Tribune Co, May 31, 2012, articles.chicagotribune.com/2012-05-31/entertainment/ct-prj-0603-naked-singularity-20120531_1_event-horizon-black-hole-glance

Kerouac, Jack. "Belief and Technique for Modern Prose." *The Portable Beat Reader*, ed. Ann Charters, Viking, 1992, pp. 58–59.

Knowlton, Jeff, Naomi Spellman, and Jeremy Hight. "34 North, 118 West: Mining the Urban Landscape," *34 North, 118 West*, www.34n118w.net/34N/

Koch, Bea and Leah Koch. "The Ripped Bodice Presents the State of Racial Diverstiy in Romance Publsihing 2017." *The Ripped Bodice*, 2017, www.therippedbodicela.com/state-racial-diversity-romance-publishing-report

Koehler, Adam. *Composition, Creative Writing Studies and the Digital Humanities*. Bloomsbury, 2016.

Konrath, J. A. "Konrath on Patterson." *A Newbie's Guide to Publishing*, April 25, 2013, jakonrath.blogspot.com/2013/04/konrath-on-patterson.html

Konrath, J. A. "Tsunami of Crap." *A Newbie's Guide to Publishing*, July 5, 2011, jakonrath.blogspot.com/2011/07/tsunami-of-crap.html

Konrath, J. A. "You Should Self-Publish." *A Newbie's Guide to Publishing*, December 28, 2010, jakonrath.blogspot.com/2010/12/you-should-self-publish.html

Koyama, Masato. "*Ucyu Renshi* (Space Poem Chain): Connecting Global People with Words." *National Aeronautics and Space Administration (NASA)*, March 7, 2012, www.nasa.gov/mission_pages/station/research/benefits/ucyu_renshi.html

Kurzweil, Ray. "The Law of Accelerating Returns." *Kurzweil Accelerating Intelligence*, March 7, 2001, www.kurzweilai.net/the-law-of-accelerating-returns

Lamott, Anne. *Bird by Bird: Some Instructions on Writing and Life*. Anchor Books, 1995.

Larsen, Michael. *How to Get a Literary Agent*, Sourcebooks, 2006.

Leahy, Anna. "Against Creative Writing Studies." *Journal of Creative Writing Studies*. vol. 1, no. 1., http://scholarworks.rit.edu/jcws/vol1/iss1/1/

LeFevre, Karen Burke. *Invention as a Social Act*. Southern Illinois University Press, 1987.

Løvlie, Anders Sundnes. "Annotative Locative Media and G-P-S: Granularity, Participation, and Serendipity." *Computers and Composition*, vol. 28, 2011, pp. 246–254.

Løvlie, Anders Sundnes. "Poetic Augmented Reality: Place-Bound Literature in Locative Media." *Proceedings of the 13th International MindTrek Conference: Everyday Life in the Ubiquitous Era*, 2009, pp. 19–28.

MacLeish, Archibald. "Ars Poetica." *Collected Poems 1917–1982*, Houghton Mifflin, 1985, p. 106.

Mahler, Jonathan. "James Patterson, Inc." *The New York Times*. January 20, 2010. www.nytimes.com/2010/01/24/magazine/24patterson-t.html?pagewanted=all&_r=0

Maran, Meredith, ed. *Why We Write*. Penguin, 2013.

Max, D. T. "The Carver Chronicles." The New York Times Archives, *The New York Times*. August 9, 1998, www.nytimes.com/1998/08/09/magazine/the-carver-chronicles.html?pagewanted=all&src=pm

Mayakovsky, Vladmir. "Order No. 2 to the Army of the Arts." *The Bedbug and Selected Poetry*, ed. Patricia Blake, Indiana University Press, 1975, pp. 145–150.

Mayers, Tim. *(Re)Writing Craft: Composition, Creative Writing, and the Future of English Studies*. University of Pittsburgh Press, 2005.

McGurl, Mark. *The Program Era: Postwar Fiction and the Rise of Creative Writing*. Harvard University Press, 2011.

"MFA Programs Database." *Poets & Writers*, www.pw.org/mfa

Miller, Laura. "When Anyone Can Be a Published Author." *Salon*, June 22, 2010, February 4, 2014, www.salon.com/2010/06/23/slush_3/

Milliot, Jim. "The PW Publishing Industry Salary Survey 2018." *Publishers Weekly*, November 9, 2018, www.publishersweekly.com/pw/by-topic/industry-news/publisher-news/article/78554-the-pw-publishing-industry-salary-survey-2018.html

Miner, Valerie. "The Book in the World." *Creative Writing in America: Theory and Pedagogy*, ed. Joseph M. Moxley, NCTE, 1989, pp. 227–236.

"Mission." *Apogee*, apogeejournal.org/mission

Moser, Laura. "Zane, the Queen of Erotica, Has a Secret." *Washingtonian*, June 15, 2015, www.washingtonian.com/2015/06/21/how-zane-the-queen-of-erotica-became-marylands-top-tax-deadbeat/

Moxley, Joseph, ed. *Creative Writing in America: Theory and Pedagogy*. NCTE, 1989.

Mura, David. *A Stranger's Journey: Race, Identity, and Narrative Craft in Writing*. University of Georgia Press, 2018.

Murphy, Annie. "Lucha Libro: Peruvian Writers 'Duke it Out' For a Book Contract in Masked Competitions." *Christian Science Monitor*, October 16, 2013, www.csmonitor.com/World/Americas/2013/1016/Lucha-Libro-Peruvian-writers-duke-it-out-for-a-book-contract-in-masked-competitions

Murphy, Annie. "Peru Makes Book Writing into a Spectator Sport and Invites Aspiring Writers into Combat." *Public Radio International*, September 30, 2013, https://www.pri.org/stories/2013-09-30/peru-makes-book-writing-spectator-sport-and-invites-desperate-writers-combat

Myers, D.G. *The Elephants Teach: Creative Writing Since 1880*. Prentice Hall, 1996.

Neary, Lynn. "To Achieve Diversity in Publishing, a Difficult Dialogue Beats Silence." *All Things Considered*, NPR, August 20, 2014, www.npr.org/sections/codeswitch/2014/08/20/341443632/to-achieve-diversity-in-publishing-a-difficult-dialogue-beats-silence

"News." Steel Toe Books, January 2, 2016, http://www.steeltoebooks.com/news

O'Neill, Tony. "Junkie Legend Jerry Stahl." *The Fix: Addiction and Recovery, Straight Up*, Clean & Sober Media, April 3, 2011, www.thefix.com/content/wicked-wit-jerry-stahl

"On the Road by Kerouac, First Edition." *AbeBooks*, www.abebooks.com/book-search/title/on-the-road/author/kerouac/first-edition/sortby/1/page-1/

"One Story." *Pro Publica*, 2017, projects.propublica.org/nonprofits/organizations/113639386/201733199349310868/IRS990

Ong, Walter. "The Writer's Audience is Always a Fiction." *Cross-Talk in Comp Theory*, pp. 55–76. Reprinted from *PMLA* vol. 90, no. 1, 1975, pp. 9–21.

Oram, Richard. "Famous Authors' Rejection Letters Surface" Interview by Liane Hansen. NPR, September 16, 2007, www.npr.org/templates/transcript/transcript.php?storyId=14453550

Ott, Martin. "Guest Blog Post, Martin Ott: Submission Season." *s [r] blog, Superstition Review*, September 14, 2013, www.superstitionreview.asu.edu/blog/2013/09/14/guest-post-martin-ott-submission-season/

"Our History and the Growth of Creative Writing Programs." *Association of Writers and Writing Programs*, www.awpwriter.org/about/our_history_overview

Paterson, James. "Who Will Save Our Books?" *Publisher's Weekly*, April 22, 2013. Full cover.

Patrick, Diane. "Sex Sells: Zane puts a new spin on an old adage." *Publisher's Weekly*, July 15, 2002, https://www.publishersweekly.com/pw/print/20020715/22893-sex-sells.html

Peary, Alexandria and Tom C. Hunley, eds. *Creative Writing Pedagogies for the Twenty-First Century*. Southern Illinois University Press, 2015.

Pettit, Emma. "The U of Missouri Press Almost Closed 4 Years Ago. Here's How it Bounced Back." *The Chronicle of Higher Education*, July 13, 2016.

Phillips, Thomas. *Sir Humphry Davy*, 1821, Public Domain Image.
Pilkington, Ed. "Amanda Hocking, The Writer Who Made Millions By Self-Publishing Online." *The Guardian*, Guardian News & Media Ltd, January 12, 2012, http://www.theguardian.com/books/2012/jan/12/amanda-hocking-self-publishing
"Poetics Program." *University at Buffalo, Department of English*, www.buffalo.edu/cas/english/graduate/poetics.html
Prose, Francine. *Reading Like a Writer: A Guide for People Who Love Books and for Those Who Want to Write Them*. HarperCollins, 2006.
Quan-Lee, Sherry, editor. *How Dare We! Write: A Multicultural Creative Writing Discourse*. Modern History Press, 2017.
Rankine, Claudia. Interview by Lauren Berlant. *Bomb Magazine*, October 1, 2014, www.bombmagazine.org/articles/claudia-rankine
Rankine, Claudia, Beth Loffreda, and Max King Cap, eds. *The Racial Imaginary: Writers on Race in the Life of the Mind*. Fence, 2015.
Rasula, Jed. *American Poetry Wax Museum: Reality Effects 1940–1990*. NCTE, 1996.
"Red Hen Press Inc." *Pro Publica*, 2017, projects.propublica.org/nonprofits/organizations/954754598/201841319349303994/IRS990
Renandya, Willy A. "Choosing the Right International Journal in TESOL and Applied Linguistics." *Academia.edu*, June 2014, www.academia.edu/2064493/Choosing_the_right_international_journal_in_tesol_and_applied_linguistics
Rendon, Fernando, et al. "An Open Letter from World-Wide Poets Addressed to World Political Leaders." *Poems for the Hazara: An Anthology and Collaborative Poem*, edited by Kamran Mir Hazar, Full Page Publishing, 2014, pp. 543–564.
Rhodes, Jacqueline. "Copyright, Authorship, and the Professional Writer: The Case of William Wordsworth." *Cardiff Corvey: Reading the Romantic Text*, vol. 8, 2002, www.cardiff.ac.uk/encap/journals/corvey/articles/cc08_n01.html
Ritter, Kelly and Stephanie Vanderslice, editors. *Can it Really Be Taught: Resisting Lore in Creative Writing Pedagogy*. Heinemann, 2007.
Robinson, Adam. "Why Did Mud Luscious Close? Getting Busy With JA Tyler." *HTML Giant*. June 6, 2013, www.htmlgiant.com/behind-the-scenes/why-did-mud-luscious-close-getting-busy-with-ja-tyler/
Sachs, Andrea. "'Queen of Erotica' Zane on how *Fifty Shades* Affects the Sexy-Book Scene." *Time*, August 1, 2012, entertainment.time.com/2012/08/01/queen-of-erotica-zane-on-how-fifty-shades-affects-the-sexy-book-scene/
Sales, Bethany. "Fifty Shades of Grey: The New Publishing Paradigm." *Huffington Post*, April 18, 2013, www.huffingtonpost.com/bethany-sales/fifty-shades-of-grey-publishing_b_3109547.html
Sample, Mark. "Location is not Compelling (Until it is Haunted)." *The Mobile Story*, pp. 95–109.
Salganik, Matthew, Peter Sheridan Dodds, Duncan J. Watts. "Experimental Study of Inequality and Unpredictability in an Artificial Cultural Market." *Science* vol 311, February 10, 2006, pp. 854–856, www.princeton.edu/~mjs3/salganik_dodds_watts06_full.pdf
Schecter, Martin. "Emily Dickinson, Madonna, Boomers, Busters, the Old Criterion, and the New Millennium—Deconstructing the Guardians of Nostalgia: A Defense of the Young Writer." *AWP Chronicle*, vol. 26, no. 1, 1993, pp. 14–20.

Schramm, Wilbur. "Imaginative Writing." *Literary Scholarship: Its Aims and Methods*, University of North Carolina Press, 1941, pp. 175–213.

Shatzkin, Mike. "A Changing Book Business: It All Seems to be Flowing Downhill to Amazon." *The Idea Logical Company*, January 22, 2018, www.idealog.com/blog/changing-book-business-seems-flowing-downhill-amazon/

Shellnut, Eve. "Notes from a Cell: Creative Writing Programs in Isolation." *Creative Writing in America: Theory and Pedagogy*, pp. 3–22.

Shelton, John. "The Autograph Manuscript of *Kubla Khan* and an Interpretation." *Review of English Literature*, vol. 7, 1966, pp. 30–42.

Shivani, Anis. *Against the Workshop: Provocations, Polemics, Controversies*. Texas A&M Press, 2011.

Silko, Leslie Marmon. "Language and Literature from a Pueblo Indian Perspective." *English Literature: Opening Up the Canon*, edited by Leslie A. Fiedler and Houston A. Baker, Johns Hopkins University Press, 1979, pp. 54–72.

"Sold! The Inscribed 1957 Presentation Copy of Jack Kerouac's On the Road Fetched $7,500 at Heritage Auctions." *The Hot Bid*, March 9, 2018, https://thehotbid.com/2018/03/09/heritage-could-sell-an-inscribed-1957-presentation-copy-of-jack-kerouacs-beat-generation-novel-on-the-road-for-8000/

Sommers, Nancy. "Revision Strategies for Student Writers and Experienced Adult Writers." *The Norton Book of Composition Studies*, pp. 323–332. Reprinted from *College Composition and Communication* vol., 31, no. 4, 1980, pp. 378–388.

Stein, Gertrude. The Autobiography of Alice B. Toklas. Harcourt, Brace and Co., 1933.

Stillinger, Jack. *Multiple Authorship and the Myth of Solitary Genius*. Oxford University Press, 1991.

Sutherland, John. "American Foetry: Pulitzer Prize Winners Accused of Fraud and Competition-Fixing—Who Ever Said Poetry was Boring?" *The Guardian*, July 3, 2005, www.theguardian.com/books/2005/jul/04/news.comment

Swiss, Thomas, and George Shaw. "The Language of New Media." *Divine Penguin*, www.divinepenguin.com/thelanguage

Thompson, John B. *Merchants of Culture: The Publishing Business in the Twenty-First Century* 2nd edition Polity Press, 2012.

Tompkins, Jane. *Sensational Designs: The Cultural Work of American Fiction*, 1790–1860, Oxford University Press, 1986.

"Top 50 Literary Magazines." *Every Writer's Resource*, 2017, www.everywritersresource.com/topliterarymagazines.html

Twine. www.twinery.org

Vincent, Alice E. "Rejection Letters: The Publishers Who Got It Embarrassingly Wrong . . ." *The Huffington Post UK*, May 17, 2012, www.huffingtonpost.co.uk/2012/05/16/publishers-who-got-it-wrong_n_1520190.html#slide=977924

Ulin, David. "George Saunders Goes Digital with 'Fox 8' E-Book." *Los Angeles Times*,April 16, 2013, articles.latimes.com/2013/apr/16/entertainment/la-et-jc-george-saunders-goes-digital-20130414

Voices of Our Nation. Voices of our Nation Arts Foundation, https://vonacommunity.org

Watts, Duncan J. "J K Rowling and the Chamber of Literary Fame." *Bloomberg*. July 19, 2013, https://www.bloomberg.com/opinion/articles/2013-07-19/j-k-rowling-and-the-chamber-of-literary-fame

Wilde, Oscar. *The Picture of Dorian Gray. The Picture of Dorian Gray and Other Writings*, edited by Richard Ellman, Bantam Books, 1982, pp. 1–193.
Williams, Mark. "Global book market valued at $143bn." *The New Publishing Standard*, October 23, 2017, thenewpublishingstandard.com/global-book-market-valued-at-143bn/
Wilson, Raymond. "Introduction." *A Coleridge Selection*, St. Martin's Press, 1966.
Winnicott, D.W. *The Child, the Family, and the Outside World*. Da Capo Press, 1992.
Woodmansee, Martha. "The Genius and the Copyright: Economic and Legal Conditions of the Emergence of the 'Author.'" *Eighteenth-Century Studies*, vol. 17, 1984, pp. 426–448.
Wonder Boys. Directed by Curtis Hanson, performances by Michael Douglas, Tobey Maguire, Frances McDormand, Paramount Pictures, 2000.
Woolf, Virginia. *A Room of One's Own*. Harcourt, 1989.
Young, Dean. *The Art of Recklessness: Poetry as Assertive Force and Contradiction*. Graywolf Press, 2010.

Deep Reading References

Introduction

Adsit, Janelle. *Critical Creative Writing: Essential Readings on the Writer's Craft*. Bloomsbury, 2018.
Ristow, Ben. *Nurturing Craft Consciousness and Artistic Practice in Creative Writing*. Bloomsbury, 2020.
Salesses, Matthew. "Pure Craft is a Lie." *Pleiades*, www.pleiadesmag.com/pure-craft-is-a-lie-part-1.

Chapter 1

Achebe, Chinua. "Africa and Her Writers." *Morning Yet on Creation Day: Essays*, Heinemann, 1975, pp. 29–46.
Hegamin, Tonya. "Inclusion and Diversity: A Manifesto and Interview." *Journal of Creative Writing Studies*, vol. 1, no. 1, 2016, http://scholarworks.rit.edu/jcws/vol1/iss1/3/.
Trotsky, Leon. *Literature and Revolution*, edited by William Keach, Haymarket Books, 2005.
Wimsatt, W. K. and M. C. Beardsley. "The Affective Fallacy." *Sewanee Review*, vol. 57, no. 1, pp. 31–55.

Chapter 2

Flaherty, Alice. *The Midnight Disease: The Drive to Write, Writer's Block, and the Creative Brain*. Mariner Books, 2005.
Mura, David. *A Stranger's Journey: Race, Identity, and Narrative Craft in Writing*, University of Georgia Press, 2018.

Mura, David. "The Student of Color in the Typical MFA Program." *Gulf Coast*, April 21, 2015, gulfcoastmag.org/online/blog/the-student-of-color-in-the-typical-mfa-program/
Mura, David. "Writing Teachers—Or David Foster Wallace Versus James Baldwin." *Journal of Creative Writing Studies*, vol. 1, no. 1, scholarworks.rit.edu/jcws/vol1/iss1/7/

Chapter 3

Emig, Janet. *The Composing Processes of Twelfth Graders*. NCTE, 1971.
Gates, Henry Louis. *The Signifying Monkey: A Theory of African-American Literary Criticism*. Oxford University Press, 1989.
Jen, Gish. *Tiger Writing: Art, Culture, and the Interdependent Self*. Harvard University Press, 2013.
Lu, Min-Zhan. "Professing Multiculturalism: The Politics of Style in the Contact Zone." *College Composition and Communication*, vol. 45, no. 4, 1994, pp. 442–458.
Macrorie, Ken. *Telling Writing*. 4th edition, Heinemann, 1985.

Chapter 4

Foucault, Michel. "What is an Author?" *Language, Counter-Memory, Practice: Selected Essays and Interviews*, edited by Donald F. Bouchard, Cornell University Press, 1977, pp. 113–138.
Iser, Wolfgang. *The Implied Reader: Patterns of Communication in Prose Fiction from Bunyan to Beckett*. Johns Hopkins University Press, 1974.
Tompkins, Jane P., ed. *Reader-Response Criticism: From Formalism to Post-Structuralism*. Johns Hopkins University Press, 1980.
Wandor, Michelene. *The Author Is Not Dead, Merely Somewhere Else: Creative Writing Reconceived*. Palgrave Macmillan, 2008.

Chapter 5

Christie, Agatha, et al. *The Floating Admiral*, HarperCollins, 2011.
Levon O.U., *Caverns*. Penguin, 1990.
Stillinger, Jack. *Multiple Authorship and the Myth of Solitary Genius*. Oxford University Press, 1991.
Trinidad, David, Denise Duhamel, and Maureen Seaton, Editors. *Saints of Hysteria: A Half-Century of Collaborative American Poetry*. Soft Skull Press, 2007.

Chapter 6

Bloomsbury, *Writers' and Artists' Yearbook 2019*, Bloomsbury Yearbooks, 2018.

Brewer, Robert Lee. *Writer's Market 2019*, Writer's Digest Books, 2018.
Burt-Thomas, Wendy. *The Writer's Digest Guide to Query Letters*, Writer's Digest Books, 2009.
Richter, David. *Falling into Theory: Conflicting Views on Reading Literature*, 2nd edition, Bedford/St. Martin's, 1999.
Sambuchino, Chuck. *Formatting and Submitting Your Manuscript*, Writer's Digest Books, 2009.
Walsh, Pat. *78 Reasons Why Your Book May Never Be Published and 14 Reasons Why It Just Might*, Penguin, 2005.

Chapter 7

Cottenet, Cécile. *Race, Ethnicity, and Publishing in America.* Palgrave MacMillan, 2014.
Greco, Albert N., Jim Milliot, and Robert Wharton. *The Book Publishing Industry.* 3rd edition, Routledge, 2014.
McHenry, Elizabeth. *Forgotten Readers: Recovering the Lost History of African American Literary Societies*, Duke University Press, 2002.
Thompson, John B. *Merchants of Culture: The Publishing Business in the Twenty-First Century.* 2nd ed., Polity Press, 2012.
Young, John K. *Black Writers, White Publishers: Marketplace Politics in Twentieth-Century African American Literature*, University of Mississippi Press, 2006.

Chapter 8

Harbach, Chad, editor. *MFA vs. NYC*, Faber and Faber, 2014.

Chapter 9

Konrath, J. A. "Konrath on Patterson." *A Newbie's Guide to Publishing*, April 25, 2013, jakonrath.blogspot.com/2013/04/konrath-on-patterson.html.
Konrath, J. A. "Tsunami of Crap." *A Newbie's Guide to Publishing*, July 5, 2011, jakonrath.blogspot.com/2011/07/tsunami-of-crap.html.
Miller, Laura. "When Anyone Can Be a Published Author." *Salon*, June 22, 2010, February 4, 2014, www.salon.com/2010/06/23/slush_3/.

Chapter 10

Bernstein, Mark and Diane Greco. *Reading Hypertext.* Eastgate Systems, 2009.
Clark, Michael Dean, Trent Hergenrader, and Joe Rein. *Creative Writing in the Digital Age: Theory, Practice and Pedagogy*, Bloomsbury, 2015.

Goldsmith, Kenneth. *Uncreative Writing: Managing Language in the Digital Age*. Columbia University Press, 2011.

Hayles, N. Katherine and Jessica Pressman. *Comparative Textual Media: Transforming the Humanities in the Postprint Era*. University of Minnesota Press, 2013.

Lang, Anouk. *From Codex to Hypertext: Reading at the Turn of the Twenty-First Century*. University of Massachusetts Press, 2012.

Perloff, Marjorie. *Unoriginal Genius: Poetry by Other Means in the New Century*. University of Chicago Press, 2012.

Index